Commerce and Its Discontents in Eighteenth-Century French Political Thought

Histories of economics tend to portray attitudes towards commerce in the era of Adam Smith as celebrating what is termed *doux commerce*, that is, sweet or gentle commerce. *Commerce and Its Discontents in Eighteenth-Century French Political Thought* proposes that reliance on this "*doux commerce* thesis" has obscured our comprehension of the theory and experience of commerce in Enlightenment-era Europe. Instead, it uncovers ambivalence towards commerce in eighteenth-century France, distinguished by an awareness of its limits – slavery, piracy, and monopoly. Through a careful analysis of the *Histoire des deux Indes* (1780), the Enlightenment's bestselling history of comparative empires, Anoush Fraser Terjanian offers a new perspective on the connections between political economy, imperialism, and the Enlightenment. In discussing how a "politics of definition" governed the early debates about global commerce and its impact, this book enriches our understanding of the prehistory of globalisation.

Anoush Fraser Terjanian is Assistant Professor of History at East Carolina University.

Commerce and Its Discontents in Eighteenth-Century French Political Thought

ANOUSH FRASER TERJANIAN

East Carolina University

CAMBRIDGE
UNIVERSITY PRESS

CAMBRIDGE
UNIVERSITY PRESS

University Printing House, Cambridge CB2 8BS, United Kingdom

Cambridge University Press is part of the University of Cambridge.

It furthers the University's mission by disseminating knowledge in the pursuit of education, learning and research at the highest international levels of excellence.

www.cambridge.org
Information on this title: www.cambridge.org/9781316608456

© Anoush Fraser Terjanian 2013

First published 2013
First paperback edition 2016

A catalogue record for this publication is available from the British Library

Library of Congress Cataloguing in Publication data
Terjanian, Anoush Fraser
Commerce and its discontents in eighteenth-century French
political thought / Anoush Fraser Terjanian.
pages cm
Includes bibliographical references and index.
ISBN 978-1-107-00564-8 (hardback)
1. France – Commerce – History – 18th century. 2. Economics –
Political aspects – France – History – 18th century. I. Title.
HF3555.T47 2012
381.0944–dc23   2012021041

ISBN 978-1-107-00564-8 Hardback
ISBN 978-1-316-60845-6 Paperback

For my parents

Contents

vii

Illustrations

Acknowledgements

It is such a pleasure finally to thank in print the people and institutions without whom I would never have completed, let alone begun, this book.

I gratefully acknowledge the financial support of the John Carter Brown Library, the Thomas Harriot College of Arts and Sciences at East Carolina University, and the East Carolina University Faculty Senate. The dissertation on which this book is based was generously funded by the Social Sciences and Humanities Research Council of Canada, the Johns Hopkins University History Department, the Brian J. Key Research Award, the Charles S. Singleton Dissertation Fellowship, and the Institut Français d'Amérique (then Washington).

Librarians at the Bibliothèque nationale de France, especially the conservateurs at the Salle des manuscrits, were most forthcoming with assistance and advice early on. I would also like to thank the conservateurs at the Bibliothèque de l'Arsenal and the archivists at the Ministère des affaires étrangères, the Centre des Archives d'Outre-Mer in Aix, the Archives de la Chambre de Commerce de Marseille, the National Archives of Canada, the Rare Books Reading Room of the Library of Congress, and the University of Ottawa's Rare Books collection. Special thanks go to the John Carter Brown Library. Its two directors, Norman Fiering and Ted Widmer, fostered this research, and its magnificent staff made it both possible and a pleasure. I am also most grateful to the staff at McGill University's Redpath and McLennan Libraries for their help during the last stages of completing the manuscript. Finally, thanks go to the relentless Inter-Library Loan staff at ECU's Joyner Library, who made it possible to work during the academic year in Greenville.

This book began as a doctoral dissertation, but it has a longer history.

The questions I have asked, and continue to hope to answer, can be traced at least as far back as my undergraduate theses in political theory and in history, supervised by James Tully and Pierre Boulle at McGill University, respectively. Their delicate nurturing of my ideas and ideals continues to stimulate this research. I also want to thank Laurette Glasgow, fearless director of the International Economics Division at the Department of Foreign Affairs in Ottawa, and Ariel Delouya, our deputy, for their example and their confidence in me and my wild idea to leave the department for academe.

The Department of History at Johns Hopkins provided not only funding for the dissertation, but also its famously challenging intellectual environment filled with sharp colleagues and extraordinary teachers with whom to discuss and debate. Anthony Pagden's *European Encounters* first inspired this project. His supervision of my M.Phil. thesis at Cambridge and my doctoral dissertation at Hopkins then shaped this book, which does not adequately reflect the pearls of wisdom he has proffered for so many years. David A. Bell generously provided a rigorous initiation into the history of eighteenth-century France. His energy and input were essential to this book's shape and completion. Orest Ranum has entertained my constant questions and drafts with his characteristic munificence and his always thoughtful and sound advice. Among so many generous gestures, he and his spouse, Patricia, went so far as to bring me to Raynal's doorstep, in Saint-Geniez-d'Olt. John Pocock discreetly offered counsel and encouragement from this project's inception, kindly sharing a draft of his writing on Raynal and making sense of my own early musings. A model feminist, teacher, and mentor, Judy Walkowitz often asked the toughest and most perceptive questions of my work. For special attention to my work in the final stages, I would like to thank Toby Ditz and Jack Greene. For their careful reading and helpful suggestions of the dissertation which inspired this book, I thank the members of my dissertation defence committee, Professors David A. Bell (again), Wilda Anderson, Mark Blyth, Toby Ditz, and Richard Kagan.

The organisers and participants of the 1998 Minda da Gunzburg conference on "Europe and Empire" listened carefully to my approach and offered encouragement in this project's earliest stages. Special thanks to Jill Casid, Caroline Elkins, Pratap Mehta, Sankar Muthu, Jennifer Pitts, and Richard Tuck.

The Centre de Recherches Historiques at the École des Hautes Études en Sciences Sociales, Paris, welcomed me into its doctoral programme, under the perceptive supervision and hospitality of Roger Chartier. Later, I was fortunate to be invited to share my work in Myriam Cottias and

Jean Hébrard's vibrant ÉHESS seminar on the "Histoire du fait colonial." The University of Ottawa's School of Political Studies twice provided a generous and probing audience for chapters presented to them: I especially thank Jacqueline Best, Linda Cardinal, Serge Denis, Dimitri Karmis, Kevin McMillan, and Paul Saurette for their helpful insights. For fruitful discussions of my work, I am also deeply grateful to my colleagues in the Triangle Intellectual History and French Cultural Studies seminar (especially Mimi Kim, Lloyd Kramer, Bill Reddy, Don Reid, Jay Smith, and Steven Vincent), as well as a long list of teachers and colleagues who have offered insights along the way: Sara Berry, Dominique Brancher, Jeremy Caradonna, Paul Cheney, Myriam Cottias, Charles-Philippe Courtois, Madeleine Dobie, François Furstenberg, Gianluigi Goggi, Istvan Hont, Vicki Hsueh, Lara Kriegel, Sheryl Kroen, Catherine Labio, Catherine Larrère, Jane Lesnick, David Marshall, Lucien Nouis, Maurice Olender, Annelie Ramsbrock, Sophus Reinert, Neil Safier, John Shovlin, Michael Sonenscher, Céline Spector, Philippe Steiner, Ann Thomson, Elizabeth Wingrove, and Amit Yahav.

Many thanks go to my colleagues and friends in the History Department at ECU. I sincerely thank Michael A. Palmer, my former chair in ECU's department of history; Gerry Prokopowicz, my current chair; Dean Alan White and Associate Dean Cindy Putnam-Evans of the Harriot College of Arts and Sciences; and the East Carolina University Faculty Senate for supporting this research and the book's production as well. Special mention goes to my dear colleagues and friends, John O'Brien and Mona Russell, who were particularly indispensable to the project's completion.

I was fortunate to be asked to join the editorial team of the first critical edition of the *Histoire des deux Indes*. I am deeply indebted to my volume editor, the erudite and prolific Gianluigi Goggi, as I am to Anthony Strugnell, Cecil Courtney, Hans-Jürgen Lüsebrink, Ann Thomson, and Muriel Brot. Key questions in this book were given an opportunity to air in the truly rich conference organised in July 2010 by Jenny Mander at Newnham College at Cambridge University. There I benefitted from the insights of William St-Clair, Stéphane Pujol, and Kenta Ohji. Though I have tried my best to offer one modest interpretation of the work herein, I am all too aware that this book does not adequately reflect the wealth of knowledge they have produced, and generously shared, concerning the *HDI*.

I am fortunate for the friends and colleagues who have sustained this project during its long gestation. Julia Holderness has stood firmly by my side, a dear friend, reader, counselor, and enlightened critic. She is by far more *dame* and more *raison* than her subject, Christine de Pizan. Anna

Krylova has offered a model for the life of a woman historian and critical thinker, with advice and encouragement.

In Paris, I experienced first-hand the ideal of the *doux commerce* of ideas. One could not ask for a finer group of historians with whom to share a writing group: For their friendship and solidarity, within and beyond the Bibliothèque nationale, I thank Charly Coleman, Andrew Jainchill, Ben Kafka, Rebecca Manley, Emmanuel Saadia, and Dana Simmons. My favourite littératrices, Natasha Lee, Anne Beate Maurseth, and Louisa Shea, nourished my fumbling in the *dix-huitième* with insight and companionship. Ariane Bergeron-Foote, *Chartiste-archiviste-paléographe*, a dear friend since we were tiny undergraduates, showed me the way to the wonderful world of Paris' libraries and manuscripts. Élodie Richard helped me navigate the corridors of the 54 blvd Raspail, and so much more. To Ken Ashworth, Francesca Feder et compagnie, and to tutti gli amici dell' Académie des Quatre Vents, I give thanks for showing me that a life outside the BnF can also be rich and wondrous.

What a joy it has been to wrap up this book (for it is not, nor perhaps could it ever be, complete) amid the marvelous collection and staff of the McLennan Library at McGill University in Montreal, where, in many ways, it began. As my deadline approached, I was fortunate to be surrounded by Pierre Boulle, Nick Dew, François Furstenberg (again), and Joanne Robertson, each of whom helped me enormously in these last stages.

I am very grateful to Eric Crahan, history and politics editor at Cambridge University Press, for taking on the publication of this book, as I am to his assistants, Jason Przybylski and Abby Zorbaugh, and to copy editors Ruth Homrigaus, Dan C. Geist, and Ami Naramor. Andrew J. Walker provided valuable research and fact-checking assistance, and Celia Braves created a beautiful index. I am also extremely grateful to the very generous manuscript reviewers for Cambridge, whose incisive suggestions I have tried my best to incorporate.

I am blessed with a large and wonderful extended family, all of whom, Fraser and Terjanian, have shown endless support. I thank Jonathan Bowling for flavouring the last phases of this book with zest. I am so grateful to James Terjanian, who kept cheering on his sister, despite his brave labours around the globe in the most difficult of conditions. And finally, without the unlimited and unwavering support, encouragement, generosity, humour, and love of my parents, Sheila and Antoine Terjanian, this book would simply not exist. I dedicate it to them, my favourite economists.

Montreal, August 2011

Introduction

Commerce and Its Discontents

On the eve of the Seven Years War (1756–63), a self-proclaimed French *philosophe* published a series of "Poetic amusements." Amid odes to "The Triumph of Poetry among all Peoples," "Love of the Fatherland," and "Idolatry," we find six pages devoted to "Commerce, a poem."[1] Firmin Douin de Caen, the poet in question, has since disappeared from the historical record, yet at the time he was awarded a certificate of merit from the French Academy for these verses on the origins and progress of commerce in France. His poem ended on a promise: that commerce would render "the Empire of the Lilies even more flourishing, / The French happier and Louis more powerful."[2]

Similarly triumphant declarations about the potential of commerce abounded during this period, though not always in poetic form. But Douin's ode represented the discourse of commerce in eighteenth-century France in yet another way: Its "hymn to commerce" also struck darker notes.[3] Midway through, Douin lamented the vile qualities of the slave trade, calling it a *"commerce odieux."*[4] This characterisation of the

---

[1] Firmin de Caen Douin, "Le Commerce, poëme. Qui a eu l'Accessit à l'Académie Françoise, en 1754," in *Amusemens poëtiques d'un philosophe, ou Poëmes académiques sur différens sujets, dont plusieurs ont été couronnés, et autres piéces fugitives* (Paris: Chez Cailleau, 1763). The author is identified in the Bibliothèque nationale de France's catalogue. All translations are my own unless I have specified otherwise.

[2] "Rends l'Empire des Lys encor [*sic*] plus florissant, / Les François plus heureux & LOUIS plus puissant." Ibid., 49.

[3] For the term "hymn to commerce," see Yves Benot, "Diderot, Pechméja, Raynal et l'anticolonialisme," *Europe: revue littéraire mensuelle* 41 (Jan.–Feb. 1963): 147.

[4] "Disgraceful objects of an odious Commerce, / hapless Negroes, what have you done to the Gods?" ("Déplorables objets d'un Commerce odieux, / Nègres infortunés,

commerce in humans as "odious" was but one example of a tension prevalent in eighteenth-century French political and economic thought, a tension between a triumphalist discourse of commerce and a foreboding sense of its destructive potential. This book aims to explore how this tension was intelligible to eighteenth-century French public intellectuals and how it manifested itself in their thought and texts.

As we shall see, Douin's ode to commerce anticipated an attitude that flourished in the aftermath of France's devastating defeat by the British in the Seven Years War. This conflict, which Winston Churchill deemed the "first world war," strained the kingdom's finances, ballooned its debt, and drastically reduced its overseas possessions.[5] It also generated a crisis of confidence among France's public intellectuals centred on the humiliating decline in their nation's power and glory, especially in comparison to victorious Britain's perceived strength.[6] This study follows the

qu'avez-vous fait aux Dieux? "). In Douin, "Le Commerce, poëme," 47, my emphasis. I have previously referred to this kind of commerce, the *commerce odieux*, as "commerce *amer*," an antonym to *doux* which means, essentially, bitter or sour. But further research has confirmed that the term *odieux*, like the term *vil*, which also qualified commerce in eighteenth-century France, emanates directly from eighteenth-century texts, whereas *amer* does not.

[5] France lost more than three-quarters of its imperial holdings in North America and West Africa, and the French debt doubled, from 1,360 million to 2,350 million livres, between 1753 and 1764 as a result of the decision to finance the war with credit and not taxes. What is more, all of this loss occurred on the tails of the already devastating French losses in the preceding War of Austrian Succession (1740–48), of which the Seven Years' War was in many ways an extension and an expansion. James C. Riley has argued against the grain of a general historiographical consensus about the war's devastating repercussions for France, stating that France's economic loss from the war has been grossly exaggerated by historians (using "dramatic language"), although he concedes that France did suffer a fiscal and political catastrophe. See James C. Riley, *The Seven Years War and the Old Regime in France: The Economic and Financial Toll* (Princeton, NJ: Princeton University Press, 1986), 191, 225. Gail Bossenga highlights that the British debt at the end of the war was greater than that of France; however with the French monarchy's mired fiscal institutions, the cost of servicing that debt was much greater for France due to its high debt servicing charges. See Gail Bossenga, "Financial Origins of the French Revolution," in Thomas E. Kaiser and Dale K. Van Kley, *From Deficit to Deluge: The Origins of the French Revolution* (Stanford: Stanford University Press, 2011), 37–66. Significant for our purposes here is the sense among public intellectuals in France during this period that the war had further crippled France's financial situation. The authoritative account of that mindset is Michael Sonenscher's "The Nation's Debt and the Birth of the Modern Republic," *Political Studies* 42 (1994): 166–231, and, most recently, *Before the Deluge: Public Debt, Inequality, and the Intellectual Origins of the French Revolution* (Princeton, NJ: Princeton University Press, 2007). For Churchill's oft-quoted assessment of the Seven Years War, see Winston S. Churchill, *The Age of Revolution* (New York: Dodd and Mead, 1957), 148–49.

[6] The term "crisis of confidence" comes from Riley, *Seven Years War*, 192. See David A. Bell, *The Cult of the Nation in France: Inventing Nationalism, 1680–1800* (Cambridge,

conceptual and ideological change the Seven Years War unleashed as it intersected with thinking about empire and what I will refer to here, in shorthand, as "Enlightenment critical practices."[7] At the time, the discourse of commerce in France was interwoven with different discourses, of politics, of empire, of justice, of equality, and of wealth. But its most common loci were histories of commerce.[8] These histories offered a perspective on commerce that ran parallel to but remained interdependent with a burgeoning "science of political economy" – what many scholars from Franco Venturi to John Robertson have considered the "unifying discourse" of the Enlightenment.[9]

This "science" was first identified as such in France by a group of theorists and practitioners clustered around the court of Louis XV in the 1750s.[10] In this period, as Voltaire famously quipped, "the nation" turned

MA: Harvard University Press, 2001), especially chapter 3, "English Barbarians, French Martyrs," for the ways in which the French defined themselves against the English in this period.

[7] This clumsy phrase aims to synthesize the plethora of critical gestures, in texts and beyond them, that self-identified agents of the Enlightenment in France deployed to advance their political and moral projects to counter and transcend despotism, including promoting agency among their readership. Reinert Koselleck offered one of the most powerful accounts of the process of "critical ferment" in sway in the eighteenth century, though he famously drew disastrous conclusions from it. See *Critique and Crisis: Enlightenment and the Pathogenesis of Modern Society* (1955) (Cambridge, MA: MIT Press, 1988), 10. Dena Goodman's *Criticism in Action: Enlightenment Experiments in Political Writing* (Ithaca, NY: Cornell University Press, 1989) offers another influential account of the practices of social and political critique I consider. Jay Smith's "Between Discourse and Experience: Agency and Ideas in the French Pre-Revolution," *History and Theory* 40 (2001): 116–42 provides an alternative approach to agency which moves beyond discourse analysis to encompass experience. Because language and texts are the tools we use to convey our understandings of our biography, our politics, and our society, I am here interested in uncovering the way people related ideas to one another and what choices of words they made to do so, with the hope of arriving at a better understanding of the foundations of ideologies governing political and economic theory and practice today.

[8] Paul B. Cheney demonstrated this early on in "History and Science of Commerce," 226, and later in chapter 3, "Philosophical History," in his *Revolutionary Commerce: Globalization and the French Monarchy* (Cambridge, MA: Harvard University Press, 2010).

[9] For the ways in which John Robertson and Franco Venturi cohere Enlightenment thought about political economy in Scotland and Italy, see Charles Withers, *Placing the Enlightenment: Thinking Geographically about the Age of Reason* (Chicago: University of Chicago Press, 2007), 42.

[10] Whereas Adam Smith later defined political economy as "a branch of the science of a statesman or legislator" (*An Inquiry into the Nature and Causes of the Wealth of Nations*. 1776. 2 vols. R. H. Campbell and A. S. Skinner, eds. [Oxford: Oxford University Press, 1976], book 4, chapter 1), it was in France that this scientific status was first attributed to political economy. See Philippe Steiner, *La 'science nouvelle' de l'économie politique* (Paris: Presses Universitaires de France, 1998). Cf. Liana Vardi's recent argument that in

its attention away from "opera" and "theological disputes" in order to "reason about wheat," as droughts and shortages focused public attention on the statutes regulating its supply.[11] Led by the king's physician, François Quesnay (1694–1774), this mix of theorists and practitioners comprised the first group of thinkers to call themselves *économistes* since their stated aim was to think analytically, arithmetically, mechanically, and graphically about the national "oeconomy."[12] Because they argued that agriculture ought to be the principal focus of attention in France, and thus that France should be ruled by (*-cracy*) nature (*phusis*), and not industry or international trade, they came to call themselves Physiocrats and their doctrine Physiocracy.[13] Their detractors referred to them otherwise, however – as a "sect" and a group of "small-frys," to name but

fact Physiocracy's "epistemological underpinnings … tied it to the realm of imagination from which it sought to escape." Liana Vardi, "Physiocratic Visions," in Dan Edelstein, ed., *The Super-Enlightenment: Daring to Know too Much* (Oxford: Voltaire Foundation, 2010), 97.

[11] Voltaire, "Blé ou Bled," *Dictionnaire philosophique in Œuvres complètes*, vol. 2 (Paris: Chez Antoine-Augustin Renouard, 1819), 241. In the eighteenth century, *blé* was translated into English as "corn, or grain for bread." Abel Boyer, *The Royal Dictionary, Abridged, In Two Parts: I. French and English, II. English and French*. Ninth edition. (London: n.p., 1755). I have opted for *wheat*, however, as it more accurately renders the sense of the term *blé* used by Voltaire into contemporary English, since *blé* is a subset of the broader term *grain*, also employed in eighteenth-century French. Voltaire's sarcasm in this quote is best heard when the passage is read in its entirety: "Around the year 1750, the nation, satiated with verses, tragedies, comedies, opera, novels, dreamy stories, even dreamier moral reflections, and theological disputes about grace and convulsions, finally turned to reason about wheat. We even forgot about vines in order to talk but of wheat and rye. We wrote many useful things about agriculture: everyone read them, except the farmers."

[12] Quesnay's *Tableau oeconomique* (Versailles, 1758) offered the first graphic conceptualisation of the forces, both "destructive" (by which he meant consumption) and "regenerative" (by which he meant reproduction), circulating within and defining the national economy. Karl Marx described the *Tableau* as "an extremely brilliant conception, incontestably the most brilliant for which political economy had up to then been responsible." *Theories of Surplus Value*, 3 vols. (Moscow: Progress Publishers, 1969–71), vol. 1, 344.

[13] Pierre-Samuel Du Pont de Nemours (1739–1817), Quesnay's promoter (and renowned co-founder of the still trading Dupont Company), coined the term *physiocratie* in his compilation of writings entitled *Physiocratie, ou Constitution naturelle du gouvernement le plus avantageux au genre humain* (Leiden, 1768). As the editors of the recent edition of Quesnay's works note, the "Doctor" never publicly acknowledged his texts. Du Pont's collection of Quesnay's writings lists the group of Quesnay's followers as "the marquis de Mirabeau, Abeille, the abbé Baudeau, and Le Mercier de la Rivière," but Quesnay is never mentioned by name. See Loïc Charles, Jean-Claude Perrot, and Christine Théré, "Introduction des éditeurs," in *François Quesnay: Oeuvres économiques complètes et autres textes* (Paris: INED, 2005), xii. Quesnay's first expressions of the thesis that agriculture was the most productive economic activity were published in his articles for the *Encyclopédie*: "Fermiers," "Grains," and "Impôt." On the ultimate failure of the

a few of the taunts.[14] Most accounts of the history of economic thought have construed this antagonism to the *économistes* as a consequence of the challenge Physiocracy posed to the long-standing principles of the *système mercantile*.[15] Yet their accounts have borrowed, intentionally or not, the categorisation of "mercantilism" first conceived by its critics. For if ever "mercantilism" existed, it was more a political system than an economic one.[16]

The policies and institutions identified with mercantilism in France were developed by Louis XIV's chief minister, Jean-Baptiste Colbert (1619–83), with the aim to counter Dutch global dominance. The operating premise of the Colbertist programme was that wealth was finite and measurable in bullion; the state should thus be the sole benefactor of trade and economic gain acquired mainly through resource extraction from the colonies.[17] This ideology has long been portrayed as bellicose – and it

---

"practice" of Physiocracy in France see Martin Giraudeau, "Performing Physiocracy," *Journal of Cultural Economy* 3, no. 2 (2010): 225–42.

[14] The terms *secte* and *fretin* are Frederick Melchior Grimm's, the co-editor of the influential *Correspondance Littéraire*. See his report dated 1 January 1770: "There has arisen since some time, in the heart of this capital, a sect as humble as the dust where it was formed, as poor as its doctrine, as obscure as its style, but soon imperious and arrogant: those who make it up have taken the title '*Philosophes économistes*.'" And later: "I defy you to draw a single drop of genius from all of the apocalypses of the Quesnays, the Mirabeaus, the de La Rivières, and all of the fastidious commentaries of the Baudeaus, Roubauds, Dupont de Nemours and other economic small-frys." *Correspondance littéraire, philosophique et critique de Grimm et de Diderot, depuis 1753 jusqu'en 1790* (Paris: Chez Furne, 1829), 322–23. Further jabs at the "sect" by the future *contrôleur-général* of France, Anne-Robert-Jacques Turgot, and by Scottish moral philosophers David Hume and Adam Smith are discussed by Emma Rothschild, *Economic Sentiments: Adam Smith, Condorcet, and the Enlightenment* (Cambridge, MA: Harvard University Press, 2001), 35–36. Possibly their greatest critic was Véron de Forbonnais, author of the *Encyclopédie*'s article, "Commerce." See Peter Groenewegen, *Eighteenth-Century Economics: Turgot, Beccaria and Smith and their Contemporaries*. (London: Routledge, 2002), 255.

[15] As Céline Spector has shown, the term *système mercantile* can be first traced to Quesnay's first convert, the marquis de Mirabeau, and his *Philosohie rurale* (1763), 329. Spector aptly locates the "birth certificate" of mercantilism as a concept in Adam Smith's *Wealth of Nations*, however: In book 4, Smith inveighs against the "popular" principle that money creates wealth, and that wealth consists of the abundance of gold and silver. See Céline Spector, "Le concept de mercantilisme," *Revue de Métaphysique et de Morale* no. 3 (2003): 290.

[16] The influential reconceptualisation of mercantilism as a political theory (rather than simply an economic one) whose contestation structured the first critiques of the absolute monarchy was Lionel Rothkrug's *Opposition to Louis XIV: The Political and Social Origins of the French Enlightenment* (Princeton: Princeton University Press, 1965), 38.

[17] On the Colbertist strategies, see Pierre H. Boulle, "French Mercantilism, Commercial Companies and Colonial Profitability" in Blussé and Gastra, eds., *Companies and Trade:*

certainly was, since the notion of finite wealth sparked a long list of wars over scarce resources.[18] In contrast, the Physiocrats were and still are characterised as pacifists, but also as "liberals," because of their second abiding principle, that goods should circulate freely *within* France – just as blood does in the body, according to the surgeon Quesnay's famous analogy.[19] This last principle did not originate with Quesnay, however. It was developed earlier by an influential *intendant de commerce*, Jacques-Claude-Marie Vincent de Gournay (1712–59), best remembered for allegedly coining the phrase still used to describe this ideology: "*laissez faire, laissez passer.*"[20] Gournay had earlier formed a circle of followers, charging them with the publication of works promoting competitive markets, and, especially, the translation of writings about commerce emanating out of England, seen as a model for France to emulate.[21]

Essays on Overseas Trading Companies during the Ancien Régime (The Hague: Martinus Hijhoff, 1981), 106.

[18] To wit Colbert's own statement of its bellicose nature, in a 1666 letter to his cousin, the intendant of Rochefort: "Le commerce est la source de la finance, et la finance est le nerf de la guerre." Quoted in Céline Spector, "Le concept de mercantilisme," 294. For one of the earliest such assessments, see Edmond Silberner's still influential *La guerre dans la pensée économique du XVIe au XVIIIe siècle* (Paris, 1939), 263. With Terence Hutchison, I suggest that it is "inadequate and misleading" to "try to force" particular thinkers into "either one compartment or the other of a mercantilist–*laissez-faire* dichotomy." Terence Hutchison, *Before Adam Smith: The Emergence of Political Economy, 1662–1776* (Oxford: Basil Blackwell, 1988), 3.

[19] Contesting this characterisation early on, Samuel Hollander has argued that the Physiocrats were in fact "as much interventionist as the mercantilists." See his "Malthus as Physiocrat: Surplus versus Scarcity," in *The Literature of Political Economy: Collected Essays II* (London: Routledge, 1998), 51.

[20] Despite its currency today, this phrase belongs to the curious history of alleged attributions. Gournay never published the phrase, but its earliest printed attribution to him is most likely by one of Quesnay's eminent followers, the marquis de Mirabeau ("the elder"), in an essay entitled "*Sur la cherté des grains*" published in 1768 in the newly founded Physiocratic journal, *Éphémérides du citoyen, ou Bibliothèque raisonnée des sciences morales et politiques*. Here Gournay's phrase is referred to as a "maxim" of great use to those interested in the "science of good legislation relative to commerce," a phrase anticipating Adam Smith's definition of political economy. See *Éphémérides du citoyen* (Tome 7, 1768): 157.

[21] Gournay and his school, which originally included key figures in the history of commerce in France such as the abbé André Morellet and Anne-Robert-Jacques Turgot, are still often identified as precursors to the Physiocrats though his project differed substantially from theirs. On Gournay's aims and strategies see Sophus A. Reinert, *The Virtue of Emulation: International Competition and the Origins of Political Economy* (Cambridge, MA: Harvard University Press, 2011), especially 199–204; Antonella Alimento, "Entre animosité nationale et rivalité d'émulation: La position de Véron de Forbonnais face à la compétition anglaise," *GIM* (2009): 125–48; Simone Meyssonier, *La Balance et l'horloge: La genèse de la pensée libérale en France au XVIIIe Siècle* (Paris: Éditions de la Passion, 1989); and a forthcoming volume by Loïc Charles, Frédéric Lefebvre, David

These ideas had been percolating since the 1720s, when a trend towards rethinking the relationship of commerce to colonialism emerged in France following the spectacular crash of the *Système* set up by charismatic Scottish financier (and gambler) John Law (1671–1729).[22] Called in by the regent Philippe duc d'Orléans (1674–1723) to repair the kingdom's finances, Law issued paper money to pay off the kingdom's debts and sought to strengthen state-run monopoly companies founded on colonial trade (to which we will turn in Chapter 4) by issuing their stock on the market. When the bubble then burst, Law's scheme crashed in a wash of panic and fortunes lost overnight. Yet it was followed in 1728 by the passing of a law in the same spirit – known as the *Exclusif* – which dictated that state companies had exclusive control over the colonial trade.[23] Both Law's *Système* and the contentious *Exclusif* spurred writings about the connection between the polity and the economy which have also been characterised as "liberal"[24] – from Richard Cantillon's *Essai sur la nature du commerce en general* (written in 1730 and published in 1755) to Jean-François Melon's *Essai politique sur le commerce* (1734). Although scholars have recently sought to introduce new frameworks for understanding the origins of classical and neoclassical economics, the narrative which paints the easy transition from mercantilism to liberal and pacific economic theories has remained powerful.[25] Yet eighteenth-century

---

K. Smith, and Christine Théré, *Commerce, société et population autour de Vincent de Gournay* (forthcoming, 2012).

[22] The most comprehensive recent account of Law's life and theories is Antoin E. Murphy, *John Law: Economic Theorist and Policy-maker* (Oxford: Oxford University Press, 1997).

[23] The still authoritative account of the *Exclusif* is Jean Tarrade's two-volume *Le commerce colonial de la France à la fin de l'Ancien Régime: L'Évolution du régime de "l'Exclusif" de 1763 à 1789* (Paris: Presses universitaires de France, 1972). Cf. Paul Cheney's important reinterpretation of the debates over the *Exclusif* in *Revolutionary Commerce*.

[24] On Cantillon, see Antoin E. Murphy, *Richard Cantillon: Entrepreneur and Economist* (Oxford: Clarendon Press, 1987).

[25] As Peter Groenewegen has noted, the view that Physiocracy was a "landmark in the beginnings of the science of economics" is widely held by "authorities as diverse as McCulloch, Marx, Marshall, and Schumpeter." *Eighteenth Century Economics: Turgot, Beccaria and Smith and their Contemporaries* (London and New York: Routledge, 2002), 56. For alternative accounts, see Richard Whatmore, who has offered a compelling account of how the sense of decline that followed the Seven Years' War structured what would eventually become a republican discourse of political economy. See Richard Whatmore, *Republicanism and the French Revolution: An Intellectual History of Jean-Baptiste Say's Political Economy* (Oxford: Oxford University Press, 2000), especially chap. 2. Other approaches tending towards a more complex view of the origins of economics include *Reflections on the Classical Canon in Economics: Essays in Honor of Samuel Hollander* (Routledge, 2002), especially Samuel Hollander's own "'Classical economics': A reification wrapped in an anachronism?" 7–26.

approaches to the economy and to its political basis were more varied than what this dualist model quiets in its simplicity.

This book seeks to broaden our perspective on these early pronouncements on the connection between politics and the economy beyond this oppositional view. By adding French voices to the pioneering literature on the Anglophone origins of political economy and economics as disciplines, it proposes that their sources were more confused and contingent than generally portrayed.[26] Including works beyond the canon and not immediately identifiable as "political-economic" also encourages us to consider attitudes towards commerce as multiple.[27] We have forgotten that there was a cacophony to eighteenth-century writings about commerce – the contests, the range of preoccupations, and, most important, the imperial experience.[28] Building on the framework of Madeleine

---

[26] This study, and all studies of eighteenth-century ideas of commerce, is necessarily indebted to J. G. A. Pocock's influential arguments first developed in *The Machiavellian Moment: Florentine Political Thought and the Atlantic Republican Tradition* (Princeton: Princeton University Press, 1975), and articulated more fully in *Virtue, Commerce and History: Essays on Political Thought and History, Chiefly in the Eighteenth Century* (Cambridge: Cambridge University Press, 1985). Developing this approach further, with special attention to the Scottish Enlightenment, Istvan Hont and Michael Ignatieff, along with Nicholas Philipson, Knud Haakonssen, and John Robertson, to name but a few, related the ideal of commercial humanism to the prevalent theories of natural law and classical republicanism. While the circulation of ideas across the Channel was continuous, some distinctions, or "exceptions," do become apparent in the French engagement with commerce in the eighteenth century. Both Catherine Larrère and John Shovlin have, in turn, pointed to the overemphasis of the historiography of eighteenth-century France on the Physiocrats. Shovlin has also called for greater notice to be given to the "din of public debate on economic questions in eighteenth-century France." See Catherine Larrère, *L'Invention de l'économie au XVIIIe siècle: Du droit naturel à la physiocratie* (Paris: Presses universitaires de France, 1992), and John Shovlin, *The Political Economy of Virtue: Luxury, Patriotism, and the Origins of the French Revolution* (Ithaca, NY: Cornell University Press, 2006), 3. The authoritative accounts of early Physiocracy are still Elisabeth Fox-Genovese, *The Origins of Physiocracy: Economic Revolution and Social Order in Eighteenth-Century France* (Ithaca: Cornell University Press, 1976) and Steven L. Kaplan's *Bread, Politics, and Political Economy in the Reign of Louis XV*, 2 vols (The Hague: Martinus Nijhoff, 1976); for its legacy in the Revolution, see James Livesey, "Agrarian Ideology and Commercial Republicanism in the French Revolution," *Past & Present* 157 (1997): 94–121.

[27] Mary L. Bellhouse offers such a model in her study of Rousseau's *Rêveries d'un promeneur solitaire* and Montesquieu's *Le Temple de Gnide*, "Femininity & Commerce in the Eighteenth Century: Rousseau's Criticism of a Literary Ruse by Montesquieu," *Polity* 13, no. 2 (1980): 285–99. Erik Thomson offers another example with his approach to uncovering economic thinking in seventeenth-century France. See especially, "Commerce, Law, and Erudite Culture: The Mechanics of Théodore Godefroy's Service to Cardinal Richelieu," *Journal of the History of Ideas*, 68, no. 3 (2007): 409.

[28] Madeleine Dobie has recently provided a compelling way of understanding these varied models and ideologies as a comprehensive discourse of "colonial political economy."

Dobie and other scholars, this study seeks to open further discussion with approaches that have generally remained distinct from each other: the history of political thought, the history of economic thought, the history of empire, and the study of the European Enlightenments. It would be anachronistic not to do so, for in the eighteenth century these now distinct academic disciplines were recognised as mutually constitutive domains of inquiry. My engagement with them joins a growing chorus of voices contending that French imperial history cannot be considered a supplement to French national history but is rather a foundational, dialectical, and constitutive element of that history.[29]

DOUX COMMERCE RECONSIDERED

One tenacious phrase in particular still lies at the centre of much writing about eighteenth-century political and economic thought: *doux commerce*, taken to mean "sweet commerce" or "gentle commerce." For

Madeleine Dobie, *Trading Places: Colonization and Slavery in Eighteenth-Century French Culture* (Ithaca, NY: Cornell University Press, 2010), 206. This book only touches on the many insights provided by Dobie's work. Her model is essential to this study in many ways because of its historical emphasis on and integration of the crucial roles of slavery and imperialism. Yet we can also note that a parallel track has been opened by international political economists with the call for a new "cultural political economy" which necessarily links politics, economics, and culture in its analyses. See the pioneering work in this field by Jacqueline Best and Matthew Paterson, eds., *Cultural Political Economy* (London and New York: Routledge, 2010).

[29] I build on Jeremy Adelman's argument that histories of empire are "necessarily entwined" with histories of nationhood and thus offer a methodological and narrative prelude to Wilder's account of the interwar French imperial nation-state. See Jeremy Adelman, "An Age of Imperial Revolutions," *American Historical Review* 113, no. 2 (2008): 339, and Gary Wilder, *The French Imperial Nation-State: Negritude and Colonial Humanism between the Two World Wars* (Chicago: University of Chicago Press, 2005), 20. With most recent works in the imperial history of France, Wilder begins by affirming the current (albeit slowly crumbling) refusal in French historiography and political discourse to recognise the living and constitutive character of France's imperial system. Ann Stoler has referred to France's "colonial aphasia" in reference to this phenomenon in *Carnal Knowledge and Imperial Power: Race and the Intimate in Colonial Rule* (Berkeley: University of California Press, 2002), 14–15. Michel-Rolph Trouillot has accentuated the "silencing of the past" in the historiography of Haiti in particular; most recently, Madeleine Dobie has delved more deeply into the problem by uncovering the absence of representations of the colonial fact in eighteenth-century France. See Michel-Rolph Trouillot, *Silencing the Past: Power and the Production of History* (Boston: Beacon Press, 1995) and Dobie, *Trading Places*, respectively. Moving beyond the imperial focus, this inquiry also shares in Sophus Reinert's project to extricate a clearer image of eighteenth-century understandings of commerce from the still calcified assumptions about Enlightenment commitments to free trade. See Sophus A. Reinert, "Lessons on the Rise and Fall of Great Powers: Conquest, Commerce, and Decline in Enlightenment Italy," *American Historical Review* 115, no. 5 (2010): 1395–425.

academic and other commentators, this phrase is often used to summarize the celebration of commerce in the eighteenth century. Yet the story of *doux commerce* in France emerges as more complex when we pay attention to its historical specificity.[30]

In French, *commerce* (without the "sweet" modifier) has always carried a broad range of meanings. Its roots are Latin: *commercium* meaning "with *merx*" or "*mercis*," meaning merchandise or the object of trade.[31] By the sixteenth century, the term had undergone a semantic shift to encompass social relationships.[32] The *Trésor de la langue française*, still the authoritative historical and etymological dictionary of the French language, begins by defining *commerce* as a series of human transactions and communications ranging from the exchange of ideas to sexual intercourse.[33] All major French lexicons and dictionaries of the eighteenth century began with this same definition.[34]

Since the nineteenth century, however, the phrase *doux commerce* has been bundled into causal narratives explaining the origins of political economy and classical economics. Perhaps the most iconic instance of this phenomenon can be traced to Karl Marx's first volume of *Capital* in 1867. Marx drew on a cemented understanding of the term when

---

[30] To be sure, Laurence Dickey has offered the most comprehensive analysis of the *doux commerce* thesis and its various mobilisations in Hirschman and Pocock, yet the theorists to whom he refers are never specified beyond the canonical list of Smith, Hume, Constant, and Defoe. See Laurence Dickey, "Doux-Commerce and Humanitarian Values: Free Trade, Sociability and Universal Benevolence in Eighteenth-Century Thinking," *Grotiana* 22–23: 272–83.

[31] Eminent linguist Émile Benveniste has shown that only in Latin did a fixed and stable expression exist to convey commerce distinct from notions of buying or selling. The origins of this vocabulary are difficult to trace, but Benveniste suggests an origin in the Greek *askholía* ("occupations") and *prâgma* ("thing"). The Romans adapted and transformed these terms to suit their adaptations and transformations of the institutions associated with them, leading to *negotium*, and, eventually, *commercium*. The roots of *commerce* are, thus, properly Roman since, for every other Indo-European language, commerce was a "trade without a name." See chapter 11, "Un métier sans nom: le commerce," in *Le vocabulaire des institutions indo-européennes*, Vol. 1 (Paris: Les Éditions de minuit, 1969), 140–46.

[32] Oscar Bloch and Walther von Wartburg, *Dictionnaire étymologique* (Paris: PUF, 2008), 144.

[33] *Trésor de la langue française: Dictionnaire de la langue du XIXe et du XXe siècle (1789–1960)* (Paris: Éditions du Centre national de la recherche scientifique, 1977–80), 1118–19.

[34] Cf. the articles "commerce" in the *Encyclopédie* (written by Véron de Forbonnais); in Furetière's *Dictionnaire de Furetière* (1690); in Académie française, *Dictionnaire de l'Académie française* (1694); in the *Dictionnaire de Trévoux* (1743); and in Savary des Bruslons, *Dictionnaire universel de commerce* (1723, 1765).

he railed against the seventeenth-century Dutch colonial administration's "system of stealing men in Celebes in order to get slaves for Java," exclaiming famously, "*Das ist der doux commerce!*"[35] Notwithstanding Marx's synthetic and sarcastic deployment of the term *doux commerce*, the origins, meanings, and uses of the term remain relatively unexplored. Not until 1977 did Albert O. Hirschman use *doux commerce* to structure one of the most influential twentieth-century works in the history of political economy, *The Passions and the Interests: Political Arguments before Its Triumph*. Largely due to Hirschman's influence, the term *doux commerce* often serves as a shorthand means of associating the origins of economic thought in the eighteenth century with a triumphalist belief in progress facilitated by free trade; indeed, it would not be an exaggeration to suggest that Hirschman's work has been the primary vehicle for the transmission and ubiquity of this notion in current eighteenth-century scholarship and beyond.[36]

Yet the term *doux commerce* is not readily traceable in the eighteenth-century French texts concerned with political economy. To be sure, the meanings ascribed to the term by Hirschman were certainly manifest in works of the period. Yet, the tendency to rely on the term to summarize the period's ideology has obscured our understanding of the theory and experience of eighteenth-century commerce. By unsettling Hirschman's oft-cited formula, this study attempts to uncover the acute tension between the sweet and the bitter, the gentle and the violent forms of commerce that existed and were represented in eighteenth-century France. I suggest that this tension indicated an ambivalence towards commerce: an awareness of its limits, a consciousness of its underbelly, and

---

[35] Karl Marx, *Capital: A Critique of Political Economy* (1867). Vol. 1. Ben Fowkes, trans. (London: Penguin Classics, 1990), 916. Ben Fowkes renders this phrase as "That is peaceful commerce!" The passage in question is drawn from pt. 8, chap. 31.

[36] Hirschman's formulation has had a wide reach and strong influence, as the reissuing of a 1997 twentieth anniversary edition attests. According to Seth Ditchik, senior editor at Princeton University Press, "several tens of thousands" of copies of *The Passions and the Interests* have been sold, and the new 1997 edition of Hirschman's work has "sold over 10,000 copies and still sells pretty steadily." Seth Ditchik, e-mail message to author, 20 October 2010. Commonly assigned in undergraduate history, politics, and economics survey courses in the United States, see, among others, the reliance upon it is evident in works such as Charles Taylor's *Sources of the Self: The Making of the Modern Identity* (Cambridge, MA: Harvard University Press, 1989), 214. Recent works by reputable historians of economic thought have also absorbed the formula. To wit, Dierdre McCloskey's assertion that "Commerce, the French said, was a sweetener: le doux commerce." See *The Bourgeois Virtues: Ethics for an Age of Commerce* (Chicago: Chicago University Press, 2006), 30.

an acknowledgement of the ease with which its deviant forms manifested themselves while coexisting with gentler ones.

So where did the term *doux commerce* come from? One early usage appears in the sceptical philosopher Michel de Montaigne's *Essais* (Bordeaux, 1588), in which he referred to the "sweet and gentle exchange" that comes of interaction with "beautiful and honest women": "*C'est aussi pour moy un **doux commerce** que celuy des belles et honnestes femmes.*"[37] In this essay, "Of three [types of] commerce," Montaigne eventually reveals his disappointment with the "commerce" of women, as with the "commerce" of friends, which he deems "noble" but ultimately impossible. Only a third "commerce," that with books, is dependable, Montaigne concludes.[38] This early association of *douceur* and *commerce* to women and femininity has gone relatively unnoticed, as our conceptual sense of the term has been distanced from this gendered valence.[39] Just as meanings of *commerce* changed considerably over time, *doux* and its substantive, *douceur*, descended from a variety of sources.[40] Originating from the Latin *dulcis*, it implied sweet to the taste, soft to the touch, and gentle.[41] This sense persisted into the eighteenth century,

---

[37] "*C'est aussi pour moy un doux commerce que celuy des belles et honnestes femmes.*" "De trois commerces," book 3, chap. 3 in Michel Equyem de Montaigne, *Essais* (1588), Pierre Villey, ed. (Paris: Quadrige/Presses universitaires de France, 1988), 824. Villey drew on Montaigne's second edition (Bordeaux, 1588).

[38] In referring to "*commerce noble*," Montaigne may have been jesting, since the nobility had been forbidden to trade since the Middle Ages. On the shifting meanings of commerce in Montaigne's work, see Philippe Desan, *Les Commerces de Montaigne: le discours économique des Essais* (Paris: A.-G. Nizet, 1992).

[39] The gendered aspect of the *doux commerce* thesis warrants further analysis and interpretation, and I encourage much-needed attention to the workings of this connection between femininity and exchange. To be sure, J. G. A. Pocock first drew attention to the gendered dimension of discourses of commerce in his *Virtue, Commerce, and History* (Cambridge, 1985), 99, 253, but researchers have not yet taken up the charge. I hope to join others in doing so in a future project.

[40] On the various uses of *douceur* in the eighteenth century, see Daniel Gordon, *Citizens without Sovereignty: Equality and Sociability in French Thought, 1670–1789* (Princeton: Princeton University Press, 1994), especially 67, 116, 123–26. As Gordon shows, the baron d'Holbach, famous for both his *salon* and his atheistic writings, went so far as to re-define *douceur* as "a flexibility that is conducive to making us liked." That a "gentleman" could and should exhibit "*douceur*" in the period was indicative of a host of gender categories in transition. Helena Rosenblatt has argued that Rousseau "pushed" the concept of *douceur* "onto the political arena" in his *Second Discourse* (1755) by associating the term with "political virtues and economic independence," and thereby "reaffirm[ing]" a classical republican paradigm against an emerging commercial ethos." *Rousseau and Geneva: From the 'First Discourse' to the 'Social Contract', 1749–1762* (Cambridge: Cambridge University Press, 1997), 85.

[41] Bloch and von Wartburg, *Dictionnaire étymologique*, 203. *Dulcis* is itself connected to the Greek *glukus, glukeros*, meaning sweet (cf. glucose), and thus connotes those things agreeable

when the two terms were again combined to refer to the sweet and gentle exchange of ideas, *le doux commerce d'idées*.[42] These multiple meanings are key to understanding commerce in eighteenth-century France, though the term is today more familiar to us in its original Latin sense, where its use is confined to the world of merchants.

In Hirschman's account, "the first mention of this qualification of commerce" appeared in Jacques Savary's *Le parfait négociant* (Paris, 1675).[43] This immensely popular how-to book for merchants seeking "perfection" served as the basis for the *Dictionnaire universel de commerce*, the first dictionary of commerce written in France, first published in 1723 and later edited by Savary's grandsons. Through meticulous explanations and examples of the mechanics and practices of commercial exchange, the *Dictionnaire* sought to teach readers not only how to trade but also how to speak commerce, that is, how to use the vocabulary of commerce.[44] In other words, it offered merchants a guide to the very terms structuring the language of commerce and to the appropriate manner in which to use them.[45] By all accounts, they used it often.[46] One passage from Savary's

---

to the taste, not bitter, and, figuratively, suave or agreeable. See Alain Rey et al. *Dictionnaire historique de la langue française* (Paris: Dictionnaires Le Robert, 1998), 1: 629.

[42] For example, in Jean-François Marmontel's account of the debates and discussions in d'Holbach's *salon*, which he called the "*côterie holbachique*." "The côterie holbachique," wrote Marmontel, "found in itself the sweetest pleasures that liberty of thought and the commerce of minds (*doux commerce d'esprits*) can procure." Quoted in Alan Kors, *D'Holbach's Coterie: An Enlightenment in Paris* (Princeton, NJ: Princeton University Press, 1976), 97.

[43] A common eighteenth-century edition was *Le Parfait négociant, ou Instruction générale pour ce qui regarde le commerce des marchandises de France et des pays étrangers* (Paris, 1713). See Jean-Claude Perrot, "Les dictionnaires de commerce au XVIIIe siècle," *Revue d'Histoire moderne et contemporaine*, 28 (1981): 36–39.

[44] As William Reddy notes, Savary was a pioneer in the "heroic effort" to systematize practical information in the eighteenth century, one factor in the "emergence of a public sphere Western Europe." William Reddy, "The Structure of a Cultural Crisis: Thinking About Cloth in France Before and After the Revolution," in Arjun Appadurai, ed., *The Social Life of Things: Commodities in Cultural Perspective*, (New York: Cambridge University Press, 1986), 264–65.

[45] See, for example, the practical advice in Savary, *Dictionnaire universel de commerce*, s.v. "Interest," 431.

[46] William Reddy has also noted how, following its first publication in 1723, the work was "hawked about Europe, not just France," having been "reissued, pirated and translated at least six more times between 1741 and 1784," indicating that "it was used by real merchants in their day-to-day dealings." Ibid., 264. The *Dictionnaire* serves as an invaluable source for this book. Yet, to be sure, my subject is not merchants, but rather the political languages and discourses that framed their and others' understanding and very experience of commerce. The pioneering study of merchant culture in eighteenth-century France is Daniel Roche, "Négoce et culture dans la France au XVIIIe siècle," *Revue d'histoire moderne et contemporaine* 25 (1978): 375–95.

dictionary implies that trade was a result of divine Providence's dispersal of its "gifts." Not only did trade foster "ties of friendship" among men, but "this continuous exchange of all of the comforts of life constitutes commerce and this commerce makes for all of the douceur [sweetness, gentleness] of life."[47]

The centrepiece of Hirschman's *doux commerce* thesis was, however, a work of extraordinary influence on eighteenth-century Europe and America: *The Spirit of the Laws*, published in 1748 by Charles-Louis de Secondat, baron de Montesquieu (1689–1755).[48] Part 4 of *The Spirit of the Laws* is devoted to a study of commerce, its "spirit," and the laws, historical and contemporary, pertaining to it. "Commerce cures destructive prejudices," Montesquieu argues, "and it is an almost general rule that everywhere there are gentle mores [*moeurs douces*], there is commerce and that everywhere there is commerce, there are gentle mores."[49] Hirschman infers that Montesquieu's use of *douces* applies to commerce, meaning at once sweet to the taste, soft to the touch, and gentle. Yet what is clearly sweet, soft, or gentle in this sentence are *moeurs*, which I render as *mores* though the term is probably best understood as "shared public morality."[50] Commerce itself is not gentle; rather, Montesquieu argues, when commerce is present, mores tend to be gentle, and vice versa.

In fact, there is not much that is *doux* about Montesquieu's commerce in this passage. Here commerce is not an end in itself. Rather, it is an agent of change. But of greater interest is what follows. Montesquieu continues by observing, "Commerce corrupts pure mores," though,

[47] Savary, *Le Parfait négociant*, cited in Hirschman, *The Passions and the Interests: Political Arguments for Capitalism before Its Triumph.* 1977. 20th anniversary edition (Princeton, NJ: Princeton University Press, 1997), 59–60.

[48] Hirschman, *Passions and Interests* (1997), 61. The first English translation of *De l'Esprit des lois* (Geneva: Barillot, 1748), by Thomas Nugent, rendered the work's title as *The Spirit of Laws* (London: Nourse, 1750), without the second definite article.

[49] "Le commerce guérit des préjugés destructeurs: et c'est presque une règle générale que, partout où il y a des mœurs douces, il y a du commerce; et que, partout où il y a du commerce, il y a des mœurs douces." "Du commerce," pt. 4, chap. 1 in Montesquieu, *De l'Esprit des lois.*

[50] As Victor Gourevitch notes, *moeurs* is "notoriously difficult to translate." The term "manners" is unsatisfactory because it elides the moral content of the French *moeurs*. It can sometimes hold the connotation of "customs" or "ways," in keeping with its Latin root, *mores*, but these terms were often distinguished by eighteenth-century writers. See Victor Gourevitch, "Note on the translations" in Jean-Jacques Rousseau, *The Discourses and other Early Political Writings* (Cambridge: Cambridge University Press, 1997), xlv. I opt for the English "mores," with Anne M. Cohler, Basia Carolyn Miller, and Harold Samuel Stone, in their translation and edition of Montesquieu, *The Spirit of the Laws* (Cambridge: Cambridge University Press, 1989), 338.

as Plato complained, "it [also] polishes and softens uncivilised mores [*moeurs barbares*], as we see every day."[51] Thus Montesquieu's essay also acknowledges the deleterious effects of commerce. Yet in omitting Montesquieu's reference to the corrupting potential of commerce upon mores, Hirschman's text seems to have limited interpretations of Montesquieu's claim.[52]

So one might say that the discontents of *doux commerce* are double.[53] On one hand, the term has been and continues to be employed to explain the ideology of commerce in the eighteenth century (and beyond), though it does not fully reflect the ideological realities of that time.[54] On the other hand, the ideal type the term describes – the idea that commerce was a sweetening, pacifying, and moralising agent – itself clashed in theory and in practice with commerce's bitterest manifestations in the eighteenth century.[55]

---

[51] "Le commerce corrompt les mœurs pures (a); c'était le sujet des plaintes de Platon: il polit et adoucit les mœurs barbares, comme nous le voyons tous les jours." Montesquieu, *De l'Esprit des lois*, pt. 4, chap. 1.

[52] Recent works have also drawn attention to this neglected aspect of Montesquieu's idea of commerce. Daniel Gordon first commented on it in *Citizens without Sovereignty*, 131. See also Elena Russo's "Virtuous Economies," which uncovers the causes of Montesquieu's fears about the destructive potential of commerce. Sophus Reinert also affirms that, despite continued historiographical contentions to the contrary, "*The Spirit of the Laws* was exceedingly clear. Unless guided by policies, commerce could lead to conquests," *Virtue of Emulation*, 192. For Hirschman's omission, see *Passions and Interests* (1997), 60.

[53] My use of the term *discontents* intentionally evokes the term used in the English translations of Sigmund Freud's influential essay, "Civilization and Its Discontents" (1930). In many ways, Freud's essay can be read as a commentary on the discontents of commercial society, in addition to being a compelling analysis of the various effects of a "well-polished Society" upon individuals and consequently on the community. More recently, Joseph Stiglitz has also named an influential work on globalisation (eighteenth-century commerce's most recent incarnation) along the same lines – *Globalization and Its Discontents* – though Stiglitz's work focuses on the failings of the international institutions responsible for global economic policy and change to assist the poorest people and countries.

[54] In an elegant article, John Shovlin has also shown how jarring it can be to read eighteenth-century French texts in the light of Hirschman's conclusions. Shovlin's reading of Sieyès reveals, for example, that "honor" and not interest was the driving desire of those engaged in economic activity. See his "Emulation in Eighteenth-Century French Economic Thought." *Eighteenth-Century Studies* 36, no. 2 (2003): 224.

[55] In a later groundbreaking article, "Rival Interpretations," Hirschman began to address this possibility. Looking backwards through a Marxist lens, he offered a diagram of the various interactions between what he termed the "DC," or *doux commerce*, and the "SD," or self-destruction, theses of capitalist theory, concluding that in some instances these two interpretations coexisted. Yet Hirschman here considered mainly nineteenth-century texts.

Turning to sources that stretch beyond Montesquieu's much-studied text, this book brings to the fore the key role of ambivalence in eighteenth-century French thought about commerce.[56] Ambivalence is a category that I draw loosely from psychoanalytic theory; it connotes the simultaneous love and hatred of the same object or phenomenon.[57] It is a term quite different from but often confused with ambiguity, which implies, simply, vagueness. Ambivalence has certainly been employed as a category of analysis by scholars as various as Homi Bhabha and Daniel Gordon to describe eighteenth-century views of colonialism and commercial society, respectively.[58] In what follows, I hope to show how prevalent this attitude was in a discourse that has, until now, been portrayed as unanimously triumphant. I do not attempt to resolve the ambivalence detected in the sources, but rather I consider their seemingly contradictory elements part of a single discourse: the discourse of commerce in eighteenth-century France.

THE *HISTOIRE DES DEUX INDES*

These contradictory aspects of commerce were evident to a cast of characters that includes Denis Diderot, the abbé Guillaume-Thomas Raynal (1713–96), and their anonymous – if hardly secret – collaborators on the bestselling *Philosophical and political history of the commerce and settlements of the Europeans in the two Indies (Histoire philosophique et politique du commerce et des établissements des européens dans les deux*

---

[56] To be sure, Daniel Gordon and the contributors to the special issue, "Postmodernism and the French Enlightenment," for *Historical Reflections/Réflexions historiques.* (1999) 25, no. 2, 180, have highlighted that "the *philosophes* were the first to make such tensions the continuous theme of their work and the essays in this volume display a fascination with the topic of ambivalence." Anthony Strugnell early on pointed to the ambivalence towards the theoretical and practical bases of commerce in eighteenth-century France. See "Matérialisme, histoire et commerce: Diderot entre le réel et l'idéal dans l' *Histoire des deux Indes,*" in Béatrice Fink and Gerhardt Stenger, eds., *Etre matérialiste à l'âge des Lumières: Hommage offert à Roland Desné.* (Paris: PUF, 1999), 296–97.

[57] The term was first introduced by Swiss psychiatrist Eugen Bleuler (1857–1939) in 1910 to describe the dominant symptom of schizophrenia. It was later adopted by Freud in *Totem and Taboo* (1912–13). In both instances, the category implied the "simultaneous presence of conflicting feelings and tendencies with respect to an object." Victor Souffir, "Ambivalence" in Alain de Mijolla, ed., *International Dictionary of Psychoanalysis* (Detroit: Thomson Gale, 2005), 56.

[58] Cf. Homi Bhabha, "Of Mimicry and Man: The Ambivalence of Colonial Discourse" *October* 28 (1984): 125–33, and Daniel Gordon, ed., *Postmodernism and the Enlightenment: New Perspectives in Eighteenth-Century French Intellectual History* (London: Routledge, 2000), 68, 209.

Indes), known to scholars as the *Histoire des deux Indes*.[59] In delving more deeply into Hirschman's genealogy of the "doctrine of *doux commerce*," we uncover the contested and contradictory ideas of commerce held by the expansive network of intellectuals and politicians involved in the composition and edition of the *Histoire des deux Indes*. In doing so, we open ourselves to the possibility of an alternative to the prevalent perspective that late-eighteenth-century economic and political thinking converged on a consensus about the emergence of liberalism.[60]

One site dominated the assembly and dispersal of ideas about the European imperial experience, the future of Europe, and the ideas of commerce in eighteenth-century France: the *Histoire des deux Indes*. This may seem like a hyperbolic claim, yet it is difficult to overemphasise the *Histoire*'s reach and influence. Born of a defeat, the *Histoire des deux Indes* is now widely recognised as an, if not *the*, influential cultural and political product of the Seven Years War. It serves, therefore, as the pivot for my analysis and arguments in this book.

From its first printing in 1770,[61] this first "philosophical and political" history of Europe's colonial experience immediately became one of eighteenth-century France's bestsellers.[62] The *Histoire des deux Indes*

[59] I will henceforth refer to this work as the *Histoire des deux Indes* or the *Histoire* in the text, and the *HDI* in the notes.

[60] See Dickey, "*Doux-Commerce* and the 'Mediocrity of Money' in the Ideological Context of the Wealth and Virtue Problem," *An Inquiry into the Nature and Causes of the Wealth of Nations*, by Adam Smith, abridged with commentary by Laurence Dickey (Indianapolis: Hackett, 1993), 245.

[61] The first version of the *HDI* (Amsterdam, 1770) appeared in 1772 and comprised seven volumes in-8°. The second version of 1774 was augmented slightly, but the greatest changes occurred to the third version, which increased to ten volumes in-8° by 1780. A fourth, posthumous edition appeared in 1821, collated and annotated by academician and journalist Antoine Jay (1770–1854) and journalist and administrator Jacques Peuchet (1758–1830). In its final form, the work was divided geographically into nineteen books – each subdivided into numerous chapters – and included an atlas and a comprehensive index. The 1780 version is considered the most complete and forms the basis of the Centre international d'étude du XVIIIe siècle's new critical edition. The first of this new critical edition's five volumes, as well as a volume of maps and charts, appeared in 2010. I draw on this third version in what follows. In using the term *version* here I follow the principles of the first modern critical edition of the work, under the direction of Anthony Strugnell, which distinguishes between four main versions of the text, of which there were several editions. See Cecil P. Courtney et al., "Bibliographie sommaire des éditions de l'Histoire des deux Indes," in Guillaume-Thomas Raynal, *Histoire philosophique et politique du commerce et des établissements des européens dans les deux Indes* (Ferney-Voltaire: Centre international d'étude du XVIIIe siècle, 2010), liii–lxxx.

[62] Robert Darnton calculated early on that the *Histoire* ranked fifth among the "forbidden" bestselling works of eighteenth-century France. See *The Forbidden Best-Sellers of Pre-Revolutionary France* (New York: W.W. Norton & Company, 1996), 63.

went through at least forty-eight editions between 1770 and 1795; it sold more copies than Adam Smith's influential *Wealth of Nations* eight times over.[63] Yet its popularity was not confined to France. Within a decade of its first printing, it was translated into English, German, Russian, Italian, Spanish, Danish, Dutch, Swedish, Hungarian, and Polish.[64] The *Histoire's* outstanding international publishing success is all the more remarkable given its length: At its most complete, the work comprised ten volumes, in octavo, and was divided into nineteen discrete "books" – more than twenty-five hundred pages of text!

Vast in scope and dense with details, the work set out to offer a comprehensive comparative historical explanation of the European imperial projects, especially the European settlements and trade in what it specified as the *two* Indies, East and West. Beginning with the travels and conquests of the Portuguese in East India and ending with the formation of the British colonies in America, the *Histoire des deux Indes* also offered readers accounts of the worlds and civilisations beyond Europe, and, crucially, an assessment of the Europeans' impact upon them. Though it sought to make its arguments by way of a historical idiom, the work was nevertheless encyclopaedic in nature; indeed, its authors deliberately sought to produce a sister volume to the *Encyclopédie* which drew attention to the connections between Europe, the East, and the West.[65] This was the first time that any work of history had privileged this relationship,

---

[63] This is not to mention the number of extracts and other abbreviated versions which appeared in pamphlets and various collections. On the work's several editions see Gilles Bancarel, "La bibliographie matérielle et l'Histoire des deux Indes," *L'Histoire des deux Indes: Réécriture et polygraphie*, Hans-Jürgen Lüsebrink and Manfred Tietz, eds. (Oxford: Voltaire Foundation, 1995), 44–45. On the *HDI*'s numerous extracts and their significance, see Hans-Jürgen Lüsebrink, "*L'Histoire des deux Indes* et ses *Extraits*: un mode de dispersion textuelle au XVIIIe siècle," *Littérature* 69 (1988), 28–41. Smith's *Wealth of Nations* was first published on 9 March 1776 and ran to six editions in 1791. R. H. Campbell and A. S. Skinner, eds., Introduction to *The Glasgow Edition of the Works and Correspondence of Adam Smith* (Oxford: Clarendon Press, 1976), 61–64.

[64] The greatest number of translations were in the English language, followed by German, Russian, and Italian. On these, and the circulation of the text in the United States and South America – especially Brasil, Mexico, and Venezuela – see Hans-Jürgen Lüsebrink, "Introduction générale," Guillaume-Thomas Raynal, *Histoire philosophique et politique des établissements et du commerce des Européens dans les deux Indes* (Ferney-Voltaire: Centre international d'étude du XVIIIe siècle, 2010), xlix.

[65] For comparisons between the *Histoire des deux Indes* and the *Encyclopédie*, see Yves Benot, *Diderot, De l'athéisme à l'anticolonialisme* (Paris: François Maspéro, 1981); Srinivas Aravamudan, "Trop(icaliz)ing the Enlightenment," *Diacritics* 23, no. 3 (1993): 51–52; and Michel Delon, "L'appel au lecteur dans l'Histoire des deux Indes," in Hans-Jürgen Lüsebrink and Anthony Strugnell, eds., *L'Histoire des deux Indes: Réécriture et polygraphie*, (Oxford: Voltaire Foundation, 1995), 53–67.

and for this reason, one is tempted to call the *Histoire des deux Indes* the first history of globalisation.

The work was not an endorsement of French or European imperial expansion, however. Quite the contrary: The *Histoire des deux Indes* more often than not recounted the failings of empires – information that threatened the French *ancien régime*. As a result, the Royal Council suppressed it in 1772; it was placed on the Index in 1774, and next formally condemned by the Parlement of Paris to be "whipped and burned in the Palace Square."[66] Adding to its notoriety, the *Histoire* was censored again by the theology faculty of the University of Paris in 1781.[67] Finally, on 25 May 1781, the Parlement of Paris decreed that the declared "author," the abbé Raynal, be "bodily apprehended" and his "goods be seized and sequestered."[68] If these bans had any impact on the reading public it was

[66] The practice of whipping and burning ("*lacérer et brûler*") books at the base of the grand staircase of the Parisian "Palace of Justice" was reserved for a select 19 of the more than 700 books condemned between 1770 and 1789. As Robert Darnton notes, authorities recognised (and feared) the publicity that this type of *autodafé* would create. Cf. *Édition et sédition*, 13.

[67] The *HDI* was the book "most frequently confiscated in the Paris Customs" (at 45 confiscations, followed by Voltaire's *Oeuvres* at 41, Rousseau's *Émile* at 12, tied with the sexually explicit *Thérèse philosophe* at 12, and d'Holbach's atheist *Système de la nature* at 8) from January 1711 to September 1789. See Robert Darnton, *The Corpus of Clandestine Literature in France, 1769–1789* (New York and London: W.W. Norton & Company, 1995), 258–59. The first censure placed on the *HDI* was by the King's State Council, which issued the *Arrest du Conseil d'état du roi, qui supprime un imprimé ayant pour titre: Histoire philosophique & politique des etablissemens & du commerce des Européens dans les deux Indes [par G.T. Raynal]. Du 19 décembre 1772. Extrait des registres du Conseil d'État* (Paris: Chez P.G. Simon, imprimeur du Parlement, 1773). The order for the *HDI* to be "*lacéré et brûlé*" is found in the *Arrest de la Cour de Parlement, qui condamne un imprimé, en dix vol. in-8, ayant pour titre, Histoire philosophique ... à être lacéré et brûlé par l'exécuteur de la Haute-Justice* (Paris, 25 May 1781). Finally, the University of Paris singled out eighty-four heretical propositions in its *Determinatio sacrae facultatis Parisiensis in librum cui titulus, Histoire philosophique et politique des établissemens et du commerce des européens dans les deux Indes par Guillaume-Thomas Raynal, A Geneve, chez Jean-Léonard Pellet, Imprimeur de la Ville & de l'Académie, 1780* (Paris, 1781). To place the academic censure of the *HDI* in perspective, we might here recall that nineteen propositions extracted from the 1750 edition of Montesquieu's *De l'Esprit des Lois* had also been censured by the Sorbonne in 1754. See Victor Goldschmidt, ed., *De l'Esprit des Lois* (Paris: Garnier-Flammarion, 1979), 8. It is also relevant to note that in the so-called liberal years of the Old Regime (1770–89), on average only four to five books were banned per year. See Robert Darnton, *Édition et sédition: L'univers de la littérature clandestine au XVIIIe siècle* (Paris: Gallimard, 1991), 13.

[68] Quoted in Kors, *Holbach's Coterie*, 228–29. Raynal was in fact allowed to plan for a rather pleasant exile from France, where he was celebrated in cities across Europe. He was allowed to return in 1784, though he was forbidden entry into Paris. Ibid.

to increase the *Histoire*'s notoriety and interest. A joke running through Paris held that Raynal must have orchestrated them, since they served to increase the already strong demand for the work.[69]

Much of the initial scholarly attention to the *Histoire des deux Indes* focused on its reception as well as on the work's authorship, demonstrating that most of the *Histoire des deux Indes* was not actually penned by Raynal.[70] A renegade Jesuit and former journalist, and later a royal correspondent and notoriously assiduous *philosophe* of the Parisian *salons*, Raynal spent twenty years of his life working on the *Histoire* in a capacity that would today be called editorial.[71] Although he contributed some writing to the enterprise and told readers, "I devoted my life to it," the finished product actually consisted of a collage of contributions by several of Raynal's contemporaries.[72] Complete sections were also borrowed from travel writings, official government correspondence and documents, and other published works.[73]

---

[69] Certainly, demand for the new editions of the work (arriving clandestinely from abroad) soared immediately after the Parlement's burning of the *HDI*. The bookseller "Esprit," for example, sold 400 copies of the in-octavo edition in ten days, for the "crazy price" of seventy-five livres. See Darnton, *Édition et sédition*, 46. Denis Diderot famously kidded: "How often would the bookseller and author of a privileged work, if they had dared, have said to the magistrates: 'Sirs, by grace, a little arrest to condemn me to be whipped and burned at the base of your grand staircase?' When a book's sentence is cried out, workers at the printer's say: 'Good, another edition!'" In *Lettre adressée à un magistrat sur le commerce de la librairie*, quoted in Darnton, *Édition et sédition*, 13.

[70] See the papers in Lüsebrink and Tietz, *Lectures de Raynal*, and Lüsebrink and Strugnell, *Histoire des deux Indes*, which opened a new phase of scholarship on the *HDI* following the still fundamental quartet of studies by Anatole Feugère (1922), Hans Wolpe (1956), Yves Benot (1970), and Michèle Duchet (1971, 1978).

[71] Raynal never called himself "*éditeur*," however. We have a remarkably limited sense of Raynal's persona and private life. For what is still the most comprehensive biography of Raynal, see Anatole Feugère, *Un précurseur de la Révolution: L'Abbé Raynal (1713–1796)* (Angoulême: Impr, ouvrière, 1922). Drawing on Feugère, Alan Kors brought Raynal and his world to life in *D'Holbach's Coterie*, especially 21–22, 160–63, and 179–85. As both a servant of the absolute monarchy and a member of the Republic of Letters, the critical movement which opposed it, Raynal belonged to an influential demographic in eighteenth-century France, where these apparently contradictory roles were quite common. See Paul Cheney, *Revolutionary Commerce*, 28–34. Cf. Norbert Elias's, *The Court Society* (1969, and 1983 in English), where he famously argued that a "civilizing process" managed by the absolute monarchy in effect subordinated elite figures and French men of letters, while allowing them to see themselves as polished superiors. Daniel Gordon offered an important revision of this thesis when he established that French authors, like Raynal, in fact carved out a "unique ideological space that was neither absolutist nor democratic." Daniel Gordon, *Citizens without Sovereignty*, 4.

[72] For Raynal's claim, see *HDI* (1780), book 1, intro, 2.

[73] See Anatole Feugère, "Raynal, Diderot et quelques autres historiens des deux Indes." *Revue d'Histoire Littéraire de la France* 20 (1913): 345.

The list of contributors – all of them anonymous – reads like a catalogue of eighteenth-century France's most famous *philosophes*: Alexandre Deleyre, Jean-Joseph Pechméja, Paul-Henry Thiry baron d'Holbach, Jean-FranÇois de Saint-Lambert, Joseph-Louis Lagrange, and, most famous, Denis Diderot, one of the principal authors of the *Histoire*'s third and most complete version, published in 1780.[74] Remembered as a dramatist, novelist, and art critic, and accepted by some as a philosopher, Diderot is perhaps most renowned as the co-editor of the work commonly referred to as the Enlightenment's *magnum opus*, the *Encyclopédie*.[75] Less known is that Diderot was also an impassioned political and economic theorist. The oversight is not surprising. The acknowledged polysemy, dissonance, multiplicity, and ambiguity of his writings have often led to his dismissal by historians of political and economic thought.[76] But Diderot's contradictions were not confusions; they were thoughtful elements of his particular epistemology and a central feature of his political project.[77]

One effect of the collage of contributions which made up the *Histoire*'s sometimes patchy narrative is that the reader encounters varying points of view throughout the work. In the light of this effect, historian Michèle Duchet called the *Histoire* "polyphonous," and one is tempted to agree that the work is more a "tissue of statements" than a unitary and coherent

[74] See Feugère, *Un précurseur de la Révolution*, 177, and Michèle Duchet, *Anthropologie et histoire au siècle des lumières: Buffon, Voltaire, Rousseau, Helvétius, Diderot* (Paris: Bibliothèque de L'Évolution de l'Humanité, 1971. Reprint. Paris: Albin Michel, 1995), 126.

[75] On Diderot's status as a philosopher, then and now, see Michel Delon's "Préface" to Denis Diderot, *Oeuvres philosophiques* (Paris: Gallimard, 2010), ix–xii.

[76] Notable exceptions are the Cambridge Texts in the History of Political Thought series, which published an edition of Diderot's *Political Writings* in 1992, edited by John Hope Mason and the late Robert Wokler, followed by Anthony Pagden's seminal *European Encounters with the New World* (New Haven, 1993). A decade later, political theorist Sankar Muthu engaged with Diderot's work in his *Enlightenment against Empire*. I share in their aim to bring to light Diderot's political and economic thought both within the *Histoire* and in texts written contemporaneously with it so as to restore Diderot's place in our understanding of eighteenth-century imperialism and commerce. Equally central to this historiographical vein are the works of Srinivas Aravamudan and Sunil Agnani.

[77] Wilda Anderson articulates this point in *Diderot's Dream*. Indeed, Diderot's contributions to the *Histoire* might be considered the paradigmatic example of what critics following Jean Starobinski have construed as his tendency to "transfer" his speech and arguments to others. See Jean Starobinski, "Diderot et la parole des autres," *Critique* 296 (1972): 10–11. On Diderot's "astonishing usage of intertextuality," and the "heteroclite treasure of the Diderotian spirit," see Barbara de Negroni, "Diderot et le bien d'autrui," in Michel Delon and Barbara de Negroni, eds., *Oeuvres philosophiques* (Paris: Gallimard, 2010), xxvii.

text.[78] Yet, as the following chapters elucidate, the endeavour did cohere in at least one important way: Amid the multiple positions it articulated, the *Histoire* mobilised powerful rhetorical strategies to project agency upon its readers and to awaken them to action. As Sylvana Tomaselli has shown, the work sought to "transform the transformers," comprising a distinctly French historical project.[79] In this way, the work clearly inscribed itself into the multidimensional mission of those who often referred to themselves as members of the "Republic of Letters," but who are now understood as protagonists in the Enlightenment.[80] Considering the *Histoire* as more than an eighteenth-century history but as a work belonging to the "enlightenment disposition," we can underline how filled with debates and contradictions that period and process were.[81] Attention to the causes and effects of the *Histoire*'s polyphony has, however, meant that, until recently, scholarly commentaries have underemphasised this latent theory of historical agency, as well as one of the *Histoire*'s central preoccupations: Let us not forget that, despite its innovative approach, the *Histoire* was, above all, a history of commerce.

---

[78] Michèle Duchet, "*L'Histoire des deux Indes*: Sources et structure d'un texte polyphonique," in Hans-Jürgen Lüsebrink and Manfred Tietz, eds., *Lectures de Raynal* (Oxford: Voltaire Foundation, 1991), 9–15, and Duchet, *Anthropologie et histoire*, 170–73. Hans-Jurgen Lüsebrink and Anthony Strugnell note the work's "kaleidoscope of registers" in their introduction to *Histoire des deux Indes*, 7. On the historian's choice to consider a document a "tissue of statements, organized by its writer into a single document, but accessible and intelligible whether or not they have been harmonized into a single structure of meaning," see J. G. A. Pocock, "The Political Economy of Burke's Analysis of the French Revolution," in *Virtue, Commerce, and History: Essays on Political Thought and History, Chiefly in the Eighteenth Century* (Cambridge: Cambridge University Press, 1985), 193.

[79] Sylvana Tomaselli, "On labelling Raynal's *Histoire*: Reflections on its Genre and Subject," (paper presented at "Raynal's 'Histoire des deux Indes': Colonial Writing, Cultural Exchange and Social Networks in the Age of the Enlightenment," Cambridge, 1–3 July 2010), forthcoming in conference proceedings. See also Gianluigi Goggi, "*L'Histoire des deux Indes* et l'éloquence politique," *SVEC* 7 (2003): 123–61.

[80] Contemporaries referred to themselves as members of the "*République des lettres*." For the history of the term, see Françoise Waquet, "Qu'est-ce que la République des Lettres? Essai de sémantique historique," *Bibliothèque de l'École des Chartes* 147 (1989): 473–502.

[81] The term and concept "enlightenment disposition" is Emma Rothschild's. See *Economic Sentiments: Adam Smith, Condorcet and the Enlightenment* (Cambridge, MA: Harvard University Press, 2001), 16. This interpretation of the Enlightenment as a space of contest and not uniformity also aligns with Mark Hulliung's *The Autocritique of the Enlightenment* (Cambridge, MA: Harvard University Press, 1998), and David W. Bates, *Enlightenment Aberrations: Error and Revolution in France* (Cambridge: Cambridge University Press, 2002).

THE *HISTOIRE*'S COMMERCE

"[C]louds will be dispelled in all parts; a serene sky will shine over the face of the whole globe … then, or never, will that universal peace arise … [and] the general happiness of men will be established upon a more solid basis."[82] This giddy "hymn to commerce" from the *Histoire*'s book 19 trumpets commerce as the agent of a potentially formidable change leading to universal happiness, peace, and sunshine.[83] At first glance, it appears that the authors of the *Histoire* cast sweet and gentle commerce as an antidote to the ills of colonialism and empire. But if we read past this and other such "hymns" in the work, we find equally impassioned narratives of the terrible potential and actual odiousness of commerce, little different from Douin's ode, woven alongside the triumphalist thread. These instances of odiousness, also qualified on occasion as "vile," pointed to the limits and the obstacles to good commerce. In particular, the text of the *Histoire* suggested three foci for understanding the underbelly of commerce: slavery, piracy, and monopoly. *Commerce and Its Discontents* is structured around this triad of limits and obstacles. And although the *Histoire* informed my choice of these points of deviation, I analyse and refract its messages through a wide range of sources, including poems, pamphlets, memoranda written for the Colonial Office, juridical treatises, and dictionaries.

THE POLITICS OF DEFINITION

Dictionaries are an important source for this book, not only because they were such an epi-phenomenon in eighteenth-century France that the renowned editor of the *Correspondance littéraire* joked about their proliferation: "the furore for dictionaries is so great among us that a *Dictionary of dictionaries* has just been printed."[84] But at a time when the "enlightenment disposition" prevailed upon a new mode of thinking about the relationship between a set of freshly-constituted categories, such as "the people" and "society," the proliferation of dictionaries also points to a politics of definition at work. First and foremost were the contestations over the very power to define key terms and the legitimacy

---

[82] *HDI* (1780), book 19, 374.

[83] Recall that the term is Yves Benot's. See "Diderot, Pechméja, Raynal," 147.

[84] This was Friedrich Melchior Grimm writing in his *Corresponance littéraire* in 1758. Cited in Gerhardt Stenger, "Introduction" to Voltaire, *Dictionnaire philosophique* (1764) (Paris: Flammarion, 2010), 8.

of other definitional projects. Indeed, most ideological power struggles in the period translated into struggles over definition. To focus on definition differs subtly from a focus on meaning. It emphasises the actors or agents engaged in defining terms over those who receive or interpret them. The eighteenth-century struggles over the definitions of terms were also inextricably linked to the project of Enlightenment. In this era when traditional norms and practices were hotly debated, there also emerged an impulse to conceive the individual and the collective human space as independent from previous *Leviathans*, or absolute powers, be they religious or secular, the church or the monarchy. So too, older categories were subject to re-evaluation and re-definition. Commerce was one such category. The revival of definitions of, and connections between, the political space and the "oeconomy" was, as we shall see, a central stage upon which the politics of definition played out.

I open the discussion of eighteenth-century commerce by considering the animated conversation about luxury in eighteenth-century France, the so-called *querelle du luxe*, for luxury was both a cause and a symptom of a growing awareness of the ubiquity and permanence of commerce. Indeed, the way people spoke and wrote about luxury tended to mirror the way they understood commerce. So the quarrel about luxury provided a conceptual training ground for the ways in which commerce was and would be represented. As a first step, writers tussled over the term's definition, ushering in the list of notions related to commerce that would become subject to the politics of definition. Through the passages in the *Histoire* dealing with luxury and Diderot's essays on the topic, we are introduced to the possibility that the discourse of commerce was ambivalent, that it was possible and intelligible to both love and hate luxury and, concomitantly, commerce and still remain within a coherent discourse. Attitudes towards luxury provide a means of understanding the shape, character, and stakes of representations of commerce; at the same time, they introduce the dialectic between the *doux* and *odieux* effects of commerce.

We begin our exploration of the collapse of the triumphalist doctrine espousing the sweet effects of commerce in Chapter 2 by focusing on the form of commerce that the *Histoire des deux Indes* famously publicized as intolerable: the "commerce of man." This analysis uncovers how the *Histoire*'s iconoclastic critique of the slave trade drew on a discourse of political slavery that implored the French to reject despotism and recognise the trade in African slaves as a species of odious commerce. In a gesture worthy of current calls for more material histories, the *Histoire* confronted the discursive and abstract uses of slavery with the practice of selling humans for profit. Here, as we shall see, rhetoric was put to an innovative and devastating challenge by experience.

Chapter 3 examines how piracy and its agents also represented a form of transgressive and odious commerce. The epithet *odieux*, in contrast with *doux*, emerged directly from the eighteenth-century vocabularies contending with piracy. The *Histoire*'s critique of the hypocrisy inherent in the supporters of the imperial system emerges here. Specifically, the imperial powers are accused of intentionally renaming their actions to avoid the sanction they enforce on others. The tendency to obfuscate definitions of piracy as a means of controlling the international trading system was, in effect, a further tactic in the politics of definition.

Another feature of critiques of both the slave trade and piracy as modes of commerce was their explicit antagonism to what are referred to as "monopolistic agents," be they the companies fuelling the slave trade or those punishing pirates while themselves engaging in piracy. The fourth and final chapter of this volume examines the explicit link different sources drew between domestic and international monopoly. But the problems with this odious form of commerce were not solely related to international trade: They were also understood to pervert the internal governance of France. The stakes and boundaries of the sweetness or odiousness of commerce lay in their power to promote or to pollute French national identity and success.

It was through the public conversation about luxury that these stakes first came to the fore, as the following chapter aims to explain.

I

Bon luxe, mauvais luxe

A Language of Commerce

Writing eight years after France had signed over most of its colonies to Britain in the Treaty of Paris, a London-based cosmopolitan well known in Paris *salons* declared that commerce had become the "craze of the century."[1] A key context for this assertion by Isaac de Pinto (1717–87) was the substantial influx of goods from the European colonies, colonies spanning from the East Indies to the West Indies, as the full title of the *Histoire du commerce ... des européens dans les deux Indes* reminded its readers.[2] With colonial "sugar, silk, tobacco, and coffee" came dramatic

---

[1] "Le commerce [est] la marotte du siècle." Isaac de Pinto, "Lettre sur la jalousie du commerce, où l'on prouve, que l'intérêt des Puissances commerçants ne se croise point, mais qu'elles on un intérêt commun à leur bonheur réciproque & à la conservation de la paix" in *Traité de la circulation et du crédit, contenant une 'Analyse raisonnée des Fonds d'Angleterre', & ce qu'on appelle Commerce ou Jeu d'Actions; un Examen critique de plusieurs Traités sur les Impôts, les Finances, l'Agriculture, la Population, le Commerce &c. précédé de l'Extrait, d'un Ouvrage intitulé 'Bilan général & raisonné de l'Angleterre depuis 1600 jusqu'en 1761'; & suivi d'une 'Lettre sur la Jalousie du Commerce', où l'on prouve que l'intérêt des Puissances commerçantes ne se croise point, &c. avec un Tableau de ce qu'on appelle 'Commerce', ou plutôt, 'Jeu d'Actions' en Hollande* (Amsterdam: Chez Marc Michel Rey, 1771), 234. Usually designating a wooden puppet's head (short for *marionette*), since the seventeenth century *marotte* has had the figurative connotation of an *idée fixe* and a mania in the French language. See Alain Rey and Josette Rey-Debove, *Le Nouveau Petit Robert, s.v. marotte* (Paris: Dictionnaires Le Robert, 1994), 1157. I have opted for the translation *craze*. A craze is at once a "crack, a breach, a flaw" and, more germane to this term of de Pinto's, "an insane fancy, a mania, a crazy condition," or a "temporary enthusiasm." *Shorter Oxford English Dictionary on Historical Principles.* 5th ed. (Oxford: Oxford University Press, 2002), 549.

[2] One symptom of this expansion was the proliferation of writings on commerce, many of which were self-identified as political-economic. See John Shovlin, "Nobility and Economy," in *The Political Economy of Virtue* (Ithaca, NY: Cornell University Press, 2006), 2. Shovlin cites Jean-Claude Perrot, *Une histoire intellectuelle de l'économie*

changes in consumption patterns, behaviour, and social norms generated by France's expanding commercial society.[3]

The influx of goods had not gone unnoticed prior to de Pinto's pronouncement in 1771. Indeed, before commerce reached the status of a craze, eighteenth-century French writers were confronting it by another means: showering attention on the manifestation of what they called *luxe*, or luxury, a related phenomenon that seemed to most observers to be occurring on an unprecedented scale. As one of the most immediate and obvious symptoms of an apparently new commercial society teeming with colonial goods, luxury captured both the imagination and the ire of many writers across a wide spectrum of professional and personal backgrounds. The flurry of printed attention to luxury can be traced to early in the century, when the power of the colonial commercial system began to make its imprint on the everyday lives of French subjects.[4] Moreover, the royal court's move to Paris under the regency of Philippe d'Orléans (1713–15) also augured an "inflationist whirlwind" of demand for luxury goods among Parisians.[5] Finally, the spectacular rise, then fall, in fortunes following John Law's *Système* compounded this interest in the repercussions of extravagant consumption.

politique, XVIIe – XVIIIe siècle (Paris: Éditions de l'École des Hautes Études en Sciences Sociales, 1992), 75, but accurately notes that the authors' own identification of their texts as political-economic does not a data set make. Christine Théré, on the other hand, draws a more comprehensive list in "Economic Publishing and Authors, 1566–1789," in Gilbert Faccarello, ed., *Studies in the History of French Political Economy: From Bodin to Walras* (London: Routledge, 1998), 1–56.

[3] This list of goods is from Jean-Baptiste Melon's *Essai politique sur le commerce* (Paris, 1734), 124. The massive increase in eighteenth-century French consumption of luxury goods has been studied most recently by Michael Kwass in "Consumption and the World of Ideas: Consumer Revolution and the Moral Economy of the Marquis de Mirabeau," in *Eighteenth-Century Studies* 37, no. 2 (2004): 187–213. Cf. Annick Pardailhé-Galabrun, *La Naissance de l'intime: 3000 foyers parisiens, XVIIe-XVIIIe siècles* (Paris: Presses universitaires de France, 1988); Daniel Roche, *La Culture des apparences: Une Histoire du vêtement, XVIIe–XVIIIe siècle* (Paris, 1989); Cissie Fairchilds, "The Production and Marketing of Populuxe Goods in Eighteenth-Century Paris" in John Brewer and Roy Porter, eds., *Consumption and the World of Goods* (London and New York: Routledge, 1993), 228–48.

[4] By 1780, a million jobs may have resulted from the colonial enterprise. Laurent Dubois, *Avengers of the New World: The Story of the Haitian Revolution* (Cambridge: Harvard University Press, 2004), 21.

[5] Dominique Margairaz, "Luxe" in Michel Delon, ed., *Dictonnaire européen des lumières* (Paris: Presses universitaires de France, 1997), 662–63. Margairaz argues that a second phase consisted of displacement of luxury from the sphere of representation to the sphere of well-being, from *faste* (essentially pomp or ornamentation) to comfort, as the title of another important work on the subject by Philippe Perrot reminds us. See *Le luxe: Une richesse entre faste et confort, XVIIIe-XIXe siècle* (Paris: Seuil, 1995).

Historians' attention to this phenomenon and its conceptualisation has grown remarkably in the last twenty years.[6] My aim here is to propose an additional and complementary perspective which suggests that luxury became eighteenth-century France's first notional site of a wide-reaching and lively contest about the shape, scope, and effects of commercial society and the locus of an evaluation of the imperial enterprise. The literature has tended, by and large, to relate the proliferation of texts about luxury in unitary terms, as a single debate between two opposing camps.[7] This narrative is not altogether surprising: The discussion shared among *philosophes* and members of the royal administration did exhibit some polarizing qualities while it was carried out in *mémoires* or essays usually prepared for the Académie des Inscriptions et Belles Lettres, in the newly founded journals of the era, and in the *salons*.[8] Yet, as I hope to show, what contemporaries referred to as the *querelle du luxe*, the luxury

[6] Recent studies on the eighteenth-century idea of luxury are too numerous to list here, except to note the pioneering works by Istvan Hont and Michael Ignatieff, *Wealth and Virtue* (Cambridge: Cambridge University Press, 1983); Donald Winch, *Riches and Poverty* (Cambridge: Cambridge University Press, 1996), and Christopher Berry, *The Idea of Luxury: A Conceptual and Historical Investigation* (Cambridge: Cambridge University Press, 1994), all of which revived Anglophone attention to conceptual questions, namely in Britain. John Shovlin's landmark study of luxury in eighteenth-century France, specifically *The Political Economy of Virtue: Luxury, Patriotism, and the Origins of the French Revolution* (Ithaca: Cornell University Press, 2006), underscored how intrinsic the concept and phenomenon was for prerevolutionary French politics and mores. The following, like all writing on the idea of luxury in France which follows Shovlin, is highly indebted to his elegant analysis.

[7] The most recent example is Jeremy Jennings, "The Debate about Luxury in Eighteenth- and Nineteenth-Century French Political Thought," *Journal of the History of Ideas* 68, no. 1 (2007): 79. John Shovlin offers the most comprehensive account of the debate in "Luxury, Political Economy, and the Rise of Commercial Society in Eighteenth-Century France," PhD dissertation, (University of Chicago, 1999) and "The Cultural Politics of Luxury in Eighteenth-Century France," *French Historical Studies* 23, no. 4 (Fall 2000): 578–84. Dena Goodman points in *The Republic of Letters: A Cultural History of the French Enlightenment* (Ithaca: Cornell University Press, 1994) to an analogous historiographical gesture whereby contemporary historiography tended to mirror the caricature of the *salonnières* put forth by Rousseau and others in the eighteenth century. Sarah Maza's astute examination of luxury's connection to French identity formation in *The Myth of the French Bourgeoisie: An Essay on the Social Imaginary, 1750–1850* (Cambridge, MA: Harvard University Press, 2003) shows that luxury had the status of Barthesian myth in the period, "an inflection of language which makes the invented seem natural," 12.

[8] The Académie des Inscriptions et Belles Lettres was founded in 1663 and comprises one of the five academies of the Institut de France. Its charter stipulated then, as it does now, that the Académie "is primarily concerned with the study of the monuments, the documents, the languages, and the cultures of the civilisations of antiquity, the Middle Ages, and the classical period, as well as those of non-European civilisations." See Blandine Barret-Kriegel, *Les Académies de l'histoire* (Paris: Presses universitaires de France, 1988).

quarrel, was by no means a Manichean dispute.[9] When we reconsider the terms of the discussion in the period following the Seven Years War and preceding the Revolution (1763–89), we discover a more faceted conversation than the oppositional term "debate" allows.

At the time, commentators on luxury certainly wrestled with the notion's very boundaries, scope, and content; in short, they struggled first of all with how to define "luxury." At the forefront of their arguments lay a shared concern – a fixation even – with definition. Indeed, nearly every text addressing the subject at the time began by specifying the connotations of the word. Diderot confronted this problem head on in the eponymous article "*Encyclopédie*" for the *Encyclopédie*, published in 1755. Among the challenges of creating a "universal vocabulary" by "fixing the significations" of terms and "defining those that can be defined," he offered "luxury" as the example of a term "we understand the least, [but] use the most."[10] "Luxury," Diderot continued, typified a term "we attribute so infallibly to so many things," though there was no "brief, exact, clear, and precise enumeration of the qualities or ideas that are attached to [it]."[11]

That luxury eluded fixed signification becomes evident when we turn to the *Histoire des deux Indes*. The work offered a dynamic engagement

[9] It was certainly another example of the "discord in the Republic of Letters" studied by Dena Goodman, characteristic, too, for its political economic substance. As Rebecca Spang and Colin Jones note, there were many facets to the experience and understanding of luxury. So too, were there many dimensions to the understanding of the concept. With their groundbreaking article, "*Sans-culottes, sans café, sans tabac*: Shifting Realms of Necessity and Luxury in Eighteenth-Century France," Spang and Jones drew on previously unmined sources such as advertisements in the pervasive *Affiches* to demonstrate how the relationship between luxury and necessity was more fluid and complicated than what they call the "republico-manichean binary" vision of the period as perpetuated by current scholarship. In other words, the practice of luxury was less polarized than its theorisation. Yet the sources in this book suggest that the intellectual polarity has perhaps been overemphasised and may blanket the truly "pantheistic" quality of the ideological discourse on luxury in the period. Colin Jones and Rebecca Spang, "*Sans-culottes, sans café, sans tabac*: Shifting Realms of Necessity and Luxury in Eighteenth-Century France," in Maxine Berg and Helen Clifford, eds., *Consumers and Luxury in Europe 1650–1850* (Manchester: Manchester University Press, 1999), 37–62.

[10] *Encyclopédie*, 5:635. Further on, Diderot sends his reader to the *Encyclopédie*'s article "*Définition*" for a definition of definition. Ibid. On the irony and epistemological significance of the fact that Diderot saw fit to represent his representation of knowledge by way of a specific article delineating "an invariable and common measure, failing which we know nothing," see James Creech, "'Chasing after Advances': Diderot's Article 'Encyclopedia,'" *Yale French Studies* 63 (1982): 183–97; Jacques Derrida, "*Hors livre / Outwork*," in *Dissemination*, trans. Barbara Johnson (Paris: Editions du Seuil, 1972. Reprint. New York: Continuum, 2004), 59; and Wilda Anderson, *Diderot's Dream* (Baltimore: Johns Hopkins University Press, 1990), chap. 3.

[11] *Encyclopédie*, 5:635A for "we attribute so infallibly" and 5:635 for "brief, exact, clear."

with the phenomenon of luxury throughout its portrayal of the global commerce resulting from European imperialisms. So, too, did luxury serve as a focal point and outlet for Diderot's post-1763 reflections on commerce (many of which were buried anonymously within the *Histoire*) and the relationship between polity and economy. When positioned among other texts and arguments about luxury of the period, both the *Histoire* and Diderot's work expose tensions present in the late-eighteenth-century French language of luxury and point to ambivalence as a central feature of this language. Within this altered French idiom, luxury was neither good nor bad; the concept was dragged through several discursive shifts and so could be "sweet" or "odious" depending on the moment or locus of its manifestation. Often it was construed as both, simultaneously, as it underwent various iterations in the hands of dexterous commentators who fashioned and refashioned the term for their own purposes.

NEW AND OLD

To the extent that luxury was understood to be an urgent moral and political crisis, eighteenth-century writers construed the crisis as a consequence of a change: the advent of a new, commercial society. In many ways, however, the problem of a new commercial society, crystallized in Benjamin Constant's essay "On the Liberty of the Ancients as Compared to the Moderns" (Paris, 1819), was, and still is, a function of its invention.[12] Stories invented and told by period writers about how the new commercial society came into being emphasised its novelty and importance, insisting that it was a force to be reckoned with. This conceptualisation of commercial society as a new phenomenon – problematic for some, encouraging for others – is all the more curious when the classical sources of its referential vocabulary are considered.[13] Yet, as we shall see, the very

[12] "De la liberté des anciens comparée à celle des modernes" was first delivered as a part of a series of lectures on English constitutionalism given by Constant to the Athénée royal in Paris in 1819 and later published in his *Collection complète des ouvrages publiés*. See Biancamaria Fontana, ed. and trans., introduction to *Political Writings / Benjamin Constant* (Cambridge: Cambridge University Press, 1988), 40.

[13] The most recent study of luxury's influence on the political thought of eighteenth-century France by Jeremy Jennings points us to the enduring classical republicanism structuring a kind of anti-luxury discourse. His compelling reading of the ways in which Charles Renouvier's *Manuel Républicain de l'Homme et du Citoyen* (Paris, 1848) extends that discourse might also specify that the terms Renouvier employed were Ciceronian – a nearly verbatim rendering of the *De officiis*. "Nothing is beautiful, nothing is noble," Renouvier remarked, "which is not useful." See Jennings, "Debate about Luxury," 102.

terms employed by the "ancients" to describe their own experience with commercial society re-emerged in the eighteenth century.

We know the concept and realities of commercial societies were not new, nor was their imperial reach.[14] Both the Greeks and the Romans lived in commercial societies, and they struggled with the moral problems related to their existence. Although the prevailing classical position was to extol the virtues of a military and agricultural society, it is clear now, as it was in the eighteenth century, that this emphatic moral and practical preference must have existed in opposition to an alternative. This alternative was a commercial society, as anxiety provoking for the ancients as it was for their eighteenth-century counterparts. The *Histoire des deux Indes*, for one, certainly emphasised the commercial nature of classical societies. Its opening pages suggested to readers that "we see by the few works of Xenophon and other writers that they [the 'ancients'] had better principles of commerce than the most part of European nations have today."[15] Consider, then, how Aristotle's *Politics* began with a reply to Plato contending that politics and economics (then referring to household management) were distinct realms, since two different terms existed to signify them, the *polis* and the *oikos*.[16] Xenophon's praise of husbandry as the gentleman's art evoked a contrast with the merchant. When Socrates compared Ischomachos's father to a merchant, the latter was duly insulted.[17] Cicero, who translated Xenophon's *Oeconomicus*, maintained this distinction as he persistently denounced the "ungentlemanly" expedience of commerce in the *De officiis*.[18] His claim that unfettered appropriation of property violated the laws of human society revealed

---

[14] As eminent linguist Émile Benveniste has noted, terms for commerce did not exist in Indo-European languages until quite late – a function, he argued, of the fact that exchange was deemed outside of society, which is why it was qualified only as the action of being "occupied," to "have to do" as *"affaires"* and "business" and *"Geschäft"* indicate. *Negotium* he considers as deriving from the Greek *askholía* ("occupations") which signifies "the fact of not having leisure." For Benveniste, this lexical silence draws attention to the newness of the activity and the category. Yet, as he notes (and as we have seen), *commercium* certainly emerged early on in Latin, building on the terms *merx* and *mercis*. The origin of these terms for "merchandise," is, however, uncertain. Émile Benveniste, *"Un métier sans nom: le commerce,"* in *Le vocabulaire des institutions indo-européennes*, vol. 1 (Paris: Les Éditions de minuit, 1969), 143–45.

[15] *HDI* (1780), book 1, chap. 1, 6.

[16] See James Booth, *Households: On the Moral Architecture of the Economy* (Ithaca, NY: Cornell University Press, 1993).

[17] See James Booth's account of this dialogue in Xenophon in "Household and Market: On the Origins of Moral Economic Philosophy," *Review of Politics* 56, no. 2 (1994): 209–10.

[18] Cicero, *De officiis*, book 2, xxiv, 87.

the moral stakes of this issue and confirmed that the life of commerce was inversely commendable to (his version of) the life of the virtuous agricultural gentleman.[19]

Viewed from this perspective, classical political thought is seen to be replete with a contrast: Profuse and emphatic praise for agricultural life, deemed most dignified, implicitly condemned the life of the merchant, and so too commerce. In other words, a keen awareness of commerce within these texts is made conspicuous by an overemphasis on its opposite. Given eighteenth-century French immersion in classical culture, the emphasis on the newness of commerce as a problem or a challenge for individuals, society, and government is all the more striking. We notice, therefore, that what is particular about the moment in question is not that commercial society was new, but that changes occurred in the scope and character of commercial society whereby observers began describing it as new. What is more, they began to write about its (perceived) newness.

THE CONTOURS OF THE *QUERELLE*

Istvan Hont addressed this classical connection when he showed that there were at least two levels of debate in the early stages of the so-called quarrel over luxury. A first set divided "ancients" and "moderns," with the ancients questioning whether luxury ought to exist at all. "Modernists" accepted the existence of luxury, but divided among themselves on the means to promote its moral and political benefits.[20] This register was in many ways an extension of the famous seventeenth-century "quarrel of the ancients and the moderns" ("*querelle des anciens et des modernes*"): the quarrel between ancient or classical virtues and a newly developing notion of modernity.

The Critique, a Sketch

As the eighteenth century unfolded, however, the critique of luxury grew. Early writers opposed to luxury tended to recommend agriculture over

[19] Ibid., book 1, vii, 21. I thank Jean Andreau, whose seminar at the École Normale Supérieure (Paris) in spring 2003 provided the tools for investigating this and other problems in Cicero's texts. On eighteenth-century representations of the gendered self see Toby Ditz, "Shipwrecked, or, Masculinity Imperiled: Mercantile Representations of Failure and the Gendered Self in Eighteenth-Century Philadelphia" *Journal of American History* 81, no. 1 (1994): 51–80.

[20] Istvan Hont, "The Early Enlightenment Debate on Commerce and Luxury," in Mark Goldie and Robert Wokler, eds., *The Cambridge History of Eighteenth-Century Political Thought*, (Cambridge: Cambridge University Press, 2006), 380.

industry, foreshadowing and then echoing a central preoccupation of the *économistes* or Physiocrats. Their theses about the value of agriculture over manufacturing shared a steady target: luxury and the society of privilege that fostered it.[21] To counter the problem of "improper employment of men and wealth in the manufacture of luxury goods," Quesnay argued, it was first necessary to free trade in order to raise agricultural prices which could be reinvested in agriculture.[22] In turn, as Renato Galliani has highlighted, the nobility actually formed an important constituency of opposition to luxury. They expressed a clear resentment and scapegoating of the new consumers of luxury. Their critiques of luxury unveil an apparent "allergy" to *paraître*, or appearance, the vexed symptom of luxury in this view.[23] John Shovlin's analysis of those antagonistic to luxury further explains how luxury was viewed as a form of spectacular consumption and therefore a threat to the social order.[24] Other opponents of luxury borrowed arguments and terms from classical antiquity to claim a causal connection between luxury and corruption, condemning it on moral grounds.[25] The most famous and emblematic articulation of this argument came at mid-century, with Jean-Jacques Rousseau's *First* and *Second Discourses* (1750, 1755), the period's most polemical critique of luxury and the commercial society it fostered.

[21] Cf. Yves Citton, *Portrait de l'économiste en physiocrate: Critique littériare de l'économie politique* (Paris: L'Hartmann, 2000), 17. For a detailed discussion of the Physiocrats' vexed relationship with luxury, see Maza, *Myth of the French Bourgeoisie*, esp. chap. 1, and Shovlin, *Political Economy of Virtue*, esp. chap. 4. The antidote to luxury the Physiocrats proposed was of course "liberty of commerce." See Baudeau cited in Shovlin, *Political Economy of Virtue*, 122.

[22] So Quesnay argued in his article "Blé" for the *Encyclopédie*. See Istvan Hont and Michael Ignatieff, *Wealth and Virtue* (Cambridge: Cambridge University Press, 1983), 16.

[23] Renato Galliani, *Rousseau, le luxe, et l'idéologie nobiliaire, étude socio-historique*, in *Studies on Voltaire and the Eighteenth Century*, vol. 268 (Oxford: Voltaire Foundation, 1989), 113–16.

[24] John Shovlin, "The Cultural Politics of Luxury in Eighteenth-Century France," *French Historical Studies* 23, no. 4 (Fall 2000): 584.

[25] Luxury and virtue were often opposed by critics in eighteenth-century France, many of whom adopted classical republican stances against it. A less-known example of this view is found in yet another poem published in the 1750s and recognised by the Académie française: "Luxury, first cause of Rome's decline." See Firmin de Caen Douin, "Le luxe, première cause de la décadence de Rome," in *Amusemens poëtiques d'un philosophe, ou Poëmes académiques sur différens sujets, dont plusieurs ont été couronnés, et autres piéces fugitives* (Paris: Chez Cailleau, 1763). Also see A. J. chevalier du Coudray's *Le luxe, poëme en six chants; orné de gravures, avec des notes historiques et critiques, suivi de poësies diverses* (Paris: Chez Monory, Libraire de S.A.S. Monseigneur le Prince de Condé, 1773).

Rousseau's Attack

At the instant when Rousseau first read the announcement of an essay
contest sponsored by the Academy of Dijon in 1749, he later recounted,
he "became another man."[26] En route to visit Diderot, then imprisoned in
Vincennes, he "scribbled" the first draft of his response, now referred to
as the *Discourse on the Sciences and the Arts*, "under an oak tree."[27] To
the Academy's question, "Has the progress of the sciences and arts done
more to corrupt mores or to improve them?" Rousseau replied provocatively that their progress corrupts. This *First Discourse* of Rousseau's
won the Academy's first prize and instantly transformed its author into
a celebrity in France and abroad with its controversial, if not entirely
original, thesis. The sciences and the arts were distractions from virtue,
Rousseau argued. They turned the attention of "civilised peoples" away
from their corruption and their figurative enslavement: In Rousseau's
words, they "spread garlands of flowers over the iron chains," and transform them into "happy slaves."[28] The most conspicuous symptom of
this state of moral and political corrosion was the taste for luxury and
ornamentation (*faste*), which, Rousseau explained, was "born" of "idleness and vanity."[29] Indeed, for Rousseau, "luxury rarely exists without
the sciences and the arts, and they rarely exist without it."[30] Society was
confounded by a paradox "worthy of being born in our day," that luxury *may* serve to "multiply" wealth, but since luxury is "diametrically
opposed to good mores," and good mores are "essential" for "Empires
to last," luxury is ultimately destructive.[31] What is more, luxury polluted

---

[26] Jean-Jacques Rousseau, *Les confessions* (1778), J. B. Pontalis, ed. (Paris: Gallimard,
1995), 430.

[27] This first section, which Rousseau referred to as "*la prosopopée de Fabricius*," formed
the basis of the discourse to which Rousseau devoted "the insomnia of [his] nights."
Diderot, then imprisoned for the publication of his *Letter on the Blind for the Use of
Those Who See* (1749), was the sole person to offer corrections on the work. Ibid., 431.
On Diderot's *Letter* see Barbara de Negroni's "Notice" in *Oeuvres philosophiques* (Paris:
Gallimard, 2010), 1100–13.

[28] Jean-Jacques Rousseau, *Discours sur les sciences et les arts*, in *Œuvres complètes*,
III, 7.

[29] Ibid., 19.

[30] Ibid.

[31] Rousseau's gesture towards the pro-luxury arguments here has been commented on by
Helena Rosenblatt, who has also shown how Rousseau's early epistles reveal a position
favourable to luxury (though not without misgivings), which she attributes to his particular "social awkwardness" about his Genevan background at the time. See her discussion of Rousseau's 1741 *Épître à Monsieur Bordes*, written while he was a tutor in
Lyon, and the similar *Épître à Monsieur Parisot* in *Rousseau and Geneva: From the First
Discourse to the Social Contract, 1749–1762* (Cambridge: Cambridge University Press,

human potential: "It is not possible for Souls degraded by a multitude of futile cares to rise to anything great; and if they had the strength, they would lack the courage."[32] Courage, and other "virtues" praised by the "ancient Politicians," contrasted with the values of his day, when politicians "speak only of commerce and money."

Rousseau's apparent worry about the endurance of empires is modulated later in the text when he identifies what "precisely" the "question of luxury" entails. It is, he replies, "to know what matters most to Empires, to be brilliant and short-lived, or virtuous and long-lasting."[33] A less surprising view of empire is made clear in his reply. They aim to be "brilliant," he says, but he goes on to rejoin "by what lustre?" Rousseau's critique thus famously rested on the contrast between classical, classical republican, and especially Spartan ideals of courage, virtue, and military strength. These damaged martial and moral qualities engendered a condition under which, as the *First Discourse* famously concluded, people knew "how to speak well" but not how to "act well."[34]

The heart of Rousseau's stance against luxury was reinforced in the letter he later addressed to the abbé Raynal in the latter's capacity as editor of the *Mercure de France* literary journal. Raynal had sent Rousseau an advance copy of "Observations" on the *First Discourse* (of which he was probably the author), and here Rousseau offered his preliminary replies.[35] To the retort that "sound policy calls for [luxury] to be prohibited in small States," Rousseau offered that the true "difficulty" to be resolved was one he had already posed in his essay: "What will become of virtue, when one has to get rich at any cost?"[36] In response to the snide comment that "the Author is not unaware" of what has already

1997), 40–41. Céline Spector has shown that, though the new science of political economy had not yet been understood as such, Rousseau's attack on luxury revealed his distillation of the "unity of the discourse" of nascent political economic writings in France into the "primacy of growth over justice." Céline Spector, "Rousseau et la critique de l'économie politique" in Bensaude-Vincent and Bernardi, eds., *Rousseau et les sciences* (Paris: L'Harmattan, 2003), 237–38.

[32] Ibid., 20. Elaborating this point about courage further, Rousseau contended that "the study of sciences is much more apt to soften and effeminate men's courage than to harden and animate it" (*Œuvres complètes*, III, 22).

[33] Here I cite Victor Gourevitch's translation in *The Discourses and Other Early Political Writings* (Cambridge: Cambridge University Press, 1997), 19.

[34] OC, III, 30.

[35] Both Rousseau's *Lettre à l'abbé Raynal* and the *Observations* to which he responded were published in the second volume of the June 1751 edition of the *Mercure de France*. Rousseau apparently cherished this letter, insisting that it be included in the first publication of his complete works. See OC, III, 1256.

[36] Ibid., 32.

"been said" on the "uselessness of sumptuary laws to uproot luxury once
it is established," Rousseau paraded one of his quintessentially jocular
remarks: "Really, no. I am not unaware that when a man is dead, one
must not call the Doctors."[37] This notion that luxury had the power to
"kill" the fundamental humanity of its "victims" was taken up again by
Rousseau in his so-called *Second Discourse*.

More radical than the *First Discourse*, the *Discourse on the Origin and
Foundations of Inequality among Men* (1755) offered an account which
began, quite provocatively again, with "casting all the facts aside."[38] The
following hypothetical or "conjectural history" of the stages in human
history, from the imagined "state of nature" to the "current" state of civilisation or "civil society" taunted Thomas Hobbes's darker notions of
humanity's earliest state.[39] In Rousseau's version, the state of nature found
happy, peaceful, and good people; "civil society" was born when the first
person said "this is mine" after "enclosing a piece of terrain," and "others
were stupid enough to believe him."[40] The resulting "Society" in which
"the People [have] purchased an idea of repose at the price of real happiness," produced four different kinds of "moral or political" inequality –
riches, nobility or rank, power, and personal merit.[41] All these ultimately
fold, in Rousseau's analysis, into one overarching category: inequality of
riches, or wealth. Though the *First Discourse* had shown how luxury was
the product of riches, the discussion of luxury in the *Second Discourse*
differs slightly. Here the attention to luxury is located in Rousseau's own
"Note IX" to the crucial moment in his text where he introduces the
"faculty of perfectibility." For Rousseau, this faculty distinguishes humans
from animals; it necessarily makes the return to the state of nature impossible, and "over the centuries, causing his enlightenment and his errors,

[37] Ibid., 33.
[38] *Discours sur l'origine et les fondemens de l'inégalité parmi les hommes* (1755) in
OC, III, 132.
[39] Eighteenth-century Scots later developed this "natural history of mankind" further.
The term "conjectural history" was coined by Dugald Stewart, Adam Smith's biog-
rapher, to explain Smith and others' recourse to this kind of fictional history. On the
eighteenth-century "stadial histories" and "four-stages theories," respectively, see Andrew
Skinner, "Natural History in the Age of Adam Smith," *Political Studies* 15 (1967), Ronald
L. Meek, *Social Science and the Ignoble Savage* (Cambridge: Cambridge University Press,
1976), and Istvan Hont, "The Language of Sociability and Commerce: Samuel Pufendorf
and the Theoretical Foundations of the 'Four-Stages Theory," in Anthony Pagden, ed.,
The Languages of Political Theory in Early-Modern Europe (Cambridge: Cambridge
University Press, 1986), 253–76.
[40] Ibid., 164.
[41] Ibid., 132 (for "the People"), and 189 (for the four types of inequality).

his vices and his virtues to flourish, eventually makes him his own and Nature's tyrant."[42]

"Note IX" first lists the myriad ways – psychological, physical, and social – that "Civilised man" has made "himself" miserable. Luxury is portrayed as "the evil which Societies have begun." Under "the pretext of providing a living for the poor who should never have been made so in the first place," luxury impoverishes "everyone else" and "oppresses and ruins both farmer and Citizen."[43] Rousseau inflames the language of the *First Discourse* further here with a dramatic analogy for the dystopia produced by luxury: It is "like those scorching south winds which, blanketing grasses and foliage with all-devouring insects, deprive useful animals of their subsistence, and carry famine and death wherever they make themselves felt." But an added danger of luxury is introduced by Rousseau: Luxury, the "remedy much worse than the evil it claims to cure [poverty]," also causes the "depopulation of the State." The spectre of depopulation, a growing concern for the eighteenth-century French, is invoked again by Rousseau later in the note when he argues that the "scorned farmer, weighed down by taxes needed to support Luxury" abandons his fields "to go look in the Cities for the bread he should be taking to them."[44] The outcome? Fallow fields and "the highways overrun by unfortunate Citizens turned beggars or thieves and destined someday to end their misery on the wheel or a dunghill." Thus, while the state "grows rich on the one hand" it "gets weak and depopulated on the other." Ultimately, Rousseau warns, a cycle is established whereby "the most powerful Monarchies, after much labour to grow opulent and become deserted" end up the "prey" of "Nations" who invade and "destroy" them. Once again, the implicit critique of empires is reframed as a commentary on monarchies. In addition to creating a subhuman, "weak, fearful, grovelling," with a "soft and effeminate" way of life which

---

[42] Ibid., 142.

[43] Ibid., 206, for this and all of the following citations until indicated otherwise.

[44] The source of much of the worry was Montesquieu's mobilisation of the threat of depopulation in his *De l'Esprit des lois* (1748) as a means of creating pressure for monarchical reform. See Carol Blum, *Strength in Numbers: Population, Reproduction, and Power in Eighteenth-Century France* (Baltimore and London: The Johns Hopkins University Press, 2002), 16. It is well known that this anxiety about depopulation, which inspired thousands of printed analyses of the perceived problem from 1760 to 1789 was delusory. France's population in fact grew from 20 million in 1661 to 28 million in 1789. See Leslie Tuttle, *Conceiving the Old Regime: Pronatalism and the Politics of Reproduction in Early Modern France* (New York: Oxford University Press, 2010), 152–53 for a recent analysis of this disjuncture.

"enervates his strength and his courage," luxury, here the synecdoche for civil society, also eroded these states.[45] And although Rousseau appeared to waiver in his portrayal of their causal relationships, the connection between them, riches, the arts and sciences, and luxury remained inextricable and mutually reinforcing in his texts.[46]

Luxury's Defenders

Rousseau's *Discourses* were written in reaction to an effervescence of pro-luxury writing in the 1720s and 1730s. In it, luxury was described as a pattern of consumption indeed spectacular; yet this feature was considered benign next to another, more important: that of satisfying individual desires and fulfilling individual pleasures. Moreover, defenders of luxury argued that luxury consumption provided an important stimulus for economic growth and ultimately for social happiness.[47] They combined an argument about the value of luxury production in generating wealth with a different kind of moral argument.[48]

These early defences of luxury in France drew quite explicitly on the works of London-based Dutch émigré and satirist Bernard Mandeville (1670–1733). The early influence of English writing on French economic thought, particularly on French reflections on luxury, is usually traced to Mandeville's provocative poem "The Fable of the Bees, or,

---

[45] Ibid., 139 for "weak, fearful, etc."

[46] While in the *First Discourse* Rousseau clearly states that luxury "is born like them [literature and the *arts*] from the idleness and vanity of men," *OC*, III, 19, later in the *Observations by Jean-Jacques Rousseau of Geneva On the Answer Made to His [First] Discourse*, he suggests another sequence: "From riches are born luxury and idleness; from luxury arose the fine Arts, and from idleness the Sciences." *OC*, III, 50. In his *Last Reply* to the critics of the *First Discourse*, he returns to his earlier sequence, concluding with a general statement of correlation: "Vanity and idleness which engendered our sciences also engendered luxury. The taste for luxury always accompanies that for Literature, and the taste for Literature often accompanies the taste for luxury: all of these things keep rather loyal company with one another, because they are all the product of the same vices." *OC*, III, 74.

[47] This part of the story tends to be sidelined by commentators. One exception is the attention given to this question in Henry C. Clark, "Commerce, Sociability, and the Public Sphere: Morellet vs. Pluquet on Luxury," *Eighteenth-Century Life* 22, no. 2 (May 1998): 83–102.

[48] Michael Kwass has conceptualised the arguments that luxury consumption was either a social good or a vehicle for "secular social progress" as "progressive consumptionism." Michael Kwass, "Consumption and the World of Ideas: Consumer Revolution and the Moral Economy of the Marquis de Mirabeau," *Eighteenth-Century Studies* 37, no. 2 (2004).

Private Vices, Public Benefits" (1714, 1723, 1728), which espoused the (then) counter-intuitive notion that "private vices," understood to mean mainly greed but also lust, hunger for power, and so forth, could lead to "public virtues."[49] With Mandeville, these pro-luxury writers reconfigured the "vice" of avarice as a social virtue. A physician by training, Mandeville used the beehive as a symbol of a productive centre of activity unbound by moral constraints. The work criticized the elite governance of England, which in his view controlled society by giving moral sanction to behaviours that might lead to increased wealth among the commoners. Mandeville praised greed and the aggressive pursuit of wealth, seeking to illustrate how it could ultimately bring about a "public virtue," the wealth of the nation.[50]

Framing Mandeville's early influence in France was a social and political context already showing signs of preoccupation with wealth and its detrimental effects upon morals and life in general. Indeed, the *sujets d'éloquence* presented by the Académie française from 1715 to 1744 speak to this concern. The subjects for these competitions of national eloquence varied from "The inconveniences of wealth" (1715) to "That the proper use of wealth makes for the glory of the Sage" (1727), "How much it matters to acquire the spirit of society" (1737), and "That the unfortunate are due a form of respect" (1741).[51]

---

[49] The "Fable" was translated into French in 1740 but had been available earlier to most *philosophes* and *encyclopédistes* through their voyages to England. In the view of influential economist and historian of economic thought Jacob Viner, for example, Mandeville was noted for his satiric aspect and was indebted philosophically to the Jansenists, especially Pierre Nicole. Jacob Viner, *Essays on the Intellectual History of Economics*. Douglas A. Irwin, ed. (Princeton: Princeton University Press, 1991), 23. Its influence peaked at mid-century; indeed by all accounts, Rousseau explicitly targeted it in his *Second Discourse*. For example, Adam Smith was "fully aware" that one of Rousseau's main targets in the *Second Discourse* was Mandeville, as seen in a letter of his published in the 1755–56 *Edinburgh Review*, where he writes: "Rousseau criticizes upon Dr. Mandeville." Quoted in Helena Rosenblatt, *Rousseau and Geneva*, 77.

[50] Discussed comprehensively in E. J. Hundert, *The Enlightenment's Fable: Bernard Mandeville and the Discovery of Society* (Cambridge: Cambridge University Press, 1994). See also his "Bernard Mandeville and the Enlightenment's Maxims of Modernity," *Journal of the History of Ideas* 56, no. 4 (1995): 577–93 and "The Thread of Language and the Web of Dominion: Mandeville to Rousseau and Back," *Eighteenth Century Studies* 21, no. 2 (1987–88): 169–91.

[51] Cited in Jean de Viguerie, *Histoire et Dictionnaire du Temps des Lumières* (Paris: Robert Laffont Bouquins, 1995), 146. On the cultural politics of the academies' competitions see Jeremy Caradonna, "Prend part au siècle des Lumières: Le concours académique et la culture intellectuelle au XVIIIe siècle en France," *Annales. Histoire, Sciences sociales* 64, no. 3 (2009): 633–62.

Yet it is with two influential readers of Mandeville that standard eighteenth-century accounts of the luxury quarrel began: Jean-François Melon's *Essai sur le commerce* (1734, 1736, 1742) and Voltaire's polemical poem "Le Mondain" (1736). The choice of author revealed a writer's approach to the concept and phenomenon called *luxe*. Those concerned with moral consequences tended to choose Voltaire, whereas those interested in luxury's positive consequences for the kingdom's wealth usually began their discussions with Melon.[52] In both instances, these authors' contentious defences of luxury were universally regarded as the spark that ignited the polemic that ensued.

Melon's Essai

If Voltaire's verses offered a more coded representation of luxury's advantages, Melon's *Essai* launched the more systematic theoretical discussion of luxury in France.[53] A former *fermier-général* (essentially a tax collector),[54] Melon is perhaps better remembered as having served as an advisor to John Law, France's notorious financial advisor in the 1720s. The ninth chapter of Melon's *Essai*, entitled "Luxe," spelled out his famous defence, beginning with the admission that the question of luxury had already been subject to debates, or, rather, "vague declamations" emanating from "a despondent and envious mind" rather than from "sound knowledge" or even "a severity of morals."[55] Thus, the immediate stake in understanding and contending with luxury lay in its definition. So Melon began with his own version, calling luxury an "extraordinary

---

[52] Rousseau famously considered that the "quarrel" was started by Melon: "It was reserved for M. Melon to be the first to publish this empoisoned doctrine, whose novelty gave him more disciples than the solidity of his reasoning." In "Dernière réponse," OC, III, 95.

[53] Melon's views were surely informed by his role as the former secretary and advisor to John Law and by his work under the service of the regent after the failure of Law's *Système*. Melon is remembered for his mixed and what we might call "bi-national" theoretical membership: The inheritor of what Eugène Daire has called the "French school," Melon also served as the translator of texts and ideas emanating from the first phases of English economic writing. According to Daire, even Adam Smith (though he was English) belonged to the French school led by Vauban and Boisguilbert. See Eugène Daire, *Economistes-financiers du XVIIIe siècle* (Paris: Guillaumin, 1843), 704–05.

[54] On the *fermiers-généraux* see Eugene N. White, "From Privatized to Government-administered Tax Collection: Tax Farming in Eighteenth-Century France" *Economic History Society* 52, no. 4 (2004): 636–63.

[55] The citation continues: "Those who find themselves in abundance, want to take pleasure in it / enjoy it [*jouir*], they have resting upon this abundance quests that the less wealthy are not in a state to pay, and this quest is always relative to the time-period, and to the people in question." Melon, *Essai politique*, 121.

sumptuousness," the source of wealth and security for the government, and the necessary consequence of a "polished" (read: civilised) society.[56] Yet with his compatriots past and future, Melon acknowledged the slippery quality of the term: "The term Luxury is an empty name" that must be banished, he continued, because it carries with it ideas that are "vague, confused, false," and therefore easily abused. The consequence of this exploitable ambiguity could be grave: "[I]ndustry itself might be stopped at its source."[57]

Luxury was, in Melon's view, a positive and inevitable result of the mores and practices of what would later be deemed "civilisation."[58] He continued with the first articulation of the notion that time is a factor in determining luxury's form and content, arguing that luxury is conditioned by and variable over time, and therefore a product of its context.[59] This notion would reappear in the *Histoire des deux Indes*, where it was combined with space, or geography, as a second related and determining factor. Where the *Essai* diverged with the *Histoire*, as we shall see, was in its fifth chapter, "Of slavery." Here Melon once again applied a principle

---

[56] "Le Luxe est une somptuosité extraordinaire, que donnent les richesses & la sécurité d'un Gouvernement; c'est une suite nécessaire de toute Société bien policée." Ibid.

[57] "Le terme de Luxe est un vain nom, qu'il faut bannir de toutes les opérations de Police et de Commerce, parce qu'il ne porte que des idées vagues, confuses, fausses, dont l'abus peut arrêter l'Industrie même dans sa source." Ibid., 129–30.

[58] The term *civilisation* was first coined by the marquis de Mirabeau in 1756 to connote the "well-polished Society" invoked by Melon. On the continuing philological debate about its origins, see Lucien Febvre, "Civilisation, évolution d'un mot et d'un groupe d'idées." 1929, in *Lucien Febvre: Pour une histoire à part entière* (Paris: Service d'édition et de vente des publications de l'Éducation nationale, 1962) (for the first positivist argument about its origins); Émile Benveniste, "Civilisation: Contribution à l'histoire du mot," in *Hommage à Lucien Febvre: Éventail de l'histoire vivante*, 2 vols. (Paris: Armand Colin, 1953); Phillipe Beneton, *Histoire des mots: Culture et civilisation* (Paris: Presses de la Fondation nationale des sciences politiques, 1975); and Jean Starobinski, "Le mot 'civilisation,'" in *Le remède dans le mal: Critique et légitimation de l'artifice à l'âge des Lumières* (Paris: Gallimard, 1989). All trace the first use of the term in print to Mirabeau's *L'ami des hommes* (1756). On the concept of civilisation in the *HDI*, see Kenta Ohji, "Civilisation et naissance de l'histoire mondiale dans l'Histoire des deux Indes de Raynal" *Revue de synthèse* 129, no. 1 (2008): 57–83.

[59] "Ce qui étoit luxe pour nos pères, est à présent commun; & ce qui l'est pour nous, ne les sera pas pour nos neveux. Des bas de soye étoient luxe du tems de Henri second; & la Fayence l'Est autant, comparée à la Terre commune, que la Porcelaine comparée à la Fayence." Melon, *Essai politique*, 123. Of course, echoes of this view exist in contemporary reflections on luxury. See, for example, Philippe Perrot, "De l'apparat au bien-être: les avatars d'un superflu nécessaire," in *Du luxe au confort*, Jean-Pierre Goubert, ed. (Paris: Éditions Belin, 1988); and Dominique Margairaz, "Luxe," in *Dictonnaire européen des lumières*, Michel Delon, ed. (Paris: Presses universitaires de France, 1997), 662–65.

of contingency, stating that "slavery has its degrees, depending on the time period and the nation." With its attempts to curb the "inhumanity, death, mutilation, tortures and all of the arbitrary excesses of a master," Louis XIV's *Code Noir* was "wise."[60] Nevertheless, Melon concluded, "Colonies are necessary for the nation, and slaves are necessary to the colonies."[61] Conspicuous by its absence is any mention of the role that slaves played in producing the list of luxury goods from the colonies that Melon discussed in his chapter on luxury.

Voltaire's Poem

These would not be Melon's last words on luxury. Shortly before his death in 1738, Melon wrote a letter to the eminent and eminently wealthy *salonnière*, art collector, and bibliophile, the countess of Verrue, which was later published in an edition of Voltaire's complete works.[62] This "Lettre à madame la comtesse de Verrue, sur l'apologie du luxe" recommended Voltaire's unique intervention in the discussion about luxury as "an excellent political lesson, disguised as pleasant banter."[63] Voltaire had just published his provocative poem praising luxury, "Le Mondain" (1736), later followed by the "Défense du Mondain ou L'Apologie du Luxe" (1739).[64] The title "Le Mondain" referred, literally, to the "man of the world," a term borrowed from a religious vocabulary and subverted to indicate opposition to Christian morals.[65] This "socialite" to whom Voltaire gave voice in verse declares outright: "[W]hoever wants to can regret the old Times ... [but] I love luxury ... all pleasures, the arts of every kind, cleanliness, taste, ornaments." This declaration of love also followed the pattern of all writings about luxury by proffering a definition. Voltaire's category is quite vast, from "all pleasures" to "cleanliness." With every *honnête homme* (essentially, gentleman), the *Mondain* shares the "sentiment" that this luxury is the source of "abundance" and "Mother

---

[60] As Madeleine Dobie has noted, Colbert's *Code Noir* was considered a "reform document" in the period, although that may not have been its intent or effect. See *Trading Places: Colonization and Slavery in Eighteenth-Century French Culture* (Ithaca, NY: Cornell University Press, 2010), 45n12, and Louis Sala-Molins, *Le code noir ou le calvaire de Canaan* (Paris: Presses universitaires de France, 1987).

[61] Ibid., chap. 5, "De l'esclavage," 51.

[62] *Oeuvres de M. de Voltaire* (Amsterdam: Étienne Ledet, 1739), 111–12.

[63] Daire, *Économistes-financiers*, 706.

[64] I draw on André Morize, *L'Apologie du luxe au XVIIIe siècle et "Le Mondain" de Voltaire* (Paris: H. Didier, 1909. Reprint. Geneva: Slatkine, 1970).

[65] Ibid., 139.

of the Arts."[66] In contrast to the society of arts and pleasures, Adam and Eve are compared to "man" in the "natural" state: "Two green Monkeys, two split-footed Goats/ Are less hideous in their bushes,/ [than you who] By the sun have scorched your face,/ Your hairy arms, your scaly hands,/ Your long, cruddy, black and crooked nails .... Here is the state of pure Nature."[67] With these barbs, Voltaire attacked both the idolaters of the state of nature – anticipating the later caricatures of Rousseau's alleged praise of the *bon sauvage* – and the "genesis" of the world according to Christianity. A caustic line of rhetorical questions demands a reconfiguration of virtue: "Silk and gold did not shine among them: / Is this why you admire our Ancestors? / They had neither industry nor comfort: / Is this virtue?" No was Voltaire's reply. Their silkless and goldless existence was, rather, one of "pure ignorance." "What Idiot," quipped Voltaire, " if he had a good bed, would sleep outside?"[68]

THE LANGUAGE OF LUXURY AFTER THE SEVEN YEARS WAR

What idiot, indeed! Voltaire's taunt received a reply thirty years later in the *Encyclopédie*'s article "*Luxe*," published in 1765. Introducing an argument that luxury is relative, the article's author, Jean-François de Saint-Lambert, rejoined: "there is luxury in all states, in all societies: the savage has his hammock which he bought with animal skins; the

---

[66] "Regrettera qui veut le bon vieux Tems, / Et l'Age d'Or et le Régne d'Astrée, ... Moi, je rends grace à la nature sage, / Qui, pour mon bien, m'a fait naître en cet âge / Tant décrié par nos pauvres Docteurs': / Ce tems profane est tout fait pour mes mœurs. / J'aime le luxe, et même la mollesse', / Tous les plaisirs', les Arts de toute espèce, / La propreté, le goût, les ornemens: / Tout honnête homme a de tels sentimens. / Il est bien doux pour mon cœur très immonde, / De voir ici l'abondance à la ronde, / Mere des Arts et des heureux travaux, / Nous apporter de sa source féconde, Et des besoins et des plaisirs nouveaux." Ibid., 133.

[67] Ibid., 135–36.

[68] "La Soye et l'Or ne brilloient point chez eux: / Admirez-vous pour cela nos Ayeux? / Il leur manquoit l'Industrie et l'aisance: / Est-ce vertu? C'étoit pure ignorance / Quel Idiot, s'il avait eu pour lors / Quelque bon lit, auroit couché dehors?" Ibid., 134–35. As Morize observes, this notion (a quote from Justinian reading "They ignored vice rather than not knowing virtue") was often cited by both Pufendorf and Grotius. Ibid., 143. Voltaire further ridiculed the rendering of primitive lifestyles and poverty as virtue in his article on luxury in the *Dictionnaire philosophique* (1770): "In a country where everyone walked barefoot, was the first to make a pair of shoes luxurious? Was he not a sensible and industrious man? Is he not the same as the man who had the first shirt? I believe the one who bleached and ironed it to be filled with genius and capable of governing a state. Nevertheless those unaccustomed to wearing white shirts took him to be a wealthy effeminate [*un riche efféminé*] who corrupted the nation."

European has his sofa, his bed."[69] Saint-Lambert's essay on luxury is an example of a shift in the language of luxury which emerged in the years of crisis and change following the Seven Years War.[70]

Luxe in the *Encyclopédie*

As we have seen, luxury had already received attention in the *Encyclopédie* as Diderot's example of a term so common, yet so unclear. Ten years later, the article devoted to luxury began with a still capacious summary: "Luxury is the use we make of riches and industry to procure ourselves a pleasant existence."[71] Its author, Jean-François de Saint-Lambert (1716–1803) would later be celebrated for two innovative works: the first "descriptive poem" in French literature, *Les Saisons* (*The Seasons*, 1769), and an equally popular "philosophical tale" named after its protagonist, *Ziméo*, which offered the first fictional account of the slave trade in eighteenth-century France (104).[72] A marquis from Lorraine, Saint-Lambert had served as an army colonel in France before turning to *philosophie*.[73] In addition to the reference to sleeping arrangements, Saint-Lambert's article may have been winking at Voltaire's work in other ways. For Voltaire was famously Saint-Lambert's mentor, but also his rival for the attentions of the physicist, mathematician, and translator of Newton, Émilie du Châtelet (1706–49).

Yet Saint-Lambert begins by agreeing with Voltaire's great critic, Rousseau. He restates the thesis of perfectibility: that "luxury has as its first cause the unhappiness of our state; this desire to be better, which is and must be in all men." Next, he outlines all of the "declamations" of the "Moralists" and the "praises" of those "politicians" who "spoke more as merchants or clerks than as philosophers or statesmen." Finding as many historical counter-examples to the list of advantages as to the list of

---

[69] *Encyclopédie*, 9:763.

[70] On the crisis, expansion, and "social malaise" of the 1760s and 1770s, see Louis M. Cullen, "History, Economic Crises, and Revolution: Understanding Eighteenth-Century France," *Economic History Review* 46, no. 4 (1993), 639–40.

[71] *Encyclopédie*, 9: 763.

[72] *Ziméo* was first published in a 1769 collection which began with Les Saisons, following a title page reading "*Contes*," or "Tales." On *Les Saisons*, see Joanna Stalnaker, *The Unfinished Enlightenment Description in the Age of the Encyclopédie* (Ithaca, NY: Cornell University Press, 2010), 127; On *Ziméo*, see Christopher Miller, 104, and Madeleine Dobie, *Trading Places*, 256–67.

[73] L. G. Michaud, *Biographie universelle ancienne et moderne … Nouvelle édition*. 45 vols. (Paris: Madame C. Desplaces et M. Michaud, 1854–1865), 37:348–53.

disadvantages, Saint-Lambert concludes that all writers on luxury to date have confused causes with effects. "Have we not seen," he prods the reader, how in the case of luxury, cause and effect "meet one another and walk more or less at an equal pace?"[74] Rather, Saint-Lambert argues, luxury is "relative to peoples' situations," to the nature of their and their neighbours' products.[75] Yet it is necessary. For without luxury, Saint-Lambert continues, "there is less exchange and commerce," and nations become less populated. Better to have "farmers, sailors and cloth-workers" than a nation of only farmers. Here Saint-Lambert introduces the prescriptive tone with which the essay concludes. A good sovereign would simply correct the "excesses" of luxury; by reforming the administration and the constitution, he could eliminate any luxury that was "without taste," "vulgar," "savage," and "vicious."[76]

This was not the first time the term *vicious* had been used to describe luxury. Saint-Lambert was certainly conscious of this fact. In an essay "On Luxury," published in 1752, controversial Scottish moral and political philosopher David Hume (1711–76) introduced a then new perspective on the issue of luxury as part of his collection of "Essays on Morals." In it, Hume posited the existence of a bifurcated luxury, manifest in two forms: one he called "innocent" and the other "blameable," "pernicious," or "vicious."[77] In later editions, the essay came to be called "On Refinement in the Arts," but it is with "luxury" in its title that it was first introduced to French speakers by way of a translation by the abbé Le Blanc, published in 1754. So popular was this translation, publishers advertised it to readers as "snapped up as fast as the most agreeably frivolous book."[78] Yet this frenzied climate calmed somewhat after the 1763 defeat. While Saint-Lambert's article appropriated some of Hume's language, it also

---

74 Ibid., 9:764.

75 *Encyclopédie*, 9:765.

76 *Encyclopédie*, 9:670, and 766 for "vicious."

77 See David Hume, "Of Refinement in the Arts," in *Essays Moral and Political*, 3rd ed. London: A. Millar, 1748. Translated into French by abbé LeBlanc as *Essais philosophiques sur l'entendement humain*, 2nd ed. (Amsterdam: J.H. Schneider, 1761) and the French translation in *Essais philosophiques sur l'entendement humain*.

78 David Hume, *Discours politiques de Monsieur Hume traduits de l'anglois*, trans. abbé Jean Bernard LeBlanc (Amsterdam: Michel Lambert, 1754). See Claude Labrosse, "Réception et communication dans les périodiques littéraires (1750–1760)," in *La diffusion et la lecture des journaux de la langue française sous l'ancien régime* (Amsterdam, 1988), cited in Shovlin, *Political Economy of Virtue*, 2. On the circulation of Le Blanc's translation, see Loïc Charles, "French Cultural Politics and the Dissemination of Hume's Political Discourses on the Continent, 1750–1770," in *Essays on David Hume's Political Economy*, Margaret Schabas and Carl Wennerlind, eds. (New York: Routledge, 2006).

introduced important modifications, balancing the praise of luxury with an historical appraisal of its relative dangers and recommendations for its potential. John Shovlin has shown how this post-war era witnessed a "properly *political* critique" of luxury, which delimited commerce from luxury.[79] These political strands are clear in Saint-Lambert's essay and beyond. But we can also detect instances in the language of luxury when the connection between luxury and commerce persisted and where the political critique Shovlin examined is complemented by a powerful voice in favour of luxury.

Butel-Dumont: Theory and Etymology

One such case – probably the most significant work in this development – was written by Georges-Marie Butel-Dumont (1725–88). His 1771 *Théorie ou Traité du luxe* offered the eighteenth century's first comprehensive work devoted entirely to a theorisation of luxury. The *Théorie* entered the public domain on the tails of Diderot's writings on luxury and as the first version of the *Histoire des deux Indes* began to reach readers. Although Butel-Dumont cited Voltaire as his model, his work clearly diverged from the "Apologie," as we shall see.[80] Awarded a prize by the Académie des Inscriptions et Belles Lettres, under whose auspices it was written, the *Théorie* served as a key theoretical reference on the topic in the period. As his fame spread to a broader public, Butel-Dumont's publishers marketed his other works by featuring the "Author of the *Théorie du luxe*," often omitting his name so obvious was the reference.[81]

---

[79] Shovlin, *Political Economy of Virtue*, 121.

[80] A citation from Voltaire's "Le Mondain," "*Le superflu, chose très nécessaire,* (The superfluous, very necessary thing)," appears on the title page of both parts of Butel-Dumont's *Théorie du luxe*. The first edition of this work, according to Cioranescu, was the Amsterdam-Paris edition in 1771. I draw on the BnF copy (1775).

[81] Louis-Sébastien Mercier refers to Butel-Dumont as the "author of the Treatise on Luxury" in his *Tableau de Paris* (1782–88), chap. 301. Cf. Jean-Claude Bonnet's edition of the work (Paris: Mercure de France, 1994), 1792. The titles of Butel-Dumont's later works also refer explicitly to it. See, for example, the *Essai sur les causes principales qui ont contribué à détruire les deux premières races des Rois de France; Ouvrage dans lequel on développe les Constitutions fondamentales de la Nation françoise dans ces anciens tems: Par l'Auteur de la "Théorie du Luxe"; Recherches historiques et critiques sur l'administration publique et privée des terres chez les Romains, depuis le commencement de la République jusqu'au siècle de Jules-César ... par l'auteur de la "Théorie du luxe."* See also the *Traité du Luxe par Monsieur Butini* (Geneva, 1774) which begins by complimenting Butel-Dumont: "Livre Premier. Des Causes du Luxe. Chapitre Premier. Définition du Luxe. 'Toute jouissance superflue est un Luxe, cette définition appartient à l'Auteur de la Théorie du Luxe, Ouvrage ingénieux.'"

Born a Parisian in 1725, the "Author of the *Théorie*" began his professional career as a lawyer but adopted in quick succession the positions of royal censor, diplomat in Saint Petersburg, and head of deposits at the *Contrôle général*, or Finance Ministry (*chargé de depots au contrôle general*). Butel-Dumont's first publication was a joint project: a translation of Josiah Child's *Traité sur le commerce et sur les avantages de la réduction de l'intérêt de l'argent* (Paris, 1754) written in collaboration with Vincent de Gournay, the influential *intendant de commerce* of "*laissez faire, laissez passer*" fame. Butel-Dumont later translated and wrote about the British Navigation Acts in 1760,[82] and finally, as Sophus Reinert has shown, Butel-Dumont's translation of seventeenth-century English merchant John Cary's *Essay on the State of England in Relation to its Trade* (1695) amplified it in such a way that the *Essai sur l'État du commerce d'Angleterre* (1755) became not only "the definite economic history of England in the period" but also "one of the most programmatic economic translations of its age."[83] As such, Butel-Dumont's oeuvre reached a wide audience in France and beyond, garnering the attention of Benjamin Franklin in Philadelphia, for example.[84]

The *Théorie du luxe*, Butel-Dumont's ninth work, garnered immediate praise in the February 1771 edition of Melchior Grimm's *Correspondance littéraire*.[85] Grimm preceded this review with five articles "in verse." Of these five, three were anonymous eulogies; two others, less laudatory, comprised reflections on the fall from royal grace of the duc de Choiseul (1719–85), once the minister of war, marine, and foreign affairs.[86] His defeat marked a key moment of political transition away from economic reform in the royal administration and consequently turned official policies away from free internal and external commerce.[87] What is more,

---

[82] Michaud's *Biographie universelle* lists his seventh work as *Acte connu sous le nom d'acte de navigation du parlement d'Angleterre*.

[83] Sophus Reinert, *The Virtue of Emulation: International Competition and the Origins of Political Economy* (Cambridge, MA: Harvard University Press, 2011), 222, 16.

[84] See Edwin Wolf and Kevin Hayes, *The Library of Benjamin Franklin* (Philadelphia: American Philosophical Society, 2006), 168–69, where we learn that Butel-Dumont sent his works to Franklin in 1778.

[85] See Diderot, Grimm et al., *Correspondance littéraire, philosophique et critique de Grimm et de Diderot depuis 1753 jusqu'en 1790* (Paris: Chez Furne, 1829–31) (1er février 1771): 51.

[86] Étienne-François de Choiseul, once the Comte de Stainville and later known as the duc de Choiseul, held various roles at court, leading some to refer to him as "prime minister" or "secretary of state." On the flexibility and interrelatedness of administrative roles in early modern France, see Orest A. Ranum's classic study, *Richelieu and the Councillors of Louis XIII* (Oxford: Oxford University Press, 1963), 1–2.

[87] As Louis Cullen has written, "the story of Choiseul remains to be teased out." "History, Economic Crises, and Revolution: Understanding Eighteenth-Century France," *Economic*

the so-called flour war, discussed in Chapter 4, had just exploded, and the lively polemic it sparked nourished the printing presses with pamphlets disputing the freedom of the internal grain trade and the liberty of commerce in general.[88] As such, Butel-Dumont's work was inscribed within the framework of the most salient political and economic news of the day.

The *Théorie* is all the more crucial for our purposes in understanding the post-Seven Years War language of luxury because Butel-Dumont was one of the first in France to write extensively about the British North American colonies. His *Histoire et commerce des colonies anglaises* (Paris, 1755) was published in the tense political climate preceding the war. In describing the history, geography, government, religion, economics, trade, and produce of the colonies, the work anticipated the form and structure of the *Histoire des deux Indes* and much writing on commerce in France at the time.[89] Indeed, it served as a key source for the *Histoire*'s book 17 and its chapters on the English presence in North America. The *Théorie* thus paired Butel-Dumont's knowledge and experience with imperialism with his analysis of luxury.

Building on Melon's thesis, the work established that luxury was both useful and profitable to the state, indeed, that luxury was indispensable to the generation of wealth.[90] The desire for material wealth acted as a stimulus to labour and production. This desire also functioned as a conduit for civilised values. Here we can detect echoes of Mandeville, for whom luxury served as the vehicle for civilisation and thus modernity.[91] Any attempt to restrict consumption, whether by sumptuary laws or other means, Butel-Dumont maintained, necessarily yielded pernicious effects.

But Butel-Dumont's treatise is also worthy of our attention for the ways in which it shared the concern with semantics of other eighteenth-century French writings about luxury. The *Théorie* is remarkable for its extensive

---

History Review 46, no. 4 (1993), 652. On the crisis, expansion, and social malaise of the 1760s and 1770s, see 639–40.

[88] See Steven L. Kaplan *Bread, Politics and Political Economy in the Reign of Louis XV*. 2 vols. (The Hague: Martinus Nijhoff, 1976), 1:xx–xxv.

[89] This argument concurs with the central claim of Paul Cheney's PhD dissertation that the "history and science of commerce" remained paradigmatic of French economic thought throughout the eighteenth century despite the prominence of the Physiocrats during the 1760s and 1770s.

[90] Butel-Dumont, *Théorie du luxe, ou Traité dans lequel on entreprend d'établir que le luxe est un ressort non seulement utile, mais même indispensablement nécessaire à la prospérité d'un état*. The work's title page cited Voltaire's poem: "Le superflu, chose trèsnécessaire," that is, "The superfluous, a very necessary thing."

[91] See Hundert, *Enlightenment's Fable*.

appeal to an etymological argument. Claiming that the real definition of luxury among the Latins was "abundance" and surplus or superfluity – expressed neutrally and without any "odious" qualifier – Butel-Dumont subverted contemporary appeals to a more "virtuous" antiquity.[92]

This brings us to a second intriguing and representative aspect of Butel-Dumont's treatise: The very act and practice of definition was deemed to be a theoretical exercise. Butel-Dumont was so intent on *defining* luxury that he added an "Appendice" to the work: the "Dissertation on the primordial sense of the word Luxury." Its aim was to "prove" that the "primitive sense of the word 'luxury' confirmed the definition given in the first part of the *Théorie du luxe* and up to the fifth chapter."[93] Butel-Dumont went so far as to argue that luxury was the ultimate generator, the motor of all production: Luxury created, in effect, "every" "thing." He defined its all-encompassing scope in this manner: "Artistic production and consequently all things man uses over and above the spontaneous presents of nature are Luxury." In conclusion, "The useful, the practical, the agreeable are variations of the same genre. Bread and inventions related to war are Luxury."[94] In this way, Butel-Dumont equated commercial society with luxury, but also deemed it as essential to the state as bread and war.[95] He repeatedly stressed, however, that his version of luxury stood in stark contrast to those "inventions" of the "protesters" against luxury or of the *économistes*.

What is more, Butel-Dumont's obvious anxiety about the correct definition of luxury was explicitly linked to his broader concern about the shape, use, and future of the emerging discipline of political economy. The *Théorie ou Traité du luxe*'s "Discours préliminaire" asked whether the study of political economy must necessarily be an "inextricable labyrinth." For Butel-Dumont, the answer was "not at all." The "science" of political economy did not contain even "thirty major truths" worth

---

[92] Butel-Dumont was later challenged by the abbé François André Adrien Pluquet (1716–90) in his *Traité philosophique et politique sur le luxe* (1786), whose two volumes denouncing the "panegyrists of luxury" were in turn challenged by the abbé André Morellet (1727–1819), who wrote but never ultimately published a lengthy defence of luxury, *Sur le luxe* (c.1786–89). For a study of the conflict between the two authors and their texts, see Clark, "Morellet vs. Pluquet on Luxury."

[93] Butel-Dumont, *Théorie du luxe*, 177.

[94] "Les productions des arts, & par conséquent toutes les choses dont l'homme fait usage au-delà des présens spontanés de la nature, sont du Luxe. L'utile, le commode, l'agréeable, sont des variétés absolument du même genre. Le pain & les inventions relatives à la guerre sont du Luxe." Ibid., 105.

[95] This gesture of Butel-Dumont's deviates from Shovlin's assessment of a trend in the 1770s which saw a growing distinction between commerce and luxe.

knowing. "But if we apply ourselves to the understanding of matters which interest the administration," he continued, "then they will be cleared up in less than a century." With new "axioms" and "principles," what he deemed "public happiness" would be protected from "incompetence and infidelity."[96] Butel-Dumont's concern with conceptual certainty and clarity thus transcended his anxious insistence about the correct definition of luxury, his drive to arrive at the definition and configuration of a new science, political economy. When based on "certain and recognised principles," this new science would ensure public felicity. According to Butel-Dumont, French society would best be served if political economy were reconfigured as a "science of administration."[97]

Butel-Dumont's belaboured attention to the correct definition of words and concepts displayed sensationalist characteristics that echoed the prevalent sensationalist philosophy warning against the confusion of signs with things.[98] His etymological emphasis was also historical. Butel-Dumont was, to my knowledge, the first eighteenth-century figure to make explicit the etymological link between *luxuria* and *luxus*, between lust and "excess, extravagance in eating and drinking, luxury, debauchery."[99] For Butel-Dumont, these were not immoral features, nor did they counter virtues, nor even fully belong within the realm of ethics.[100] Once again, this etymological "generosity" supported a single aim: to insist that luxury equalled surplus, surabundance, and nothing more. By repeating this aim, Butel-Dumont structured his argument as a response to the anti-luxury writers.

For Butel-Dumont, therefore, the sense attributed to the word *luxus* and its co-derivatives related to incontinence was "another sensible proof

96 "L'étude de l'économie politique est-elle donc un labyrinthe inextricable? point du tout. Il n'y a peut-être pas dans cette science trente vérités majeures à connoître. Si l'On s'appliquoit sérieusement à pénétrer les matieres qui intéressent l'administration, elles seroient toutes éclaircies en moins d'un siecle. On auroit alors des axiômes, au lieu de questions; & chacun étant guidé par des principes certains, reconnus, l'impéritie ni l'infidélité ne pourroient nuire au bonheur public." Ibid., xx.

97 Among Scottish contemporaries, Adam Smith being the most central figure, this obligation was the purview of the "science of the legislator." See Donald Winch, *Adam Smith's Politics: An Essay in Historiographic Revision* (Cambridge: Cambridge University Press, 1978), 159–60, and Knud Haakonssen, 1981, 97–98.

98 See John Shovlin's excellent summary of the sensationalist programme in "Cultural Politics of Luxury," 578.

99 Charlton T. Lewis and Charles Short, *A Latin Dictionary* (Oxford: Clarendon Press, 1880), 3:93. Cf. Anne Robert Jacques Turgot's article "Étymologie" for the *Encyclopédie*, 6: 98–111.

100 The double meaning was also reflected in the famous *Dictionnaire de Furetière*'s definition of *luxe*, which was followed alphabetically, but also thematically, by *luxure*.

that *luxus, luxuries* & *luxuria* signify surplus (*surabundance*)." Butel-Dumont tapped into another key topos of the period which deserves further exploration: the semantic connections between the concepts related to economy and those related to sex. He argued that that "the vigour which drives the frequent search for women's caresses and which lead to the Sin of *luxure,* has at its source the *surabundance* of juices that cannot be contained, as the French word *incontinence* indicates." His work encourages an examination of the ways in which writers outside of the "*économiste*'s sect" formulated and confronted the idea of luxury. In particular, the following considers works which we know reached an audience beyond the *philosophes* in the Parisian *salons.*

Mercier's Old Man

One intervention about luxury we know reached readers far beyond the *salons* is found in the various prose portraits of Paris written by the notorious journalist, dramatist, and novelist Louis-Sébastien Mercier (1740–1814). The first such work, *L'An 2440, rêve s'il en fût jamais* (*The Year 2440, dream if ever there was one*) (1771) was, according to Robert Darnton, *the* forbidden bestseller in eighteenth-century France.[101] In this account of Paris as it might look in the year 2440, a 700-year-old dreamer awakens to find himself transported by time to a new world. Mercier's observations are organised thematically, but one of the recurrent themes is luxury. Luxury is the focus of the chapter "On Commerce," which has as its theme the ills of colonialism. "It was agreeable," the old man's "guide" tells him, for you to "take chocolate, savour spices, eat sugar and pineapples, drink cream from Barbados, dress in bright cloths from India." To do so, however, was to partake in a "destructive luxury" and deteriorate into a people that was "blind and barbaric!"[102] For the "thirst for gold" led them to "break the sacred ties of blood and nature on the Guinean coast, arming fathers against sons."

In this new world, a Physiocratic paradise of sorts emerged: "We only practice internal trade" founded on agriculture which "satisfies the needs of man, and not his pride." The old man later notes that indeed, ornamentation has not disappeared in this utopian future – people wear "braided

---

[101] *L'An 2440* tops all of Darnton's lists best-selling clandestine literature in the period, undergoing twenty-five editions between 1769 and 1789. See Robert Darnton, *The Forbidden Best-Sellers of Pre-Revolutionary France* (New York: W.W. Norton & Company, 1996), 63.
[102] Ibid., 374–75.

FIGURE 1. "The accursed hunger for gold ..." This frontispiece to vol. 3 of the
1774 edition of the *Histoire des deux Indes* (La Haye: Gosse, fils, 7 vols., in -8)
was described in the work's "Explanation of the Engravings" as "A Philosopher,
with a gesture of indignation, traces, on a column, these words: AURI SACRA
FAMES, &c. We see in the distance, some vessels." Virgil's famous lament about
the effects of the "accursed hunger for gold" on the "hearts of mortals" (*Aeneid*
III, 56–57) represents one of the perspectives on gold and luxury in the *Histoire*.
*Courtesy of the Rare Books and Special Collections Division of the Library of
Congress, Washington, DC.*

hats," for example, but these are harmless in comparison to when "in my time, a puerile and ruinous luxury had deranged all brains; a body without a soul was overloaded with gilt, and the robot thus resembled a man."[103] The effect of ornamental goods in the year 2440 is portrayed as rather anodyne in comparison to the eighteenth-century phenomenon. The luxury of the old man's epoch not only deranged brains and emptied souls, but caused the poverty of nations by engendering new needs and costs.[104] Mercier's inflammatory language evokes Rousseau: "burning caustic," the guide remarks in reply to the old man's query about where the hospital had gone; luxury had "gangrened the healthiest parts of your State, and your political body was covered with ulcers. Rather than gently closing these wounds, you envenomed them further."[105] In the "new Paris," however, the "art of creating debts and not paying them was no longer the science of the beautiful people."[106] The "barbarian luxury" which "fattened people with lackeys and horses" disappeared along with the "golden, painted and varnished" carriages. Instead, carts carried goods and furniture and people remembered that they had legs with which they walked the streets in an orderly manner.[107] The old man's guide to the future reassures him that "since, politics is more enlightened ... it unites and enriches citizens rather than ruins them."[108]

Mercier's later portrait of the capital, *Tableau de Paris* (1781), similarly expressed consternation at the devouring effects of luxury upon eighteenth-century Parisian life, and also upon equality and morals in France. With constant appeals to the glorious and virtuous past of the ancients, Mercier's Paris had become, to his regret, a space corrupted by the effects of a destructive luxury. Viewed through the lens of the language of luxury, Mercier's entire portrait of Paris can be seen to be about the shape and effects of *luxe*: We can understand it as a depiction of a newly transformed space. But it is a language that carries with it a level of contingency, similar to that in Saint-Lambert's *luxe*.

[103] Louis-Sébastien Mercier, *L'An 2440: Rêve s'il en fut jamais*. Edited by Christine Marcandier-Colard and Christophe Cave. Paris: La Découverte (1999). The work was begun in 1768 and first published in 1771. See note b of chap. 2: "J'ai sept cent ans." See also Everett C. Wilkie, "Mercier's *L'An 2440*: Its Publishing History during the Author's Lifetime," *Harvard Library Bulletin* 32 (1984).
[104] See Ibid., chap. 40, "Du commerce."
[105] Ibid., chap. 8, "Le nouveau Paris," 118.
[106] Ibid., chap. 4, "Les portefaix," 96.
[107] Ibid., chap 5, "Les voitures," 100–01.
[108] Ibid., chap. 40, "Du commerce," 378.

Voltaire's Old Man

In a similar vein, consider the voice of another old man, Voltaire's *L'Homme aux quarante écus* (*The Man with Forty Crowns*) (1768), who argued, "[a]nother cause of our poverty lies in our new needs." Though Voltaire served as the public face of pro-luxury discourse in France, a closer reading of this later text reveals a more complicated stance and points again to ambivalence within the discourse of luxury. Voltaire's "forty-crown man" continued: "We need to pay our neighbours 4 million for an article, and five or six for another, in order to fill our noses with a stinking powder from America; coffee, tea, chocolate, cochineal, indigo, spices cost us more than 60 million per year. All this was unknown in the time of Henri IV." This remark of Voltaire's suggests the possibility of an alternative reading of the earlier "Le Mondain" in which the famous poem's "pleasant banter" in favour of luxury is tinged with irony, presenting the reader with a not so subtle critique of imperial trade and its "stinking," expensive goods. *L'Homme aux quarante écus* also accentuates a deep connection between popular conceptions of the manifestation of luxury and the material presence of the colonial experience. Regarded in this light, the critique of bad luxury in the post-war period is seen to be entrenched in negative views of the rampant imperial and colonial experience of the period.

BOTH INGENIOUS AND BARBAROUS: LUXURY IN THE *HISTOIRE*

As we have seen, by far the most influential narrative on the causes and effects of this imperial enterprise in eighteenth-century France was the *Histoire des deux Indes*. But as a self-declared history of commerce, the work is also a key source for the examination of representations of luxury in eighteenth-century France. Part and parcel of its multiple narratives about the commerce and customs of the European empires, luxury was represented in the *Histoire* as contingent on both time and space.

The discussion of luxury in the *Histoire* was predominantly characterised by its plural nature, or "pantheism."[109] In its opening books, amid accounts of the discoveries and conquests and wars of the main European empires, the references to luxury are mainly favourable. It is discussed in laudatory terms; its effects are consistently construed as advantageous.

---

[109] I draw this term from Jones and Spang, "Necessity and Luxury," 55.

In "Ormuz," "the most beautiful and pleasant city in the Orient," an "ingenious luxury" (*un luxe ingénieux*) combined with abundant wealth and "polished" inhabitants.[110] An "immense commerce" and the presence of "flirtatious women" meant that one could "taste" all "delights." In this commercial paradise, good manners prevailed:

Men from almost every part of the earth could be seen there, conducting their business with a politeness and consideration little known in other places of commerce. The port's merchants who communicated a part of their courtesy to the foreigners set this tone. Their manners, the good order that they maintained in their city, the conveniences, and the pleasures of every sort that they gathered, all converged with the interests of commerce to attract traders.[111]

The *Histoire*'s discussion of Ormuz provides an excellent example of the work's assumption about the inextricable link between luxury and commerce. You could not have luxury without commerce. Furthermore, the places in which commerce flourished were ones where the life of the merchant was made pleasant: You could not have commerce without luxury.

Luxury, in this account, was at once an indicator, a symptom, a cause, and an effect of a healthy commercial society. Although it may have resulted from morally undesirable roots on occasion, luxury yielded positive effects as early as the fourteenth century: At that time in France, the *Histoire* related, vanity generated industry by creating a need for luxury items unavailable for import: "The custom of wearing their arms on their clothes made for some progress in their manufactures, because the woollen coats [*draps*] covered in arms were a luxury that could not be taken from abroad."[112] At the same time, a "grand and tasteful" luxury generated opulence in Venice, resuscitating the architecture of Athens, where what was considered noble was at once "economical and sumptuous." Foreigners bought vessels, silk and gold, and silverware. The inhabitants of Venice were criticized for using utensils and dishes of gold and silver. Although sumptuary laws existed, these "permitted a sort of luxury which

---

[110] This portion of the text warrants further analysis of its Orientalist qualities. Among the first to address this question as it relates to the *HDI* was Srinivas Aravamudan in *Tropicopolitains: Colonialism and Agency, 1688–1804* (Durham, NC: Duke University Press, 1999). Madeleine Dobie has since drawn attention to the ways the Orient offered a displacement of colonial anxiety in eighteenth-century France, in *Trading Places*.

[111] *HDI* (1780), book 1, chap. 14, 83–84.

[112] Ibid., book 1, 11. As we shall see, this vanity also inspired luxury in the colonies, especially among the Marylanders. This same point had been made earlier by the abbé Galiani in his *Dialogues sur le commerce des blés* (1770).

conserved funds in the state" – a state whose finances were well administered and whose people were content. The Venetians were the first to have imagined "tying wealthy subjects to the government by committing them to placing a part of their fortunes in the state's funds." Combined with the great population and its "immense treasures," Venice's commerce was the greatest in all of Europe.[113]

The reverse was also true: The English lived without luxury and did not have "arts and advancements."[114] The Germans lived without commerce or industry, and "if the peaceful possession of one's inherited goods can compensate man for his lost liberty, then the people of Germany were happy," the *Histoire* remarked, not without irony.[115] The opening sections of the *Histoire* thus set the stage for understanding the mixed foundations of the European nations that would become the maritime empires of the seventeenth and eighteenth centuries via conquest and war.

In the non-European world, luxury was also represented as both cause and sign of refinement, yet here the valence is less positive. In China, the "arts of luxury" were so advanced that the prince did not need to pay homage to the labourers of the soil, but he did "nevertheless" and in so doing enhanced his status in "public opinion."[116] The very first mention of *luxe* in the *Histoire* appeared in an account of how the nobles of Constantinople learned the arts and luxury of the "Arabs and the Chinese" during the "crazy" crusades."[117] These nobles quickly became dependent on luxury and on the arts it generated, such that they could not easily deprive themselves of it.[118] A pattern of dependency emerged: The nobles' conquests generated wants soon transformed into needs. This conception of a self-perpetuating system of luxury reoccurs later in the *Histoire*, as well as in Diderot's writings on luxury.

The *Histoire*'s discussion of the luxury of the ancient world resembled its premodern variety: Luxury led to progress among the ancient Egyptians. Roman luxury grew with conquest, and Rome's consumption could hardly be satisfied by the Egyptians' drawing goods out of

---

[113] *HDI* (1772), book 1, 13–14.

[114] *HDI* (1780), book 1, 18.

[115] "Si la possession paisible de son héritage peut dédommager l'homme de la liberté, le peuple d'Allemagne étoit heureux." Ibid.

[116] *HDI* (1780), book 1, chap. 20, 104.

[117] "La noblesse de l'empire prit dans les folles expéditions des croisades quelque chose des moeurs des Grecs et des Arabes." *HDI* (1780), book 1, 11.

[118] "Elle connut leurs arts et leur luxe ; il lui devint difficile de s'en passer." Ibid.

India, among them incense. "Nothing equalled the frenzy that was generally had over this perfume," the *Histoire* remarked. "It served equally for the worship of the gods, for magnificence, and for voluptuousness." The Egyptians surrendered to this abundance, such that "Cleopatra, with whom their empire and their history ended, was as magnificent as she was voluptuous."[119] Citing Pliny, the *Histoire* sustained the thesis that the Romans possessed sufficient virtue to preserve the power that their ancestors had acquired, and Egypt contributed to the majesty of the empire by way of the riches that it brought from India.[120] This connection of virtue to majesty and the grandeur of voluptuousness to metaphors of surrender, submission, and addiction or compulsion conjoined a productive thesis to a pathologizing discourse of luxury. This mode of speaking about luxury construed it as both creative and destructive – and in both cases almost a natural force with powers over human agency.

There are two moments in the *Histoire*'s account of early modern Europe, however, at which luxury's effects are deemed wholly negative. In medieval France, the barons are described as having a "barbarous *faste*" and a "savage luxury" that did not encourage the "useful arts."[121] In a similar vein, luxury paired with desires (*jouissances*) caused the disappearance of "noble passions" among the Portuguese. The effect of this evaporation of virtue was both corporal and moral. Working in tandem, luxury and desires "weaken the body's strength and the soul's virtues." Corrupted by wealth and by the aim of their conquests, the generosity of the Portuguese was weakened further by their "cupidity," the *Histoire* argued.[122]

The *Histoire*'s representation of luxury changed significantly as the record of the European encounter with the New World progressed. Whereas we find a generally productive and favourable notion of luxury in the Old World – both in its ancient and early modern periods – its functions and effects were different on the far side of the globe. Luxury's influence is clearly negative in the final books of the *Histoire*, which tell the story of the European colonial presence and settlements in the Americas.

Two principal lines of critique reveal the preoccupations of the *Histoire*'s authors. The first is anxiety over the need to increase the

[119] *HDI* (1780), book 1, chap. 11, 73.
[120] Ibid., 74.
[121] *HDI* (1780), book 1, 17.
[122] Ibid., 80–81.

population through the establishment of solid family structures. Thus, in North America, the absence of luxury, which "drags misery in its path," encourages a "desire to please one another" and to "assemble," leading to good health and fecundity.[123] No longer was voluptuousness a regal trait, as it had been under Cleopatra; rather, only those "wealthy and voluptuous colonists" were distracted from their purpose when "attracted to the metropolis by its luxury" and consequently neglected the responsibilities of family life and agriculture.[124]

Instilling this form of dependency was a metropolitan strategy, the *Histoire* explained in its second line of critique. The spread of the taste for luxury was a way of ensuring that the colonies remained dependent on metropolitan manufactures and that they did not become rivals in the cured meat and wheat markets.[125] A vain finery (*vaine parure*) was encouraged among Canadians, while the sedentary arts were discouraged by the French court. Virginians and Marylanders were contaminated by the Old World's luxury, resulting in an "unfortunate indebtedness" that yielded dependency once again.[126] Here, the *Histoire*'s language of luxury is characterised by metaphors of contamination, contagion, and surrender. The *éclat*, or lustre, encouraged among Canadians by Europeans in fact masked the colonists' poverty and distracted them from success in both agriculture and lives of health and virtue.

The critique of luxury's power to corrupt came to a head in book 17 in an intervention by Denis Diderot, inserted as chapter 4 and entitled "Comparison of polished peoples and savage peoples." Echoing Rousseau's famous critique in the *First and Second Discourses*, among others, Diderot here announced that luxury made civilised man "more barbarous than the savage." At this moment, the *Histoire* spoke of how the "spectacle of luxury," equated with *faste*, both "humiliates and crushes" all whom it touches.[127]

The language of luxury had changed. Through its travels from the Old World to the New, luxury now resembled servitude. The representations of luxury in the *Histoire* thus reflect a polyphony of views that is representative – especially those views that may at first strike us as contradictory but upon closer examination can better be understood as ambivalent. Let us now turn to Diderot's writings on commerce, for it is

---

[123] Ibid., book 18, chap. 34, 363.
[124] Ibid., book 18, chap. 35, 370.
[125] "les marchés des salaisons & des bleds." Ibid., book 18, chap. 28, 345.
[126] Ibid., book 16, chap. 18, 143.
[127] *HDI* (1780), book 17, chap. 4, 347.

in the writings of this key contributor to the discourse of luxury – and indeed to the *Histoire* – that this ambivalence is best exhibited.

DIDEROT: *BON LUXE, MAUVAIS LUXE*

Diderot's various interventions in the discussion about luxury further collapsed the polarized constructions of luxury publicized by the eighteenth-century "quarrellers" while sustaining their concern with definition. He argued that there are two types of luxury: *bon luxe* and *mauvais luxe* (good luxury and bad luxury).

As we have seen, his was not the first such argument. Leblanc's translation of Hume's essays had presented a similar concept to the reading public, and Saint-Lambert had appropriated it but reconfigured it for his *Encyclopédie* article. Diderot probably read Hume's essay, though we do not know for certain. Even if he did not, the similarities between their positions are notable and point to a shared, though not identical, language in circulation. Recall that by most historiographical accounts, LeBlanc's translation of Hume is considered the high point of the apology for luxury in France.[128] In this account, the power of Rousseau's critique in the *First and Second Discourses* quieted those arguments in favour of luxury. Yet sources outside of the familiar cursus of texts in the history of eighteenth-century political and economic thought allow for an additional interpretation.

An example of an alternative locus for these views is a piece of art criticism, one of the first. In 1767, Diderot inserted his first commentary on luxury within his review of that year's art *salon*, written for Grimm's *Correspondance littéraire*. The *Satire contre le luxe à la manière de Perse* ("Satire against luxury in the style of Perseus") promised a lampoon, but Perseus's style, in Diderot's version, offered a more nuanced appraisal. Although Diderot was then allegedly sympathetic to the Physiocrats' reverence of agriculture and therefore might have been expected to be critical of luxury, the "Satire" posed the problem in Humean terms: He drew a distinction between useful and vicious luxury.[129] This first expression of Diderot's two-sided model of luxury was later augmented in his philosophical rebuttal of his sensualist fellow *philosophe*, Claude Adrien

---

[128] See Shovlin, *Political Economy of Virtue*, 23. In his "Translator's preface," Leblanc refers to Melon as his "friend" and notes the symmetries between Hume and Melon's texts. See p. xv.

[129] For further analysis of Diderot's rendition of luxury in the *Salon* of 1767, see Anderson, *Diderot's Dream*.

Helvétius (1715–71), the "Réfutation d'Helvétius," written in 1773 but first published as fragments in the *Correspondance littéraire* from January 1783 to March 1786.[130]

Diderot's most elaborate discussion of the subject lies, however, in a work best described as a mirror of princes not unrelated to Fénelon's *Télémaque*. In this case, however, it was a mirror of empress text. Published posthumously, this collection of memoranda and counselling essays is now referred to as the *Mélanges pour Catherine II (Assortments for Catherine II)*.[131] The collection consists of a compilation of texts believed to be memoranda prepared by Diderot for the empress of Russia, who invited him to St. Petersburg in 1773–74 to infuse her political practice and court with French *philosophie*. Widely acknowledged as illustrations of Diderot's political thinking in the mid-1770s, these texts represent a key source for our understanding of Diderot's assessment of luxury but also of the second edition of the *Histoire des deux Indes* (1774), the first to which Diderot contributed.

Lodged between an essay on public schools and another on private education, we find memorandum no. 26, called simply "Luxe," though it covers far more than that.[132] Luxury provided Diderot with a framework to develop a broader diagnosis of the social and political situation followed by a stunning plan of action for an "enlightened" minister of France.[133] The memorandum began with a satirical description of what Diderot referred to as the "bizarrely complicated" contemporary writings on luxury.[134] According to his report of the *querelle*, two groups had

---

[130] Diderot "refuted" Helvétius's hyperbolic sensualism and his "reduction" of the "wealth and diversity of humanity" into a single essentialist model of "man." See Diderot, *Oeuvres* (1994), 1:774.

[131] I am citing from Laurent Versini's edition: Diderot, *Oeuvres*, vol. 3. See also Georges Dulac, "Pour reconsidérer l'histoire des *Observations sur le Nakaz* (à partir des réflexions de 1775 sur la physiocratie)," in *Éditer Diderot: Études recueillies par Georges Dulac* (Oxford: Voltaire Foundation, 1988), 467–514 and "Observations sur le Nakaz," in *Dictionnaire de Diderot*, Roland Mortier and Raymond Trousson, eds., (Paris: Honoré Champion, 1999). Wilda Anderson offers a careful analysis of how *repos*, the "Tahitian site of jouissance," is the only manifestation of luxury amid Diderot's Tahitians in the *Supplément au Voyage de Bougainville* (1772). See her *Diderot's Dream*, chap. 4, esp. 149.

[132] Although the order of the manuscripts of these texts is not entirely certain, we can discern a semblance of their structure in part thanks to an embryonic "Plan" of Diderot's for his manuscripts. See Diderot, *Oeuvres*, 200. At the time of writing, we look forward to Georges Dulac's edition of the *Mélanges* for volume 21 of the authoritative edition of Diderot's complete works, the *DPV*.

[133] See Diderot, *Oeuvres complètes*, vol. 3, "Politique," 200.

[134] Diderot, *Mélanges pour Catherine II*, in *Œuvres*, 3:282–92, 308.

formed: one comprised Jean-François Melon and the "attacks" on luxury by the "sect of the Economists"; the other backed Voltaire's "defence." This distinction is itself remarkable, given Melon's arguments in favour of luxury. Helvétius (whose *De l'Esprit* Diderot had earlier rebutted) had no place in this scheme, Diderot wrote, because he "drowns the true principles of luxury in such a prodigious luxury of details" that "his ideas were not very clear." Yet luxury was "plain to see," Diderot declared. One had only to proceed empirically and sensually, with one's eyes, to recognise that "the history of luxury is written on all of the doors of the capital's residences" and "in such bold type that I cannot conceive how, with such good eyes, they did not read it readily."[135] The history of luxury was not to be found in texts but was decipherable through a "reading" of the material world.

Taking up the challenge he posed twenty years earlier in the article "*Encyclopédie*," Diderot began the memorandum in a manner that had to be familiar to readers of works on luxury by then – by staking a claim to the true definition of luxury, founded on a critique of existing stances and the identification of an obvious, if ignored, sign. In this version, luxury was the effect of a historical situation whereby an "incredible inequality of fortune among citizens ha[d] come to be established" in France, a "centre of true opulence" surrounded by a deep, vast misery. The implications of this centripetal wealth were devastating, by his account: "In this nation," he continued, "merit, good education, enlightenment and virtue lead to nothing," while gold "leads to everything." Gold had become the "god of the nation." With religion usurped by gold, virtue too had been reconfigured in the France he depicted: The only virtue was wealth, the only vice, poverty. The consequence of this condition was a "ruinous emulation" of upper-class lifestyles,[136] and the result was a nation that Diderot deemed best represented by "three symbolic animals" (probably the three orders or Estates into which prerevolutionary France was organised) who, like Lafontaine's fabled frog, swelled themselves continuously out of "envy of the others" and finished by collapsing.[137]

---

[135] Ibid., 293. This second jab at his sensualist foe would have been obvious to his readership.

[136] "Il inspire une ruineuse emulation aux conditions supérieures, et l'exemple des uns et des autres entraîne le reste de la nation." Ibid., 293. On the structural force of emulation in the eighteenth century, see Reinert, *Virtue of Emulation*.

[137] Diderot was clearly making a point with a long history. Cf. Lafontaine, "The Frog Who Wants to Be as Fat as the Bull" (*La Grenouille qui veut se faire aussi grosse que le bœuf*): "Envieuse, s'étend et s'enfle, et se travaille.... La chétive pécore / S'enfla si bien qu'elle creva. / Le monde est si plein de gens qui ne sont plus sages; / Tout bourgeois veut

Now the narrative shifted to the first person to find Diderot asking "all of the philosophers" and "all of the politicians" if his portrait of their miserable state was loyal. These politicians and philosophers were made to exclaim: "But that is where we find stables, horses, statues, and paintings, wines from all regions, parks, castles, and masterpieces from the Gobelins and the Savonnerie!" That is, they replied with the now familiar argument of Melon and Hume that luxury produced wealth. To this, Diderot retorted with his first direct attack on the status quo: "So much the better; where would you like for them to be?" "What," he prodded, "would you like people to do with their gold?" In his assessment, those who spent less than they earned were wise, whereas the poor who emulated the wealthy were crazy. Thus, he also put forward an argument in favour of savings and a tirade against emulation. Wealth was not the problem in and of itself. Rather, "in a society poisoned by bad luxury," the French had become the worst species of bugs: "scrawny insects that surround these puffy and portly bodies to attach themselves, and to sting them and suck them and to spread drop by drop a little portion of the blood that they have drained from the veins of their co-citizens."

This "bad luxury" not only assaulted the integrity of the individual, it also corrupted *moeurs* (mores), fine arts, sciences, and the mechanical arts in a spiral of empty emulation and dissimulation "at the centre of wealth by wealth itself, mother of all vices; in the state superior to this one by baseness; in the inferior states by prostitution and bad faith; in each state, by the indifference about the choice of means of acquiring more than one has, or of masking one's poverty." This may be read as a self-contradiction or a form of ventriloquism – standard practice for Diderot. Here, "the great lord court[s] the sovereign's courtesan," the fine arts found more advantages in "working more" rather than "working well," such that "Vien only sculpts the tops of doors." The mechanical arts had degenerated so much that superficial glosses were coveted more

bâtir comme les grand seigneurs, / Tout petit prince a des ambassadeurs, / Tout marquis veut avoir des pages." Jean de La Fontaine's *Fables choisies, mises en vers par J. de La Fontaine* underwent seven editions, according to Cioranescu (1709, 1715, 1743, 1755, 1796, 1796, 1797), and four illustrated editions, according to Alain-Marie Bassy. See *Les Fables de La Fontaine*, 261. Marc Fumaroli, *Le poète et le roi: Jean de La Fontaine en son siècle* (Paris: de Fallois, 1997) offers an explanation of how this fable related to the plight of Fouquet, whose château Vaux-le-Vicomte was confiscated by Louis XIV, and who was himself imprisoned for posturing as more luxurious, more sumptuous, and, in effect, more royal than the king. See also the reference to frogs and bulls in Isaac de Pinto's *Essai sur le luxe* (Paris: Michel Lambert, 1762), 23–24: "Mais comme il y a plus de grenouilles que de boeufs, le nombre de ceux qui crèvent est grand."

than quality. In short, the "entire society is full of fatuous gluttons" or "lavish misers": "a grande dame has 20 dresses, six shirts, much lace, and no underwear," and "the first loge at the Opera is rented, and the libretto borrowed. Two or three stables are kept and the children's education is neglected."

In this state of affairs, French heads "spin" with the "drunkenness of gold," and in this moment of "vertigo," their fortune "passes more rapidly than it was acquired." So Diderot wound his readers towards a clear conclusion – only to jolt them. For this dizziness, Diderot claimed, saved "the nation" ("*Ce vertige sauve la nation*"). With his characteristically agile rhetoric, Diderot pushed the classical argument of the anti-luxury spokespeople even further by turning it on its head. The "vertigo" of bad luxury saved the nation by triggering a vertiginous cycle of social and individual destruction, which in turn generated more bad luxury. The self-generating spiral of degeneration destroyed the nation, but in so doing also saved it. For a destroyed nation could be rebuilt, this time on proper foundations. Striking here is how Diderot resorted to the concept of nationhood to make his claim fifteen years before the abbé Sièyes's provocative pamphlet "What is the Third Estate?"(1789) armed the Third Estate with this political category which liberated them from the absolute monarchy's stranglehold on "the state."[138]

What were readers – and the French as victims – meant to make of this social paradox? For Diderot, *le remède est dans le mal* (the cure is the ailment). That is to say, the remedy for luxury lay within luxury itself – but a different kind.[139] By encouraging the "rebirth of another sort of luxury," Diderot argued, that was no longer the "mask of misery" but instead "the sign of public ease, and of general happiness," one could restore "the *moeurs* [and] the sparkle of life to this poor nation."

Who better than Diderot to lead the charge? Crowning himself "King Denis," he offered Catherine II and his fellow nationals a programme for total social transformation.[140] The conviction was that this would

---

[138] For the evolution of the concept of the nation in eighteenth-century France, see David A. Bell, *The Cult of the Nation in France: Inventing Nationalism, 1680–1800* (Cambridge, MA: Harvard University Press, 2001).

[139] Jean Starobinski uses the same phrase to describe his reading of Rousseau's social thought: In essence, the cure for civilisation's ills lay within civilisation. *Le remède dans le mal: Critique et légitimation de l'artifice à l' âge des Lumières* (Paris : Gallimard. 1989), 170.

[140] As Dena Goodman has so carefully reconstructed, this was apparently not the first time Diderot had been crowned "King." Dealt the *fève*, or bean, at a celebration of the "Fête des Rois" on 6 January 1770 at the rue Royale home of the baron d'Holbach, Diderot proclaimed "Le Code Denis," in verse no less, extolling a love of liberty and unity in a

lead towards a healthier society, a "redressed and enriched nation."[141] The self-proclaimed "philosopher-king" first delineated eighteen prag- matic remedies for France's ills, ranging from the "reduction in num- ber of royal residences" to the "cessation of tribute payment to Rome" to the "reduction of middle operators in tax collection." He suggested "precautions" be taken to ensure that "gold does not become the god of my country" and to ensure that rewards for merits and virtue would exist only "*through competitions*" ("*par le concours aux places*" – his empha- sis). Under these conditions, King Denis would be able to promise that "the peasants of Brie will have a chicken in their pot on Sunday."

But once the monarch had fulfilled the condition of a chicken in every pot, "what then must be the conditions for material ease and well-being in society?" he asked.[142] For Diderot, the wealth of the nation could not be achieved by merely satisfying subsistence conditions; the fulfilment of necessities was a necessary but insufficient condition. Rather, in the first instance, the ruler should have the intention to "no longer entangle myself in anything, and to believe that every one of [his] citizens under- stands their interests better than [he does]." Here, King Denis displayed a penchant for a kind of laissez-faire policy that translated into abstention from any involvement in commerce other than to assist it in supporting the "great faltering *maisons de commerce*," abstention from regulation of manufactures, and the rewarding of inventors not by exclusive rights but by "money and honours," freedom of the press, and so forth.[143] Most important, however, his plan would ensure the people's happiness.[144]

A second phase of social transformation would ensue once "talent and virtue lead to something," once "the only inequality of fortunes are those from industry or happiness," once he had "banned all of these

---

speech Goodman reveals to be a defence of the "values of the Republic of Letters, in contrast to those of monarchy." *The Republic of Letters*, 185–86.

[141] Although Versini does not make any remarks to this effect, this seems to be a little joke about Plato's philosopher-kings. The exact citation reads: "Me voilà couronné par les mains de Votre Majesté Impériale, et le philosophe Denis proclamé par Melchior Grimm." Diderot, *Oeuvres*, 3:295.

[142] The term Diderot uses is *aisance des conditions*. According to *Le Nouveau Petit Robert*, *aisance* denotes affluence as well as grace; it means the easy life assured by wealth (*une situation de fortune*), and it also carries a corporal meaning: grace and the absence of effort.

[143] In an earlier memorandum to Catherine II, Diderot praised "Houses of commerce" as one of the few French successes in the economic realm. See "Maisons de commerce" in *Oeuvres*, vol. 3.

[144] For Diderot, true *bonheur* was not innocence but the product of the exercise of virtue. See "Réfutation suivie de l'ouvrage d'Helvétius intitulé L'Homme," in *Oeuvres*, 2:432.

corporations which condemn millions of industrious citizens to die of hunger or to enter a prison," and once he had encouraged agriculture, "the nourishing mother [*la mère nourrice*] of an entire empire." The contempt for corporations and the monopolies expressed here by Diderot had crystallized in the debate over the Company of the Indies, discussed in Chapter 4 of this book. Only at this juncture in the transformation, he continued, were "wealthy citizens" ensured.

"What then," asked King Denis, "will these wealthy citizens do with their gold?" The problem, he emphasised, was that "gold is not edible." [145] The nation's rescue lay thus in the cultivation of the "other" luxury: By devoting themselves to "multiplying their pleasures," the pleasures of "all of the senses," poets, philosophers, sculptors, and "treasures from China" would abound. This other luxury was a luxury of sensual pleasures. Cultivation of pleasure came at a small price: These were all of the "charming vices" that made for the happiness of man in this world and, Diderot added sarcastically, for his "eternal damnation" in the other. The "inconveniences" of libertine mores, such as the existence of "courtesans," "kept women," "seduced girls," and "husbands and wives with little loyalty," were, on balance, "petty" or "small." Though "many voluptuous pleasures of every kind, lots of pride, lots of envy, lots of lust, and many lazy people" would abound, there would no longer be any crime.

For Diderot, these conventional vices were preferable to those produced by "misery, the taste for splendour, and destitution." By minding that "gold and more gold cannot give one all of the prerogatives of merit and virtue," King Denis also maintained that the fine arts would necessarily "make great progress." Here he revisited the examples provided in the description of the society corrupted by bad luxury and showed how, under the "other" luxury, these instances would transform, and would encourage not only sound mores but also the growth of French industry. In this transformed France, the young woman (*femme du peuple*) who in an earlier scenario sought vainly to buy a gold watch that did not function would reply instead to the watch maker: "Sir, I would like a good watch, with a strong box made in Paris; no Geneva, please, I would prefer to do without." [146] To the cloth merchant, she would say: "Rubbish! Madam,

---

[145] "L'or ne se mange pas." This is an extraordinary measure or standard of value – consumption in the most literal sense. Was it also, perhaps, a nod to the "*Auri sacra fames*" (deplorable hunger for gold) of the *Aeneid* (III, 56–7)?

[146] The example of watches is a highly revealing indicator of the extent to which Diderot's discussion reflects a social reality. Cissie Fairchilds provides a table listing "selected items" she characterises as "populuxe" goods. She deduces an increasing presence of

this is but a rag; show me something better or I shall go elsewhere." And finally, recognition for the author would ensue: "When Denis passes in the streets of the capital, there is a tumult, a noise, acclamations, never ending 'Vive Denis!' And Denis, who has a tender soul ... is embraced on the Pont Neuf as Catherine Second is in her convent and will be one day in the streets."

In Diderot's idealised vision, luxury was inevitable, but it was also a phenomenon that could produce social good and happiness, provided it took a carefully circumscribed form. The fruit's core was not completely rotten. In this system, good luxury could perpetuate itself – and did. So did bad luxury. The difference between the two was that the cycle of bad luxury ultimately destroyed the nation. Their functioning was not dissimilar from the operation of the invisible hand. But in this text, at least, society switched from good to bad luxury through the reforms of an enlightened monarch. In the end, King Denis's programme for redressing a society caught in a vicious cycle was not so different from how Emma Rothschild and others have portrayed Adam Smith's reform strategy.[147] Smith's dominant definition of luxury as the opposite of necessity and his call for sumptuary laws stood in contrast to Diderot's account of the anxiety-provoking phenomenon that was the state of luxury in France. The alternative vision offered in the *Mélanges* argued that a new France had first to acknowledge this state of luxury and then work with it. Instead of obliterating luxury and excoriating it as anathema to a certain notion of classical virtue, Diderot preferred that monarchs seek ways to welcome the inevitability of human vanity by encouraging its least perilous manifestations. In this way, to paraphrase Albert Hirschman, Diderot adjoined a richer dimension to the intended consequences of his programme, the programme of Catherine II, and the programme of

these "populuxe" items in the "lower-class inventories" from 1725 to 1785. These goods were desired as symbols of an aristocratic lifestyle rather than for their own usefulness: "Had they wanted watches only for their usefulness as timepieces, lower-class Parisians should have been content with cheap pinch-beck or silver ones. Gold watches were a symbol of aristocracy; no *petit maître* aping the *gens de mode* would have considered his ensemble complete without one." Indeed "cheap" watches nearly disappeared from "lower-class inventories" whereas gold watches show a "spectacular rise." She shows that 5.1 per cent of "lower-class inventories" contained gold watches in 1725, whereas 54.7 per cent did so in 1785. This increase took place against a backdrop of stable value. Cissie Fairchilds, "The Production and Marketing of Populuxe Goods in Eighteenth-Century Paris," in *Consumption and the World of Goods*, John Brewer and Roy Porter, eds. (London: Routledge, 1993), 229–30.

147 Emma Rothschild, *Economic Sentiments: Adam Smith, Condorcet and the Enlightenment* (Cambridge, MA: Harvard University Press, 2001), esp. 64–72.

Louis XV for a new commercial society guided by an enlightened monarch's hand. For Diderot, the invisible hand was detached neither from the political body nor from the effects of imperial commerce.

When we consider the many quarrels about luxury in eighteenth-century France in tandem with the assessment that commercial society was new, we see how these notions emerged from classical sources, but also how they moved beyond them. Reaching a wide audience through a range of genres, they shared at their core a preoccupation with defining the key categories. Examined alongside one another, Diderot and the *Histoire*'s accounts reveal a generalized ambivalence about luxury – it was often loved and hated simultaneously – but they also reveal a more complex attitude towards the social and political repercussions of commerce, the "craze of the century," than allowed for by traditional reflections on the Enlightenment. Writing and thinking about luxury conditioned the languages of commerce developing in France during this period, especially in the crucial period of political change after the Seven Years War. The ambivalent tendency revealed here also exhibited itself elsewhere: the dual nature of commerce also emerged in discourses about piracy and monopoly. Most violent among them, however, was the limit to the ideal of *doux commerce* presented by slavery and the slave trade, the subject of the chapter that follows.

2

Doux commerce, commerce odieux

The Commerce in Humans

THE RHETORIC OF SLAVERY

"Man is born free, and everywhere he is in chains. One believes himself the others' master, and yet is more a slave than they. How did this change come about? I do not know."[1] With these now familiar lines, Jean-Jacques Rousseau opened his *Du contrat social (Of the Social Contract)* (1762) and introduced his powerful reconfiguration of the "principles of political right" and the bases of legitimate political authority. These principles he explicitly contrasted with the theories of Hugo Grotius (1583–1645) and, by extension, the jurisprudence of Thomas Hobbes (1588–1679) and Samuel Pufendorf (1632–94). According to Rousseau, these three "abettors of despotism" had grounded political authority in submission.[2] Their theories had

This chapter was presented to the Johns Hopkins University European History Seminar (1998), the Europe and Empire Conference held at the Minda da Gunzburg Centre for European Studies, Harvard University (1998), the Johns Hopkins Interdisciplinary Forum on Political Thought (1999), Professor Toby Ditz's Workshop in Early American History (2003), and the Carolina Seminar in French Studies (2005). I thank participants in each of these helpful settings for their constructive comments. In particular, I am grateful to David Bell, Paul Cheney, Toby Ditz, Madeleine Dobie, Gianluigi Goggi, Julia Holderness, Matthew Klemm, Lloyd Kramer, Catherine Larrère, Natasha Lee, John Marshall, Anne-Beate Maurseth, Pratap Mehta, Sankar Muthu, Anthony Pagden, Jennifer Pitts, J. G. A. Pocock, Orest Ranum, Louisa Shea, Jay Smith, Philippe Steiner, Ann Thomson, Richard Tuck, and Steven Vincent for their helpful comments.

[1] Jean-Jacques Rousseau, *Du contrat social* (1762), book 1, chap. 1. As we saw in Chapter 1, Rousseau's claim that he "does not know" was a rhetorical ruse, since he had provided an account of this phenomenon in his *Discourse on the Origin and Foundations of Inequality among Men* (1755).

[2] Rousseau referred to "Grotius and the others" (book 1, chap. 5) as "*les fauteurs du despotisme*" (book 1, chap. 4).

established the prevailing relationship between illegitimate governors and their subjects, which Rousseau famously cast as a form of slavery.

While this metaphoric use of slavery to describe a political relationship was central to the *Social Contract*, it was by no means exclusive to it. Rousseau's influential treatise was but one example of a broader trend in eighteenth-century French writings on politics, in which we can note how slavery metaphors dominated the language of protest against unjust political rule. This rhetoric provided a powerful tool for conceptualising relations to absolute authority in France as despotism, the Frenchman's "chains."[3] A systematic analysis of the uses of the metaphor of slavery to portray relations to despotic authority in broader contexts lies beyond the scope of this chapter. Yet a search of one of the largest available databases in the French language suggests a significant increase in the use of the term *esclave* in eighteenth-century writings across several genres.[4]

To be sure, the metaphor of political slavery was not new. In France, it derived from a rich heritage that can be traced through, for example, Henri comte de Boulainvilliers's *Histoire de l'ancien gouvernement de la France, avec les XIV lettres historiques sur les Parlements ou Etats-Généraux* (1727), the anonymous *Soupirs de la France esclave, qui aspire après la liberté* (n.p., 1689), and Étienne de la Boétie's *Discours de la servitude volontaire* (c.1548).

We can also locate this rhetorical strategy in prerevolutionary journalism. For example, several articles in Pierre Rétat's *Révolutions de Paris* referred to the need to break "the chains of despotism" and argue, for

---

[3] This is just one of many ways that the metaphor of slavery was used in eighteenth-century France. The notions of being slaves to passions, to luxury, or, especially poignant in Rousseau, to civility or civilisation were also pervasive and warrant further exploration. Whereas despotism was a central preoccupation of the Physiocrats, especially Chinese despotism (cf. Quesnay's "Despotisme de la Chine" [1767]), they and their fellow *économistes*' views on slavery and the slave trade have received little scholarly attention. Michèle Duchet's detailed account of the *anti-esclavagisme* or anti-slaveryism of the Physiocrats and the *philosophes* was the first comprehensive study of the ways in which a neocolonialist politics of a metropolitan bourgeoisie was formulated. See her *Anthropologie et histoire au siècle des lumières: Buffon, Voltaire, Rousseau, Helvétius, Diderot* (1971; Reprint, Paris: Albin Michel, 1995). Since Duchet, there are three principal studies of the physiocratic approach to slavery: Philippe Steiner's "L'Esclavage chez les économistes français;" Yves Citton's *Portrait de l'économiste en physiocrate* (Paris, 2000); and Madeleine Dobie's *Trading Places* (Ithaca, NY, 2010).

[4] Here I emulate Keith Baker's study of the occurrence of *révolution* in the same eighteenth-century corpus – the American and French Research on the Treasury of the French Language (ARTFL) at the University of Chicago (with the Institut national de la langue française, CNRS) database. Although ARTFL is not a fully representative sample of French published works from the period, it can suggest a term's prevalence. From 1700–89, the database retrieves 1,696 references to the term *esclave* and 886 to the term *esclavage* in 436 documents. This compares to 708 references to *esclave* and 141 to *esclavage* in 349 documents from 1600–99.

example, that "each day decides whether France will be 'enslaved or free,' whether the French will be the happiest or the unhappiest of people."[5] Finally, in one of its most potent formulations, the metaphorical use of slavery to describe politics was manifest in Jean-Paul Marat's *The Chains of Slavery, A Work wherein the Clandestine and Villainous Attempts of Princes to Ruin Liberty are Pointed Out, and the Dreadful Scenes of Despotism Disclosed* (1774).[6] First written to urge English voters to support Wilkes and parliamentary reform in Britain, the tract was revised and published in French by the "friend of the people" himself in 1793 as the Revolution turned to Terror.[7]

In one parallel account of this problem, Thomas Kaiser's study of the orientalisation of despotism in eighteenth-century France explains how the content of prerevolutionary French references to despotism was informed by reactions to Ottoman society and Franco-Turkish diplomatic relations.[8] When we read his sources further, we can also note that, in them, despotism was described as a form of "enslavement," and France a "slave" to despotism. Consider the article's opening citation from Jean-Louis Carra: "to enslave this beautiful nation [of France] under the ruins of her *moeurs*, her fortune, and her liberty." Kaiser also draws upon the "celebrated anonymous Huguenot attack on Louis XIV's monarchy, *Soupirs de la France esclave*," which, as he shows, "explicitly drew from contemporary accounts of the Ottoman Empire."[9] Of interest to us here, however, is the coincident status of these accounts as metaphorical.

---

[5] Cited in Keith Michael Baker, *Inventing the French Revolution: Essays on French Political Culture in the Eighteenth Century* (Cambridge: Cambridge University Press, 1990), 223.

[6] On Marat's text, see Rachel Hammersley, "Jean-Paul Marat's the Chains of Slavery in Britain and France, 1774–1833" in *The Historical Journal* 48, no.3 (2005): 641–60.

[7] Keith Michael Baker has argued that this text exemplifies the "metastazization" of the discourse of classical republicanism and that it is "an extreme version of the idiom of classical republicanism." See his "Transformations of Classical Republicanism in Eighteenth-Century France," *Journal of Modern History* 73, no. 1 (March 2001): 43–47. Whereas studies of classical republicanism have rightfully emphasised this central discourse's concern with liberty, the goal in countering despotism, little attention has been brought to the study of the language used to represent despotism. To put it another way, because existing scholarship tends to accent the aim of reform – liberty – its foil – slavery – has received scant attention in this discourse.

[8] Cf. Madeleine Dobie's latest work which brings to light the pervasive influence of Orientalist gestures in French absolutist cultural norms and practices. See *Trading Places: Colonization and Slavery in Eighteenth-Century French Culture* (Ithaca, NY: Cornell University Press, 2010) 9, and especially Chapter 3.

[9] Thomas E. Kaiser, "The Evil Empire? The Debate on Turkish Despotism in Eighteenth-Century French Political Culture," *Journal of Modern History* 72, no. 1 (2000): 8 and 13.

In her work on slavery in France's "old regime," Sue Peabody points further to the rhetorical strategy linking slavery to despotism in legal discourse of the period.[10] Her study of lawyers' petitions to the Paris Admiralty Court calling for the freedom of slaves brought to France demonstrates that some legal arguments employed the symbol of the African slave to criticize the perceived tyranny of the French crown. One example was the legal deposition, or *mémoire*, in which soon to be famous lawyer Henrion de Pansey pleaded for the freedom of a slave called Roc by making explicit the connection between despotism and slavery in France.[11] Henrion followed most lawyers arguing for the freedom of slaves brought to France when he began his *mémoire* with a history of the abolition of medieval slavery manufactured to justify a freedom principle, the notion that any slave setting foot in France was free.[12] Such histories explained the abolition of slavery in Europe as a consequence of the advent of Christianity and the moral system it allegedly espoused, which made the enslavement of fellow Christians morally unacceptable.[13] The briefs also drew on the symbol of the African slave to represent their audiences' own perceived enslavement to the tyranny of Louis XV and the attempts of Chancellor Maupeou to control the Parlement of Rennes and restrict the authority of the Parlement of Paris.

Not unlike the rhetoric of political tract writers like Rousseau, these lawyers arguing before the Admiralty Court remained focused on what one might call a *static* form of slavery on the French territory, be it

---

[10] Sue Peabody, *There Are No Slaves in France: The Political Culture of Race and Slavery in the Ancien Régime* (New York: Oxford University Press, 1996).

[11] Pansey, *Mémoire pour un Nègre*.

[12] Robert Harms draws on Peabody's work in *The Diligent*, wherein he discusses the case of Pauline Villeneuve's enfranchisement and the legal arguments made by Gérard Mellier and Pierre Lemerre Le Jeune for and against this former colonial slave's freedom.

[13] See Mallet and Le Clerc du Brillet's opening arguments in the case of the slave Jean Boucaux versus his master Bernard Verdelin, *Mémoire pour Jean Boucaux*. In their view, a "Christian" spirit of charity caused the French to release their slaves through several methods of manumission. See Peabody, *No Slaves in France*, 27. In a slight departure from these arguments, Henrion's historical account of the rise of slavery is more "secular" because, although it links Christianity with liberty, it does not credit it with the decline of slavery in medieval France. Rather, it "hints that Christian missionaries may have been responsible for introducing modern slavery to French territories." Peabody, *No Slaves in France*, 100. It is important to note, however, that there is no mention in Peabody – nor is there any mention in Henrion's *mémoire* – of what, then, was responsible for the decline of medieval slavery in France.

of "Nègres" to former masters or of "François" to a despotic king *in France*.[14] The *traite négrière*, as the massive displacement of captive Africans by Europeans to serve as slaves in the Americas was then called, did not figure in these texts. Nor did other writers using the rhetoric of slavery, including Rousseau, address it.

French historian Jean Ehrard pointed early on to the paucity of references to the slave trade in mid-eighteenth-century works. Among the seventy-two thousand articles of the *Encyclopédie*, only thirty-three made explicit reference to the slave trade.[15] Louis Sala-Molins has in turn criticized modern scholarship of the eighteenth century for continuing to "read" without slaves, and blacks, in view.[16] Yves Benot noted that this "lacuna in memory" was "helped if not incited by intellectual historians," dating as far back as the famed nineteenth-century historian of the French Revolution, Jules Michelet (1798–1874), who for generations construed the slave revolt in Saint-Domingue as "the most appalling war of savages ever seen" without any mention of the abolition of slavery it spurred in 1794.[17]

---

[14] At this period, the terms *Nègres* or *noirs* were often used as shorthand to describe African slaves. The *HDI* uses *Nègres*, *noirs*, and *esclaves* interchangeably. For a good overview of the social and legal implications of this racial language, see Pierre H. Boulle, "In Defense of Slavery: Eighteenth-century Opposition to Abolition and the Origins of a Racist Ideology in France," in Frederick Krantz, ed., *History from Below: Studies in Popular Protest and Popular Ideology* (Oxford: Basil Blackwell, 1988). For a more general discussion, see Carminella Biondi, *Ces esclaves sont des hommes: Lotta abolizionista e letteratura negrofila nella Francia del Settecento* (Pisa: Ed. Libreria Goliardica, 1979).

[15] "L'esclavage devant la conscience morale des lumières françaises: indifférence, gêne, révolte." Jean Ehrard, "L'Encyclopédie et l'esclavage: Deux lectures de Montesquieu," in *Enlightenment: Essays in Memory of Robert Shackleton* (Oxford: Voltaire Foundation, 1988), 143.

[16] Louis Sala-Molins, *Les Misères des lumières: Sous la raison, l'outrage* (Paris: R. Laffont, 1992), 15.

[17] "La plus épouvantable guerre de sauvages qu'on ait vue jamais." Yves Benot, *La Révolution française et la fin des colonies* (Paris: La Découverte, 1988), 10, 205–16. Paul Gilroy's *Black Atlantic* encourages an approach to the period which takes into account the influence of events such as the revolution in Saint-Domingue on the shape of democratic ideas under development in Europe at the time. Other recent works seeking to "re-read" the history of Europe in this period with attention to events and ideas emanating from the colonies include, especially, Laurent Dubois's *Les esclaves de la République: L'histoire oubliée de la première émancipation, 1789–1794* (Paris: Calmann-Lévy, 1998); Marcel Dorigny ed. *Les Abolitions de l'esclavage de L.F. Sonthonax à V. Schoelscher, 1793, 1794, 1848* (Paris: Éditions UNESCO and Presses universitaires de Vincennes, 1995); Michel Vovelle ed., "Révolution aux Colonies," *Annales historiques de la révolution française*, no. 293–94 (1993): 345–509; and Alain

Yet, as Benot and Sala-Molins have noted, no reader of the *Histoire des deux Indes* can ignore that in it "the *commerce in man*" as a social practice was clearly targeted.[18] Under the title "The Europeans go to Africa to purchase cultivators for the Antilles; Manner in which this commerce is carried out," book 11 explicitly announced that it would investigate how the "tragedy" of the "commerce in man sold & bought by man" came about and of what it consisted.[19] This subject was in and of itself remarkably original for the period. Book 11, and consequently the *Histoire des deux Indes*, also brought to bear the contemporary realities of the slave trade upon the pre-existing rhetoric of metaphorical slavery in historical and political texts of the period. To be sure, the metaphorical use of slavery to describe a politics of oppression also figured in the *Histoire*. But the work's novelty and polemical force stemmed largely from the innovative manner in which it historicised that rhetoric and, in doing so, harnessed its power to bolster an argument against the iniquitous "species of commerce" that was the triangular slave trade.[20]

Yacou and Michel Martin, eds., *De la Révolution française aux révolutions nègres et créoles* (Paris: Éditions Carribéennes, 1989).

[18] *HDI*, book 11, 157. Let us recall here the full title of the work: *Histoire philosophique et politique des établissements et du commerce des Européens dans les deux Indes* (my emphasis). The "commerce in man" is at the centre of the *HDI*'s concerns and not simply a veiled attempt to show that "the condition of the Frenchman under a despotic ruler was linked metaphorically to that of a slave," as Peabody has contended, *No Slaves in France*, 97. Here I depart from her portrayal of the *HDI* as one of a canon of Jansenist *parlementaire* critiques seeking to advocate "a radical equality whereby all social hierarchies [in France] would be levelled."

[19] The *malheur*, that is, "*le commerce de l'homme, vendu & acheté par l'homme.*" *HDI*, book 11, 157.

[20] Cf. Michèle Duchet, *Anthropologie et histoire au siècle des lumières: Buffon, Voltaire, Rousseau, Helvétius, Diderot.* (Paris: Maspéro, 1971. Reprint. Paris: Albin Michel, 1995), 125–33, 151–72. This first and important study of the colonialist ideological context in which the *HDI* was produced maintained that the *HDI*'s arguments against the slave trade were in fact disingenuous. Duchet contended that the work actually consisted of a thinly veiled defence of the interests of French imperialism. Louis Sala-Molins, among others, followed suit in *Les misères des lumières*, 19. If we turn to the works of Émilien Petit or Jean-Baptiste Dubucq, both senior officials in the colonial administration, we can notice their highly critical remarks of the disparaging descriptions of the slave trade in the *HDI*. See Émilien Petit, *Observations sur plusieurs assertions extraites littéralement de l'Histoire Philosophique des Etablissements des Européens dans les deux Indes, édition de 1770* (Amsterdam and Paris: Chez Knapen, Imprimeur de la Cour des Aides, au bas du Pont Saint Michel, 1776). See Michel Antoine, "Le Conseil du Roi sous la règne de Louis XV." In *Mémoires et documents publiés par la Société de l'École des Chartes.* Vol. 19. (Geneva and Paris: Droz, 1970), 154, 558, for what little is known about Petit.

THE COMMERCE IN HUMANS

Book 11 of the first version of the *Histoire des deux Indes* (1770) began by promising its readers an account of the "climate, soil, agriculture, animals, birds, fish, plants, fruit, minerals, mores, customs, superstitions, prejudices, sciences, arts, commerce, government and laws" of Africa and Africans, declared the necessary components of "good" history.[21] The account of slavery in Africa and the details about the culture and politics of life on its west coast were for the most part written by Jean-Joseph Pechméja, with Raynal adding or removing sections.[22] A fellow Aveyronnais living in Paris, Pechméja (1741–85) was later celebrated as an author, publishing a well-received didactic "voyage-and-exploits" novel, *Télèphe*, in 1784, after winning honourable mentions from the Académie française for two of his essays.[23]

We learn from these initial accounts by Pechméja that slavery existed in Africa before the arrival of Europeans. But this slavery was here characterised as innocuous and as yet uncommercialized.[24] In time, however (no dates are mentioned), a number of "piracies" were "committed upon the eastern coasts of Africa." This was the *Histoire des deux Indes'* principal explanation for the rise of the commerce in slaves. Exiled from Spain,

[21] *HDI*, book 11, 200–01. This list comprised a description of the proper pursuits of "good" history – one that gives us "information upon those points which it most concerns us to know; upon the true glory of a sovereign, upon the basis of the strength of nations, upon the felicity of the people, upon the duration of empires" – a fragment of Diderot's added in 1780, but it nevertheless offers an adequate summary of Raynal's original aim in launching the *HDI*. Michèle Duchet suggests this piece is a fragment of an unpublished tract of Diderot's entitled "Sur les Beaux-Arts et Belles-Lettres." See her *Diderot et l'Histoire des deux Indes ou l'Écriture Fragmentaire* (Paris: A. G. Nizet, 1978), 84.

[22] In a letter dated "ce 3 août 1786," Naigeon writes (probably) to Monsieur Vandeul: "Mr. Diderot n'a rien mis du sien dans la 2e Edit. de l'abbé raynal.[*sic*] le morceau sur les negres qu'on trouve dans cette seconde Edit. est comme le premier de mr. Péméga [*sic*].... Diderot a fort ajouté à ce morceau sur les negres dans la dernière Edition, mais il a plutôt étendu les raisonnemens de péméga et fortifié ses preuves." Reprinted in Herbert Dieckmann, *Inventaire du Fonds Vandeul et inédits de Diderot* (Geneva: Droz; Lille: Giard, 1951), 93–94.

[23] For what little is known about Pechméja, see L. G. Michaud, *Biographie universelle ancienne et moderne ...* Nouvelle édition. 45 vols. (Paris: Madame C. Desplaces et M. Michaud, 1854–1865), "PEC," 338–39, and Gianluigi Goggi, "Pechméja, Jean-Joseph" in Roland Mortier and Raymond Trousson, eds., *Dictionnaire de Diderot* (Paris: Honoré Champion, 1999). Jeffrey Merrick has recently analysed the novel *Télèphe* in "Male Friendship in Pre-revolutionary France," *GLQ: A Journal of Lesbian and Gay Studies* 10, no. 3 (2004).

[24] The Mameluc dynasty in Egypt was "composed of ten or twelve thousand slaves, brought from Georgia and Circassia when they were very young"; Algiers was "well cultivated by slaves"; and the despotic ruler of Morocco maintained "a feeble guard of negroes." *HDI*, book 11, 163, 182, 183.

a group of "suspicious subjects" sought refuge along the Barbary Coast, and their "spirit of revenge made them pirates." These "sea monsters" began to attack ships laden with "spoils" from the New World and made "some desert islands" their "country." With gold and silver in short supply, and farming "under a burning and unwholesome sky" too burdensome, their "self-interest, ever fruitful in expedients, suggested the plan of seeking cultivators in Africa." The "civilised nations" then "adopted this infamous scheme without hesitation."[25] Thus the "shocking" commerce in humans began. This extreme synthesis is almost comic in its terseness: In one paragraph, the *Histoire* accounts for the Black Legend, the history of settlement on the African coast, the creation of the filibusterers, settlement in the Caribbean, and the slave trade "plan."

The chapters that follow, in contrast, offer the many details devoted to providing a description of the "Western Coast of Africa, known by the name of Guinea," promised in book 11's title. Although slavery "is of very high antiquity" in Guinea, Raynal and Pechméja explain that many of the beneficent rules governing it had been rendered "ineffectual" ever "since the Europeans established luxury on the coasts of Africa." It was then that "corruption" spread and slave procurement led to armed conflict. Nevertheless, the trade gained the complicity of princes and chiefs, who began to encourage it; indeed, the authors allege that "injustice has known no bounds or restraints."

Later sections discuss not only the "colour of the inhabitants" but also the "nature of the soil," the "idea of the several governments," the "manner of making war," the "modes of worship," and the "manners, customs, and occupations of the people of Guinea."[26] They describe early Guinean trade

[25] These citations are drawn directly from the three sections in book 11 where the pirates, or *flibustiers*, are discussed: Ibid., 157–59, 188–93, and 276–77.

[26] Ann Thomson has carefully demonstrated that the first two versions of the *HDI* drew on Cornélius de Pauw for their contemptuous accounts of the Guineans deemed, like Pauw's Americans, to be a "particular species of man." But, as Thomson argues further, one of the important changes to the *HDI*'s third version was the "overturning of the perspective" on the Africans undertaken by Diderot, who incorporated the more moderate theses and language from the abbé Demanet's *Nouvelle Histoire de l'Afrique françoise* (Paris, 1767), and especially from Volume 12 of the abbé Pierre-Joseph-André Roubaud's *Histoire générale de l'Asie, de l'Afrique et de l'Amérique*, published from 1770–75. See "Diderot, Roubaud et l'esclavage" *Recherches sur Diderot et sur l'Encyclopédie* 35 (2003): 71, 75–80. The *HDI*'s descriptions of Africa warrant further systematic attention. The critique offered by Hédia Khadhar in "La description de l'Afrique dans *l'Histoire des deux Indes*," in Hans-Jürgen Lüsebrink and Anthony Strugnell, eds., *L'Histoire des deux Indes: Réécriture et polygraphie* (Oxford: Voltaire Foundation, 1995), the only one available to date, suggests that Africa is portrayed as a terrain ripe for European control, development, and enlightenment. Cf. Jean-Claude Halpern, "L'Africain de Raynal," in

as consisting primarily of "certain exchanges of salt and dried fish" for "stuffs made of a kind of thread"; small in scale, it was unable "to cause a material alteration in the manners of its inhabitants." Early European arrivals fixed prices for wax, ivory, and other trade goods and attempted to exploit the area's gold, but they were "unmercifully repulsed." The search for gold was then "abandoned," and "the attention of all men ... turned to the slave trade."[27] Thus, the *Histoire des deux Indes* traced the beginnings of commercial society in Guinea to the trade in slaves.

The account that immediately followed, however, focuses less on the slave trade's "injustice" than on its fundamental inefficiency. The result of these "infamous arts" was that the "people of the coast" had "found it impossible to supply the demands of the merchants." This predicament meant that the Guineans themselves had become "the currency of the state of Guinea," and every day "this currency [was] carried off and nothing is left them but articles of consumption."[28] Consequently, "their capital gradually vanishe[d]." These conditions necessarily impoverished and indebted the Guineans further. The "trade for blacks" would have been "entirely lost," the *Histoire* argued, if "the inhabitants of the coast had not imparted their luxury to the people inland, from whence they now [drew] the greatest part of the slaves that [were] put into [their] hands."[29] This other form of commercial society, of which luxury was symptomatic, had thus embedded itself into the coastland.

The result was that the price of slaves was augmented to "four times the former cost." The profits received by the proprietor were "intercepted" by different hands for the expenses of transport and taxes, such that the amount received was far less than European traders paid. These expenses, continually increasing as the distances at which slaves were sold increased, could, the *Histoire* predicted, become so great that potential sellers would decide to keep their slaves rather than sell them. The implication was that the end of the slave trade might come about as a result of, on one hand (to impose a not yet fully theorised economic vocabulary), the opportunity cost calculation in the mind of the trader, and, on the other, the depletion of what was (curiously) construed as a non-renewable resource. But the *Histoire* predicted that that time was a long way off, because in

---

Gilles Bancarel and Gianluigi Goggi, eds., *Raynal, de la polémique à l'histoire* (Oxford: Voltaire Foundation, 2000), 235–42.

[27] *HDI*, book 11, 218–20.

[28] "Les têtes de negres [*sic*] représentent le numéraire des états de la Guinée. Chaque jour ce numéraire leur est enlevé, & on ne leur laisse que des choses qui se consomment." Ibid., 221–22.

[29] "C'est de cette manière que le commerce des Européens a presque épuisé les richesses commerçables de cette nation." Ibid., 222.

the near future at least the colonists would continue to find people willing to purchase and sell slaves.[30]

A further iniquitous detail of the trade in African captives, according to the *Histoire*, lay in the way that slave merchants collected themselves into "companies" and formed "caravans" by which they drove several files of thirty or forty slaves through "barren deserts."[31] These slaves were secured in a manner "ingeniously contrived"[32]: "a fork of wood, from eight to nine feet long, is put round the neck of each slave. A pin of iron, riveted, secures the fork at the back part in such a manner that the head cannot disengage itself." However, the text argued, it was not this cruel device but "the public faith" that "secure[d] to the proprietor the possession of his slave," and that same public faith was "silent with regard to a slave and a trader who exercises the most contemptible of all professions." The French were thus with their silence perpetuating the trade in slaves, though they simultaneously protested their metaphorical slavery to despotism. This perceived double standard lay at the core of the *Histoire*'s critique.

Thus, in the 1770 version of the *Histoire des deux Indes*, book 11 offered a detailed account of the iniquitous contemporary realities of the slave trade, that "infamous commerce of crimes and misfortunes, of men exchanged for arms, of children sold by their fathers!"[33] Although the authors of the *Histoire* claimed not to have "tears sufficient to deplore such horrors," it would seem that by the 1780 version, the details of the slave trade provided by the original book 11 were deemed insufficient rhetorical ammunition against the trade.

FROM "DETAILS" TO "WAR MACHINE"

The *Histoire des deux Indes* changed in 1780. Though attributed to Raynal in 1770, his engraved frontispiece first appeared in the 1774 La Haye edition, portraying the engraved profile (by Charles-Nicolas Cochin) of a sober abbé in full ecclesiastical dress. The motto read, "G.ME T.MAS RAYNAL, / De la Société Royale de Londres et de l'Académie / des Sciences et Belles-Lettres de Prusse."[34] In 1780, however, the abbé's

[30] Ibid., 222–23.

[31] No commentary on the nature of these companies follows, however. In fact, other than mentioning that most of the Europeans on the coast of Guinea maintained companies, there is no discussion of their worth (or, rather, deleterious effect) in book 11.

[32] "assez heureusement imaginée." *HDI* (1772), book 11, 146.

[33] *HDI* (1772), book 11, chap. 20, 286.

[34] Compare *Histoire* ... [*des*] *deux Indes* (A Amsterdam, 1770 (and 1772), 6 vol. in-8) with the *Histoire* ... [*des*] *deux Indes* (A La Haye: Chez Gosse fils, 1774, 7 vols. in-8)

religious garb was replaced by the *négligé* of the quintessential eighteenth-century man of letters, and a cloth head wrap took the place of the curled wig. He was shown writing at his desk, on which stood three volumes of the *Encyclopédie*. The pedestal beneath depicted an allegorical scene containing a number of figures, including the goddess of liberty (holding a spade on which there is also a Phrygian bonnet) attentively surveying slaves liberated from their chains. The motto now read, "To the Defender of Humanity, of Truth and of Liberty."[35]

The transformation of the frontispiece signalled an equally important transformation in the text. In the 1780 version, the *Histoire des deux Indes* became what one influential commentator has called a "war machine."[36] In large part, this change was a result of Diderot's revision of the second version and subsequent augmentations of the work. For Diderot, the *Histoire* had become a prolongation of the spirit and function of the *Encyclopédie*. He used it as a vehicle to expand upon ideas on which he was working and to win them public attention in the hope of affecting popular opinion without drawing the authorities' attention to himself.[37]

We can now ascertain with confidence which sections of the *Histoire* were drawn from fragments of Diderot's other, often unpublished, writings. Recent accounts of Diderot's contributions attribute the greater part of the "philosophical" content of the *Histoire philosophique ... des deux Indes* to him, that is, those sections of the text comprising more general

and Histoire ... [*des*] deux Indes (A Maestricht: Chez Jean-Edme Dufour, Imprimeur et Libraire, 1775, 7 vols. in-8).

35 "Au Défenseur de l'Humanité, de la Vérité, de la Liberté." This frontispiece, appearing in Vol. 1 of the in-4 1780 edition by Pellet, was signed twice: It was drawn by Charles-Nicolas Cochin and engraved by Nicolas de Launay. For a more detailed comparison of this portrait with the previous one, see Ottmar Ette, "La mise en scène de la table de travail: poétologie et épistémologie immanentes chez Guillaume-Thomas Raynal et Alexander von Homboldt," in Peter Wagner (ed.) *Icons, texts, iconotext: Essays on Ekphrasis and Intermediality* (Berlin: De Gruyter, 1996), 175–212. On the pedestal, see Lise Andries, "Les illustrations dans *l'Histoire des deux Indes*," in Hans-Jürgen Lüsebrink and Anthony Strugnell (eds.) *L'Histoire des deux Indes: réécriture et polygraphie* (Oxford: Voltaire Foundation, 1995), 34.

36 The term is Hans Wolpe's from his *Raynal et sa machine de guerre*. Indeed, as discussed in the Introduction, it is the 1780 version that caught most of the attention of the book censorship authorities.

37 In a letter from Mme de Vandeul to her mother dated 11 April 1777, she writes that the last days of Diderot's life were spent writing for and reviewing the *HDI*; he sometimes worked "fourteen consecutive hours" ["*quatorze heures de suite*"] on it. Thus, the *HDI* appears to have replaced the *Encyclopédie* as Diderot's central preoccupation. See J. Massiet du Biest, *La Fille de Diderot* (Tours, 1949), cited in Duchet, *Diderot et l'Histoire*, 10.

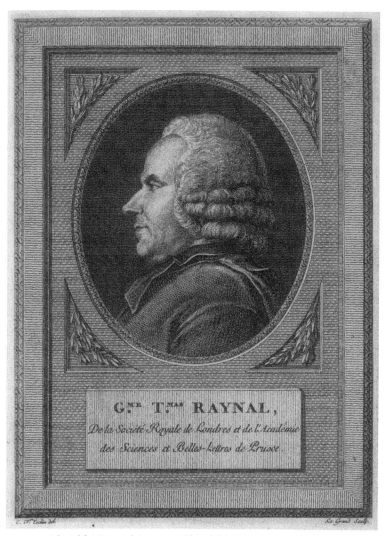

FIGURE 2. The abbé Raynal in 1774. The abbé Raynal in ecclesiastical dress by C. N. Cochin (drawing) and Le Grand (engraving). Frontispiece to vol. 1 of the 1774 edition of the *Histoire des deux Indes* (La Haye: Gosse, fils, 7 vols., in 8). *Courtesy of the John Carter Brown Library at Brown University.*

FIGURE 3. Raynal the *philosophe* in 1780. Raynal as *philosophe* by N. Cochin,
"Secretary of the Royal Academy of Painting and Sculpture" (drawing), and
N. De Launay, "Of the same Academy and That of the Arts of Denmark"
(engraving). Frontispiece to vol. 1 of the 1780 edition of the *Histoire des
deux Indes* (Geneva: J. Pellet, 1780, 3 vols, in-4).
*Courtesy of the Rare Books and Special Collections Division of the Library
of Congress, Washington, DC.*

and theoretical reflections.[38] Book 11, in particular, was so expanded, but also radicalised.[39] To the description of the cruel fetters binding the African captives, for instance, a passionate appeal to the reader was added: "Reader, while you are perusing this horrid account, is your soul not filled with the same indignation I experience in writing it? Do you not, in your imagination, rush with fury upon those infamous conductors? Do you not break the forks with which these unfortunate people are confined? And do you not restore them to their liberty?"[40] Most curious, however, was the change to chapter 24: To the details on the origins and progress of the triangular slave trade, Diderot inserted a polemical history of the origins and development of slavery *in Europe*. This addition has been afforded minimal attention, but I suggest that it alters book 11's overall effect and heightens its moral and political significance.[41]

Against Rousseau's claim that he did not know *how* "man" born free came to be "everywhere in chains," Diderot's 1780 addition explicitly set out to offer an account of that process. As we shall see, the aim of this history within a history was both didactic and moralising. Chapter 24 began by announcing that "some considerable revolution" would be necessary to make "the evidence of the great truth felt" by the promoters of the slave trade, that is, that their commerce was "reprobated by morality." Meanwhile, to encourage those writers who justified the trade to reconsider their actions, it provided an account of how European slavery came to its end as "proof" that "there is no reason of state that can authorise slavery."[42]

---

[38] Our ability to do so is due largely to the meticulous work of Gianluigi Goggi. The principal writings are found in the *Fragments politiques* and the *Fragments échappés* published by Assénat-Tourneux (Diderot, *Oeuvres*, vols. 4 and 5) and are formally attributed to Diderot in the *Correspondance littéraire*. For identifications of Diderot's texts, see Gianluigi Goggi, *Denis Diderot, Pensées détachées, Contributions à 'L'Histoire des deux Indes.'* 2 vols. (Siena: Tip. del Rettorato, 1976–77), *Denis Diderot*, but also, previously, Duchet, *Diderot et l'Histoire*; Hans Wolpe, *Raynal et sa machine de guerre: "L'Histoire des deux Indes" et ses perfectionnements* (Paris: M. Th. Litec, cop., 1956) *Raynal et sa machine de guerre*; Dieckmann, *Inventaire du Fonds Vandeul*; and Feugère, *Un précurseur de la Révolution*.

[39] That is to say, the text was transformed into a political tool, critical of the political status quo and aiming to instigate reform. The term is Yves Benot's. See "Diderot, Pechméja, Raynal et l'anticolonialisme," *Europe; revue littéraire mensuelle* 41 (Jan.–Feb. 1963): 147.

[40] HDI (1780), book 11, chap. 17, 149.

[41] In her pioneering discussion of Diderot's "anthropology and history," for example, Michèle Duchet mentions the fact that Diderot added the history of slavery to book 11, but she does not discuss its implications. See *Anthropologie et histoire*, 175. Recent studies have revisited the construction of chapter 24. See Ann Thomson, "Diderot, Roubaud et l'esclavage" *Recherches sur Diderot et sur l'Encyclopédie* 35 (2003): 69–93, and Gianluigi Goggi, "Diderot-Raynal, l'esclavage et les Lumières écossaises" *Lumières* 3 (2004): 53–93.

[42] HDI, book 11, chap. 24, 267.

The proof Diderot offered was historical. It begins with a definition of slavery, the first in book 11: "Slavery is a state in which a man has lost, either by force or by convention, the property of his own person, and of whom a master can dispose as his own effects."[43] This definition is encompassing enough to include both metaphorical and real slavery. Next, he delineates the different stages of the development of this "odious state," from "the first ages" when it was "unknown" through to its "end." The history that follows is generic, in stark contrast to the exhaustive and detailed accounts of the slave trade that precede it.

The reader first learns that the "natural equality" of men in the first ages did not endure, as the weakest and "less cunning" were soon obliged to submit to those "who were able to feed and defend them." Soon those in command came to see themselves as superior to those who obeyed them, and they began to consider their subordinates as slaves. When societies "acquired a knowledge of the arts and of commerce," the weak found support in the magistrate, the poor found resource in industry, and "both emerged, by degrees, from the kind of necessity that they had experienced of submitting to slavery, in order to procure subsistence." At this point, although liberty came to be considered "as a precious and unalienable property," the laws continued "to impose the penalty of servitude." At a fifth stage, as armies "became mercenary," wars led to the "necessity" of procuring slaves, as was "the practice of the Greeks and Romans and of all people who chose to increase enjoyments by this inhuman and barbarous custom."

This narrative of the development of European slavery would have been familiar to eighteenth-century readers. Up to this point, it was highly derivative in many ways, perhaps most obviously of the four stages theories of the rise of commercial society.[44] The account also paralleled those proffered

---

[43] Ibid., 268.

[44] As Gianluigi Goggi has shown in meticulous detail, one of Diderot's key sources for this account was the Scot John Millar's *Observations Concerning the Distinction of Ranks in Society*, published in London in 1771 and translated by J. B. Suard in 1773. Goggi argues that Millar, in turn, drew from and reconfigured Simon-Nicolas-Henri Linguet's *Théorie des loix civiles*. Gianluigi Goggi, "Diderot-Raynal," 56–93. This version of the stadial history of human origins also closely resembled William Robertson's account of the rise of commercial society in his *Histoire du règne de l'empereur Charles-Quint, précédée d'un Tableau des progrès de la société en Europe depuis la destruction de l'Empire Romain jusqu'au commencement du seizième siècle [...] ouvrage traduit de l'anglois.* (Amsterdam and Paris, 1771). On the four-stages theory of history and commercial society and its theoretical foundations most famously articulated by Adam Smith in *An Inquiry into the Nature and Causes of the Wealth of Nations* (1776), see Istvan Hont, "The Language of Sociability and Commerce: Samuel Pufendorf and the Theoretical Foundations of the 'Four-Stages Theory,'" in Anthony Pagden, ed., *The Languages of Political Theory in Early-Modern Europe* (Cambridge: Cambridge University Press, 1989). See also Ronald L. Meek, *Social Science and the Ignoble Savage* (Cambridge, MA: Cambridge University

by the lawyers pleading before the Admiralty Court and seized more generally on the concomitant rhetoric of political slavery. The section's most obvious reference was, however, to Montesquieu. Indeed, Charles Louis de Secondat, baron de La Brède et de Montesquieu, famously a *président à mortier* of the Bordeaux Parlement and author of *The Spirit of the Laws* (1748), was explicitly targeted in the work's opening chapter and represented one of its central interlocutors.[45] The *Histoire's* account of the "origins and progress of slavery" paralleled Montesquieu's accounts of the "origin of the right of slavery" in book 15 of *The Spirit of the Laws*.[46]

These two works diverged on a crucial point, however: their explanation of how slavery ended. For Montesquieu, as for the lawyers pleading the cases of French slaves in the Admiralty Court, it was Christianity that "in our climates" had "brought back that age" when slavery "has so fortunately been abolished."[47] In the historical account added by Diderot in 1780, by contrast, it was *commerce* that had ended both "personal" and "real" slavery in Europe.[48] Returning to Diderot's addition, we find a description of two different but concurrent episodes that took place at some point in the "Middle Ages" wherein commerce acted as the catalyst for the elimination of slavery. First, Italian city-states acquired sufficient wealth through commerce to become "ashamed" of the era's "humiliating vassalages" and responded by "shaking off the yoke of their feeble despots."[49] Meanwhile, in the rest of Europe, the Germans invaded and appropriated lands so vast that their proprietors could not "retail all his slaves under his own inspection"; instead, they had to "disperse them over the soil they were to cultivate."[50] Since this distance prevented their

Press, 1976); Ronald L. Meek, "Smith, Turgot, and the 'Four Stages' Theory," in *Smith, Marx and After: Ten Essays in the Development of Economic Thought.* London: Chapman & Hall, 1980; and Harro M. Höpfl, "From Savage to Scotsman: Conjectural History in the Scottish Enlightenment," *Journal of British Studies* 17 (1978): 19–40.

[45] *HDI*, book 1, chap. 1, 16. This reference is discussed in greater detail later.

[46] So does the article "Esclavage" in the *Encyclopédie*, of which the *HDI* was in many ways an extension. See Ehrard, "L'Encyclopédie et l'esclavage."

[47] *The Spirit of Laws* (1748), book 15, chap. 7. See also book 15, chap. 8. On the ways in which Montesquieu's Christianity thesis was already under challenge by Voltaire and Linguet, as Diderot revisited the *HDI*'s third version, see Goggi, "Diderot-Raynal, l'esclavage et les Lumières écossaises," 59.

[48] The distinctions are Montesquieu's in *The Spirit of Laws.* Book 15, chap. 10 explains that there are "two sorts of slavery: real and personal. The real one is the one that attaches the slave to the land," whereas personal slavery "is service in the household, and it relates more to the person of the master."

[49] *HDI*, book 11, chap. 24, 272. Emphasis added.

[50] "Des lors, le propriétaire ne pouvoit pas retenir sous ses yeux ses esclaves [*sic*], & il fut forcé de les disperser sur le sol qu'ils devoient defricher." It is important to note this use of the term *esclaves* to describe serfs. Ibid., 273–74.

being managed, "it was thought proper to encourage them by rewards proportioned to their labour." By this account, "personal slavery" ended when lords "universally adopted" the situation that eventually developed, whereby they accumulated more wealth when they were able to "offer a fixed rent" for the land being worked upon, and the slaves began to cultivate the land at their own expense.[51]

The catalyst for the end of both personal and real slavery, then, was a commercial transaction, the institution of a system of exchange of labour for income, which, recalling the definition of slavery provided at the beginning of the history, meant that slavery ended when man regained the ability to "dispose of his own effects." The role of commerce as the catalyst for the end of slavery was made more explicit in the introductory section of the work, when, *pace* Montesquieu, Diderot wrote, "It was through that sound policy, which commerce always introduces, and not through the spirit of the Christian religion" that this end of slavery came about.[52] This "great change," he argued in book 11, was "brought on in a manner by itself"; it was an auspicious and beneficent development.[53]

There was, however, one additional agent that hastened this development: We could call it politics. Diderot explained that it was "the chief of every republic" who, "perpetually at war with his barons" but "unable to resist them by force," used "artifice" to protect the slaves against the tyranny of their masters and to "undermine the power of the nobles, by diminishing the dependence of their subjects." Although the "motive of general utility" may have inspired some, "most of them were visibly induced to adopt this fortunate policy, more on account of their personal interests, than from principles of humanity and benevolence."[54] Thus, the history of slavery first added to book 11 in 1780 explained slavery's end in Europe as deriving from two coterminous agents: commerce in combination with or precipitated by politics, or, the "visible hand" of political authority with its "self-interest rightly understood."

While this history of slavery in Europe challenged the traditional Christianity thesis postulated by Montesquieu and others, its alternative

---

[51] Again, these are Montesquieu's terms: *servitude personelle* and *servitude réelle*. Ibid., 274.

[52] *HDI*, book 1, 16. We know that this section is Diderot's as well; it too appears to have been added in 1780. See Duchet, *Diderot et l'Histoire*, 65.

[53] "Ce grand changement, qui se faisoit, pour ainsi dire, lui-même." *HDI*, book 11, 274.

[54] Ibid., 275. Again, this point is partially reiterated in the introduction to the work cited previously, where "the honour of having abolished slavery" is attributed to "that sound policy, which commerce always introduces" and which in turn "induced" kings to "bestow freedom upon the slaves of their vassals." Ibid., book 1, 16.

causal explanation for the end of slavery, commerce, was in itself modelled on Montesquieu's theory of commerce, what Albert Hirschman has conceptualised as *doux commerce*.[55] As we have seen, for Montesquieu, commerce was sweet or gentle because it "cures destructive prejudices" and "polishes and softens barbarous mores." Its "natural effect" is "to lead to peace" and to "unite nations," and it "produces in men a certain feeling for exact justice."[56] But another look at *The Spirit of Laws* reveals that commerce alone could not achieve these ends. Book 20, chapter 12 argues that states and their laws play an important role in facilitating commerce and ensuring that it is free. Montesquieu explained: "Liberty of commerce is not a faculty granted to traders to do what they want.... What hampers those who engage in commerce does not, for all that, hamper commerce." Here, he offered the example of England, which forbade the export of wool or ungelded horses: "It hampers the trader, *but it does so in favour of commerce*."[57] In his next chapter, Montesquieu added that if one sought to enjoy "the liberty of commerce," then the state had to "be neutral between its customs houses and its commerce and must arrange that these two things never thwart one another." Thus, according to Montesquieu, the potential of commerce to liberalise and civilise could be realized only with the help of government guidance or leadership.

In the history of slavery added by Diderot to book 11 of the *Histoire*, the auspicious development of commerce was spurred by the "fortunate policy" of heads of state acting with a heightened sense of their self-interest. This development brought an end to political, real, and personal slavery in Europe. Diderot's challenge to the traditional account of slavery's abolition is significant but not surprising in this context. In contrast

[55] Montesquieu may have been the first to coin the phrase and is its most authoritative exponent, but the theory runs large. See, for example, J. G. A. Pocock, *Virtue, Commerce, and History: Essays on Political Thought and History, Chiefly in the Eighteenth Century* (Cambridge: Cambridge University Press, 1985), 103–56; Anthony Pagden, *European Encounters with the New World* (New Haven, CT: Yale University Press, 1993), 169–71, and *Lords of all the Worlds: Ideologies of Empire in Spain, Britain, and France c.1500-c.1800* (New Haven: Yale University Press, 1995), 178–81. It is important to note here that while Montesquieu discusses slavery, he does so without reference to the *trade* in slaves. Conversely, there is no discussion of the "commerce in humans" in all of part 4 of *The Spirit of Laws*, the section on commerce, other than an oblique reference in chapter 21 of book 21, "On laws in their relation to commerce considered in the revolutions it has had in the world." In this chapter, he lists one of the "consequences of the Discovery of America" to be that "voyages to Africa became necessary; they furnished men to work the mines and lands of America."

[56] Montesqieu, *The Spirit of Laws*, part. 4, book 20, chaps. 1–2. This is where most traditional readings of Montesquieu's theory of commerce tend to stop.

[57] Ibid., emphasis added.

to the approach of most universal histories of the time, the *Histoire des deux Indes* was, above all, a history of commerce.[58] For Diderot, the changes brought on by commerce and politics at the end of the Middle Ages consisted in a "revolution [that] was ... so complete" that "liberty became more general *throughout the greatest part of Europe* than it had been in any climate, or in any age."[59]

DOUX COMMERCE, COMMERCE ODIEUX

But as the first twenty-three chapters of book 11 documented, the story of European slavery did not end with its Old World abolition: "[H]ardly had domestic liberty been reborn in Europe than it was buried in America."[60] It was the "Spaniard, the first to be vomited up by the waves onto the shores of the New World," who "called for slaves in Africa," and "all the nations, free or subjected," had "without remorse sought to increase their fortune in the sweat, blood and despair of these unfortunates."[61] Unlike Rousseau, contemporary lawyers arguing in the Admiralty Court, or even Montesquieu, here the *Histoire des deux Indes* explicitly tied the story of European slavery to the "horrible system" that was the "commerce in man." In the *Histoire*'s account, no sooner did slavery end in Europe than it was absorbed in Atlantic commercial relations. In this way, the Old World's past was shown to be indelibly linked to the New World's

[58] Voltaire began his own popular "French" universal history, the *Essai sur les moeurs*, by stating the aim of continuing where the Bishop Bossuet left off in his *Discours sur l'histoire universelle*, to write a universal history with attention to the "mores," "customs," and "spirit" of "men." Ibid., 196. J. G. A. Pocock's recent *Barbarism and Religion. Volume I: The Enlightenments of Edward Gibbon, 1737–1764* (Cambridge: Cambridge University Press, 1999) offers the most comprehensive analysis to date of the varying methodologies and philosophies of this trend – what he has called "Enlightenment historiography."

[59] *HDI*, book 11, 275. Emphasis added. This assertion is followed by the claim that "[s]ince it [slavery] has been abolished among us the people are a hundred times happier, even in the most despotic empires, than they were formerly in the best-ordered democracies." It appears that, once again, Diderot engages the rhetoric of slavery by confronting its metaphorical quality and asserting that in the "real" social life of Europeans, no institutionalised social relation like the slavery of the "Middle Ages" and before exists any longer. This statement ignores the "domestic slavery" of women in Europe, to which Montesquieu devoted an entire book (book 16) in *The Spirit of Laws*.

[60] Ibid.

[61] *HDI*, book 11, 276. This abridged version of the slave trade's initiation, provided at the end of the "history of slavery," differs slightly from the accounts provided elsewhere in the *HDI*, where it is the "pirates," called Spanish "refuse," who initiate the "traffic of man." It is probable that "Spaniards" was shorthand for pirates here, a significant conflation worth further study.

future. This appears to be the first time that any French work explicitly made that connection.[62]

Yet, as we have seen, the accounts of the slave trade provided in the first part of book 11 contrasted with the history of slavery added by Diderot by revealing that New World slavery was by most counts even more abominable than its Old World analogue.[63] The material conditions differed significantly, making for differences in the degree and kind of captivity experienced by New and Old World slaves. The slave of Europe's Middle Ages was under the command of a master who "disposed of his own effects"; this slave had, according to the *Histoire*'s account, lost "the property of his own person."[64] The African slave brought to the New World, by contrast, was fettered; he was also "disgraced" by being branded with "the name or the mark of his oppressor."[65] A second iniquitous feature of the New World commerce in humans was its status as a trade. As a "species of commerce" wherein humans were both subjects and objects of trade, slavery in the New World worsened the condition of the Africans held captive because it in effect sullied and thwarted the panacean potential of commerce.

This potential was repeatedly invoked outside of book 11. The *Histoire des deux Indes* was replete with references to the awesome powers of commerce as an essentially civilising, liberalising, and pacifying agent. That is why the idea of *doux commerce* is so often considered to be the work's central leitmotif. Some of its praise of the panacean virtues of commerce was unrestrained and bordered on the phantasmagorical: It was commerce that had "dug canals," "drained plains," "founded cities," and "collected, clothed and civilised" entire populations.[66] Moreover, the progress of commerce across the globe ensured nothing less than that "clouds will be dispelled in all parts; a serene sky will shine over the face of the whole globe.... [T]hen, or never, will that universal peace arise ... [and] the general felicity of men will be established upon a more solid basis."[67]

[62] Later works explicitly refer to the *HDI*'s forceful claim while making the same rhetorical point about the hypocrisy of the Frenchman's repugnance for the "enslavement" of despotism and simultaneous support of the enslavement of the "Negroes." See, e.g., Febvé, *Essai philanthropique sur l'esclavage des nègres. Par Mr. L'abbé Febué Chanoine de Vaudemont: Membre de la Société du Philantrope* (S. l. n. d. 1778), 27.

[63] "Non, quoi qu'on en puisse dire, la condition de ces infortunés n'est pas la même que la nôtre." *HDI*, book 11, 284.

[64] Ibid., 268.

[65] Ibid., 224, 257.

[66] Ibid., book 1, chap. 1, 4.

[67] *HDI*, book 19, 374. For more on the passages in the *HDI* extolling commerce as the instrument of world peace, see Marian Skrzypek, "Le commerce instrument de la paix

The "commerce in man" provided a foil for this celebratory and essentialist understanding of the powers of commerce: This was book 11's influence on the work as a whole. The account of the slave trade, of commerce described in all of its "shocking" and "horrid" detail, inadvertently challenged the assumed coherence of the theory of commerce as a vehicle for liberty, civility, and morality around the globe. First, as evident in the history of European slavery, commerce was portrayed as unable to achieve its magnificent ends independently of the direction of the "chief of every republic" or the "sovereigns of the earth."[68] Second, the account exposed the idea that commerce was not uniform. Whereas some commerce may indeed have been liberalising, civilising, and pacifying, other forms of commerce, namely, the commerce in humans, were fundamentally immoral and intolerable.

While the "commerce in man" was indeed a "species of commerce," it constituted the very antithesis of *doux commerce*. It was, rather, a *commerce odieux* on at least two levels. First, it was inefficient, turning humans into non-renewable capital and exhausting supplying nations' "only saleable commodities."[69] Still worse, the commerce in humans was inimical to any universal sense of humanity: It was fundamentally immoral. This is a point that the eighteenth-century French *esclavagistes*, apologists for slavery, ignored at their peril.[70] When they participated in the *commerce odieux*, when they listened "coolly and without emotion" to accounts of African slaves "tyrannised, mutilated, burnt, and put to death," Europeans in effect jeopardised their own humanity.[71] Thus, while a version of the *doux commerce* thesis was posited as the universal "soul of the moral world," the account of the slave trade in book 11 complicated that seemingly uniform concept and established that some forms of commerce were in fact less sweet, less efficient, and less moral

---

mondiale," in Gilles Bancarel and Gianluigi Goggi, eds., *Raynal, de la polémique à l'histoire* (Oxford: Voltaire Foundation, 2000), 243–54.

[68] *HDI*, book 11, 275, 287.

[69] *HDI* (1780), 222.

[70] This is a point Diderot made later in a dialogue with an imaginary slave merchant (an *armateur*). See *HDI* (1780), book 11, chap. 24, 277–87.

[71] Ibid., 277. See also book 11, 264, where, in a description of the colonial "masters," Raynal claimed that "by committing such outrages against humanity, they injure themselves." This notion of the contagion of diseased commerce is likely informed by Montesquieu, who remarked that "[slavery] is useful neither to the master nor to the slave: not to the slave, because he can do nothing from virtue; not to the master, because he contracts all sorts of bad habits from his slaves, because he imperceptibly grows accustomed to failing in all the moral virtues, because he grows proud, curt, harsh, angry, voluptuous and cruel." *The Spirit of Laws*, book 15, chap. 1.

than others. The ultimate effect was to furnish the idea of commerce with an important moral and political dimension.

THE ANTIDOTE?

Given, then, that the slave trade was a diseased form of commerce that not only thwarted the potential of *doux commerce* but also tainted the moral fibre of all Europeans who sanctioned it, what was to be done with it? The *Histoire des deux Indes* was ambivalent on this point. Certain passages suggested that the mechanisms that put an end to slavery in Europe should be revived to purge it in the New World.[72] Thus, we find a call for the "sovereigns of the earth" to "overturn the whole system of slavery":

If you do not sport with the rest of mortals, if you do not regard the power of kings as the right of a successful plunder, and the obedience of subjects as artfully obtained from their ignorance, reflect on your own obligations. Refuse the sanction of your authority to the infamous and criminal commerce of men turned into so many herds of cattle, and this trade will cease. For once unite, for the happiness of the world, those powers and designs which have been so often exerted for its ruin.[73]

Just as the abolition of slavery in Europe was "hastened" by the intervention of "chiefs of every republic" acting in their own self-interest, so too could the New World slave system be stopped, making way for sweet commerce.[74]

In a similar passage, the *Histoire* called for "all the maritime powers" to work together to bring an end to piracy.[75] Through "salutary laws and examples of humanity," the maritime powers could ensure that these "sea monsters" would be "changed into men." Their plunder curbed, the pirates would see fit to grow "corn and various fruits" on the coasts of Africa they had once pillaged, which they would exchange for European goods. This would establish a communication "so natural" between the European and African coasts and clear the way for a "new kind of conquest" that would "amply compensate for those which, during so many centuries, have contributed to the distress of humankind." Thus,

---

[72] *HDI*, book 11, chap. 24, 277.

[73] Ibid., 287.

[74] Ibid., 275.

[75] We can here recall that in an earlier passage, the *HDI* attributes the initiation of the slave trade to this "*peuple de pirates, ces monstres de mer*," that is, "this people of pirates, these sea-monsters." Ibid., 190.

the proposed plan for the eradication of the illicit *commerçants*, the pirates, also followed the pattern set in the history of European slavery: Self-interested political intervention would necessarily clear the way for "the spirit of commerce," the antidote to the *commerce odieux*, leading to universal peace and happiness.

From these passages, then, one might conclude that the history of European slavery provided a formula that, if repeated, could put an end to the slave trade. But the *Histoire des deux Indes* was not so consistent. In reading book 11, it is important to measure these calls for "politics" and "new commercial conquests," this apparent *remède dans le mal*, against the text's equally passionate calls for reform.[76] We find, for instance, passages recommending ways of improving the slaves' voyage from Africa to America.[77] The work also suggested a six-step programme to alleviate the slaves' suffering and improve their morale once in America.[78] Finally, it advocated a plan by which to eventually "ease them from their chains" into liberty by "subjecting them to our laws and manners" and providing the newly freed men and women with cabins and plots of land.[79]

While the text is in this sense ambivalent, if not contradictory, about what to do with the slave trade, it is quite clear about the risks involved in not taking any action: "There are so many indications of the impending storm, and the Negroes only want a chief, sufficiently courageous, to lead them on to vengeance and slaughter."[80] Once this chief appeared,

---

[76] This is Jean Starobinski's phrase describing Rousseau's social thought: in essence, that the cure for civilisation's ills lay in civilisation itself. See *Le remède dans le mal*, 170. The "reform track," as Laurent Dubois has called it, increasingly came into vogue later on in the decade. Dubois, *Les esclaves de la République*, 59–62. See also, "L'esclavage est-il réformable? Les projets des administrateurs coloniaux à la fin de l'Ancien Régime," in *Les Abolitions de l'esclavage*, 133–41.

[77] *HDI*, book 11, chap. 24, 248–50. As Gianluigi Goggi has elucidated, these ideas had been circulating in Physiocratic circles, especially in the works of Dupont de Nemours and the abbé Baudeau, and were already present in Roubaud's *Histoire générale de l'Asie, de l'Afrique, et de l'Amérique*. But they reached the corridors of power by way of a colonial official, the baron of Bessner, whose memorandum, *De l'esclavage des nègres* (1774) sparked a great debate in the Bureau des colonies, and notably fierce opposition from Malouet. According to Goggi, Raynal's decision to broadcast Bessner's memorandum through the *HDI* suggests a reading of the text as an imperial voice box. See Goggi, "Diderot-Raynal, l'esclavage et les Lumières écossaises," 72–73. The puzzle of how to interpret Diderot's decision to leave these controversial theses in the text remains, however.

[78] Chapter 22 discusses "the wretched condition of slaves in America" and how each nation "treats the slaves differently," as do the different religions. Chapter 23 offers detailed suggestions as to "how we could render the state of the slaves more tolerable." Ibid., 261–65.

[79] Ibid., 287.

[80] Ibid., 288–89.

"Spaniards, Portuguese, English, French, Dutch, all their tyrants will become the victims of fire and sword."[81]

It is on this foreboding note that chapter 24 ends. The reader is left with a clear sense of inaction's dangers but confusion about what action would be appropriate.[82] The history of European slavery added by Diderot in 1780 offered no strategy for ending the slave trade. This begs the earlier question of what its purpose actually was.

The answer may lie in the realm of rhetoric. This history of European slavery could, in effect, be seen as an additional form of rhetorical ammunition against the slave trade. At a time when "history still provided the essential ideological resources for political contestation," to borrow Keith Baker's formulation, Diderot's addition served to "alert moral recognition in the reader," who, previous to the 1780 version, had not in either Raynal or Diderot's view been sufficiently moved by the accounts of the slave trade to contest or reform it.[83] By juxtaposing an account of how their ancestors had eventually been freed from their state of slavery with detailed descriptions of contemporary slavery, the history within the history encouraged European readers to make a causal connection between an enslaved past thought buried and a present that propagated that enslavement in its most iniquitous form. In this way, the *Histoire* derided the deplorable situation wherein "the torments of a people to whom we owe our luxuries, can never reach our hearts" but "even imaginary distresses draw tears from our eyes, both in silent retirement of the closet, and especially at the theatre."[84]

By drawing on a familiar story – that of their own sense of enslavement and slavery, historical and contemporary – and juxtaposing it to accounts of the trade in slaves, Diderot in effect elicited readers to draw a parallel that, in turn, took the metaphorical rhetoric of political slavery used by theorists such as Rousseau and lawyers such as Henrion to

---

[81] There is agreement among most scholars studying the *HDI* that this passage was "borrowed" from Louis-Sébastien Mercier's *L'an 2440*, chap. 22. The language is almost identical. Anatole Feugère was the first to remark on this in his *Un précurseur de la Révolution*, 204–05.

[82] David B. Davis has argued that this ambivalence and apparent "narrowing of alternatives" is a sign of increasing moral uncertainty in the mind of the Enlightenment. See David B. Davis, *The Problem of Slavery in Western Culture*. (Ithaca, NY: Cornell University Press, 1966), 422.

[83] Baker, *Inventing the French Revolution*, 32. The phrase "alert moral recognition" is Judith Shklar's. She used it to describe the role of utopias, but I suggest it also aptly describes one of the functions of the history of European slavery added by Diderot in 1780. See *Men and Citizens*, 2.

[84] *HDI*, book 11, chap. 24, 256–57.

task for its obliviousness to the slave trade. The effect was to unsettle the politics of defining slavery in abstract terms. In combining this challenge to both metaphorical slavery and the slave trade, the *Histoire des deux Indes* constituted one of eighteenth-century France's first wholly anti-slavery tracts.[85] Its accounts of slavery and the slave trade also hold hermeneutical importance for our interpretation of the idea of commerce in the *Histoire*. Not only do they amplify the work's critical force, they provide a lens through which the idea of *doux commerce* is revealed to be fundamentally unstable, though commerce is also clearly understood as a deeply moral and political force. This moral and political nature of commerce also comes to the fore in the representation of piracy, a second site of collapse of the doctrine espousing the sweet effects of commerce

---

[85] Indeed, the *HDI* served as one of the foundational texts upon which the soon-to-be Girondin *député*, Jacques-Pierre Brissot (de Warville, 1754–93), founded the Société des Amis des Noirs, the first abolitionist society in France, in 1788.

3

Cette odieuse piraterie

Defining Piracy

War, commerce, and piracy / Are an indivisible trinity.
  – Goethe, *Faust* II, act 5, ll. 11184–88

All of Europe knows that the King of England had been in 1754 the aggressor against the King's possessions in North America, and that last June, the English Navy, in contempt of the right of peoples [*droit des gens*] and of faith in Treaties, began to carry out the most violent hostilities against His Majesty's Vessels, and against the navigation and commerce of his subjects.[1]

With this declaration, Louis XV officially initiated the Seven Years War. The specific cause provided was the "seizure at Dunkerque of His Majesty's ships," attacked "in full peace-time by a squadron of thirteen English vessels." Although Louis had proposed that this assault might be forgiven if England made restitution for the French vessels, the refusal of the English king "obliged" him to "repel force with force." In this way, a "bad seizure" was revealed to be a dangerous provocation and a justification for war. The eighteenth century's global war began, then, with an act of piracy re-defined as a legitimate basis for imperial belligerence.

Among the types of odious commerce identified in the eighteenth century, only piracy was censured by the courts and the royal administration. Carefully circumscribed, the act of piracy became illegal in this period, whereas monopoly was legally protected by the state until the Revolution and the trade in slaves was not fully banned until 1831.[2] The

---

[1] *Ordonnance du Roi, Portant déclaration de guerre contre le Roi d'Angleterre, Du 9 Juin 1756.*
[2] Whereas colonial slavery was banned in Saint-Domingue in 1793, and later in Paris as part of the Convention's general declaration of liberty on 16 Pluviôse, Year II (4 February

juridical framework around piracy took shape with the first comprehensive maritime ruling in France, Colbert's Ordonnance de la Marine du mois d'aoust 1681. Article 10 of title 9 explained that ships and goods of French subjects or allies reclaimed from pirates would be returned to their owners upon their payment to the state of one-third of the value of the ship's goods "as fees of reprisal."[3] A further ruling in 1718 allowed acts of piracy by the king's subjects to be forgiven if their agents were willing to "repent sincerely" and live in the colonies of America. Those who did not repent were "to be punished by death, and their goods confiscated as well as those of their abettors, accomplices and members, who would be condemned to the gallows in perpetuity."

In this way, pirates, sometimes represented in the literature of the period as romantic anti-heroes and at other times as criminals, officially became outlaws in eighteenth-century France. Yet the 1718 Ordonnance also enacted the crucial distinction that the seizure of goods from ships of other nations was carefully reconfigured when exercised by agents of the imperial state. "Piracy" became "good seizure" when those who acted against the state's enemies had a commission. A long history of reclassifying the practice of piracy can be traced as far back as a famous story first told by Cicero and popularised by Augustine in his *City of God*. Confronting a pirate, Alexander the Great once asked what he "meant by infesting the seas." The pirate responded defiantly, "The same as you do when you infest the whole world. But because I do it with a little ship, I am called a robber. Because you do it with a great fleet you are called an emperor."[4] The re-description of piracy in eighteenth-century France shared the attitude of the pirate-emperor tale. I would like to suggest that in this case, it drew more specifically on a legacy of international

1794), this abolition was revoked by Napoleon in 1802. Later, the trade in "Blacks" was abolished in fits and starts (1818, 1827, and 1831). Slavery in France, in the colonies, and the slave trade were not finally abolished until 1848, by decree of the Provisional Government of the IInd Republic. See Marcel Dorigny, ed., *Les Abolitions de l'esclavage de L.F. Sonthonax à V. Schoelcher, 1793, 1794, 1848.* (Paris: Éditions UNESCO and Presses universitaires de Vincennes, 1995).

3 "Les navires & effets de nos sujets ou alliés repris sur les pirates, & réclamés dans l'an & jour de la déclaration qui en aura été faite à l'Amirauté, seront rendus aux propriétaires, en payant le tiers de la valeur du vaisseau & des marchandises, pour frais de recousse." The article was reprinted in Valin's *Nouveau commentaire*, 2:263.

4 Augustine, *The City of God against the Pagans* (4:4), trans. and ed. R. W. Dyson (Cambridge: Cambridge University Press, 1998), 148. As Dyson notes, Augustine probably drew this story from Cicero, *De re publica* (3:14–24). See Cicero, *On the Commonwealth and On the Laws*, trans. and ed. James E. G. Zetzel, (Cambridge: Cambridge University Press, 1999), 119.

jurisprudence that began with Hugo Grotius (1583–1645) and his seventeenth-century treatise on the "right of prize," the *De iure praedae* (1604–06). As a study of dictionaries of jurisprudence and legal commentaries shows, the reworking of the definition of piracy was reinforced in seventeenth-century France through Colbert's Ordonnance de la Marine and persisted well into the eighteenth century.

In the previous chapter, we saw how the *Histoire des deux Indes* confronted the *doux commerce* thesis by challenging complacency about the slave trade and provoking its readers to recognise the analogy between freedom from feudal servitude and the end of the African slave trade. The example of piracy offers a connected perspective on the nature and representation of commerce in imperial France. Interspersed throughout the *Histoire* are various accounts of pirates, alleged disruptors of imperial commerce, that draw on a confused idiom of piracy to provide a devastating critique of the hypocrisy of the European powers. These imperial states the *Histoire* charged, manipulated jurisprudence to justify their practice of piracy at the same time that they condemned its practice by individuals. This influential reading picked up on that powerful imperial tool: definition. In this instance, the crucial category was *prise*, a term that designates both the act of seizing and the prize seized.[5]

To reveal how the French state was able to redefine its commercial piracies as good seizures, this chapter first establishes the eighteenth-century semantic field for "pirate" by examining the definitions of piracy in dictionaries of the period. A careful reading of the meanings of "piracy" and its conceptual cognates brings to light the varied understandings of the term at the time, and consequently highlights subtle ways in which it was reconfigured to blur its relationship to the imperial commercial enterprise. My principal source is, predictably, the *Reasoned Dictionary of the Sciences and the Arts*, or the *Encyclopédie*, but I also draw upon Savary de Bruslons's *Universal Dictionary of Commerce* (*Dictionnaire universel de commerce*) (1723), a key source for the *encyclopédistes*.[6] Savary's

---

[5] The eighteenth-century French term *prise* poses problems for translation, as does the term *course*, discussed in a later footnote. In French, the term *prise* (as with its Latin counterpart, *praeda*) is used both to describe an action, that of capturing or storming or seizing from a ship, and to refer to the goods gained in a capture or storm or seizure. Not only does it belong to at least two different parts of speech, it is often accompanied by the transitive "to do," or *faire*. In short, there is no single equivalent term in English. I have opted for the unsatisfactory and somewhat clumsy rendering of the term as *seizure* because *seizure* evokes both the action of seizing and the thing seized.

[6] The extent to which Savary's *Dictionnaire universel* was drawn upon (often verbatim) by the *encyclopédistes* is evidenced in the content of the article "Nègre." See Andrew

extensive compilation of legal, agronomic, financial, and other facts and advice served as an important reference for merchants and policymakers alike in the period. Augmented in its second edition by articles from the *Encyclopédie*, the *Dictionnaire* also represented a dominant perspective within the culture that widely considered it as an authoritative text.

A foray into lexicography offers just one perspective on the idiom of piracy.[7] To flesh out the reach of this semantic field, I narrow in on legal or juridical questions and turn to Hugo Grotius's seminal treatise on the "right of prize," the *De iure praedae*. This treatise offered the first example of the state itself manipulating definitions of pirates and piracy to defend actions condemned when they were performed by transient individual agents, pirates. It is in dictionaries of jurisprudence that the legacy of Grotius prevails and provides a context that foregrounds the practical applications of these definitions. But I also turn to the work of an overlooked eighteenth-century legal theorist, René-Josué Valin, whose well-circulated *Commentary on the Maritime Ruling of 1681* (1759, 1766) reinforced the right of prize confirmed by Colbert. Valin's work remained a core reference in most studies of international law in the eighteenth century and continued to be cited until the twentieth century, as we shall see.

With this framework we can better understand the contrast between the juridical concern and the intrigue and fantasy of pirates as romantic anti-heroes manifested in the *Histoire des deux Indes*. In this text, the authors developed a critique of the disjuncture between legal theory and state practice. The *Histoire* called the distinction between piracy and good seizure into question on two fronts. First, its narrative was one of the participants in the emerging genre of pirate histories that idealised pirates, glorifying them as shrewd leaders and celebrated filibusterers (the literal pirates of the Caribbean), as pioneers of a free and egalitarian society.[8] In

Curran, "Diderot and the *Encyclopédie*'s Construction of the black African" in *SVEC* 2006:09, 41.

[7] Marcus Rediker's influential corpus on piracy refers to the "pirate idiom." See especially *Between the Devil and the Deep Blue Sea: Merchant Seamen, Pirates and the Anglo-American Maritime World, 1700–1750* (Cambridge: Cambridge University Press, 1987). Here I discuss the idiom and semantic field of *piracy*, highlighting the differences between the two terms.

[8] As Hans Turley has argued, the "earliest sustained and complete history of the 'golden-age' pirate" was Charles Johnson's *General History of the ... Pyrates*. This work, in fact written by Daniel Defoe under a pseudonym, was reprinted many times after its initial appearance in 1724. See Hans Turley, *Rum, Sodomy and the Lash: Piracy, Sexuality, and Masculine Identity* (New York: New York University Press, 1999), 32. Manuel Schonhorn reports that Defoe's authorship was not discovered until 1932. See the introduction to his edition of *A General History of the Pyrates* (Columbia: University of South Carolina Press,

this way, the *Histoire* refused the vilification of the pirate formalised in jurisprudence and elsewhere. On a second front, the *Histoire* called the bluff of the maritime jurisprudence that justified the state's dubious commercial practices by vilifying pirates and reconfiguring the state's own acts of piracy as legal. The *Histoire* demonstrated to its readers that this hypocrisy ultimately underlay the foundation of France's imperial enterprise and structured a system of commerce far more odious than sweet.

THE POLITICS OF DEFINITION (BIS)

Historians of piracy tend to begin their texts discussing, and often complaining about, the semantic slippage between terms in the pirate vocabulary. From Philip Gosse – still the classic reference for the history of pirates in France – to Gérard Jaeger to Patrick Villiers (to mention only key French historians of piracy in France), virtually all writers on the subject address the difficulty of arriving at a stable definition of "pirate".[9] The legacy of this politics of definition remains an issue for international law and commerce to this day: There continues to be no universally accepted definition of "piracy" in international law.[10] By bringing forward the

1999), xxiii. As Turley notes further, the "image of the fearless, bloodthirsty sea dog – the piratical 'character' that subsequent generations of readers imagine – can be traced to Exquemelin's volume." Ibid., 162. Here, Turley refers to Alexandre-Olivier Exquemelin (whom he refers to as John Exquemelin), whose *Bucaniers of America* (1684) served as a central source for the authors of the *HDI*.

[9] See Philip Gosse, *The History of Piracy* (London: Longmans, Green, 1932); Gérard A. Jaeger, ed., *Vues sur la piraterie: Des origines à nos jours* (Paris: Librairie Jules Tallandier, 1992); and Patrick Villiers, *Les corsaires du Littoral: Dunkerque, Calais, Boulogne, de Philippe II à Louis XIV (1568–1713)* (Paris: Presses universitaires du Septentrion, 2000). For example, Marcus Rediker, one of the most prolific Anglo-American scholars of piracy, begins a recent work by providing his own definition: "I define a pirate as one who willingly participates in robbery on the sea, not discriminating among nationalities in the choice of victims." See *Devil and the Deep Blue Sea*, 256n3.

[10] See Afua Hirsch, "Efforts to Tackle Epidemic Hindered by Lack of Internationally Agreed Definition," *Guardian*, 20 November 2008. Although the UN Convention on the Law of the Sea (UNCLOS), which entered into force in 1994, offers a definition of piracy (Article 101 specifies that piracy consisted of "illegal acts of violence or detention … committed for private ends, and directed: (i) on the high seas, against another ship or aircraft, or against persons or property on board such ship or aircraft; (ii) against a ship, aircraft, persons or property in a place outside the jurisdiction of any State" as well as "any act of voluntary participation in the operation of a ship or of an aircraft with knowledge of facts making it a pirate ship or aircraft."), the resurgence of piracies in 2008 brought to light its limits. As Joseph M. Isanga argues, the UNCLOS definition is "premised on a traditional understanding of piracy – one that assumes that the state system works effectively and that a state can enforce its own laws in the territorial sea." Yet "pirates have become organized, technological advanced, and versatile – a development that explodes

multiplicity of meanings and semantic slippage between the terms used to describe pirates and piracy in eighteenth-century France, it is possible to paint a truer, if more complex, portrait of the period and its engagement with commerce in all of its manifestations. It also draws attention to the ways in which obfuscation became a broader political strategy in a charged political space, beyond official sites of sovereignty.

THE ENCYCLOPÉDIE

An analysis of the crazy quilt of definitions offered in the *Encyclopédie*, the vehicle of a changed and changing political space, provides an obvious starting point for an understanding of the vocabulary of piracy in eighteenth-century France. By examining the definitions in the sequence suggested by the articles themselves we can simulate the gestures of eighteenth-century readers and approach the meanings available to them.

It is surprising to learn that there is no article for "piracy" per se in the *Encyclopédie*. This absence is of course especially curious since it is well known that throughout the seventeenth and eighteenth centuries the European empires engaged in a steady stream of minor combats at sea.[11] In contrast, the term "pirate" was offered a definition by the chevalier de Jaucourt (1704–90), the generalist charged with penning many of the *Encyclopédie*'s articles. Classified as "Maritime," Jaucourt's pirate is "the name given" to "bandits" who command ships and attack merchant vessels to "pillage and steal" from them; they afterwards "withdraw" to "far away and isolated" places, where they "can be sheltered from the punishment they deserve."[12] It is later within the article devoted to the agent, the pirate, that the action, piracy, is finally addressed. Jaucourt offers a historical account of piracy, interrupted by judgements about it. Jaucourt first claims that "it is hard to believe" that piracy has ever been "honourable," much less the practice of the Greeks and Barbarians. Yet Jaucourt then cites Thucydides's account of how these very Greeks and Barbarians undertook "the profession of pirates under the command

---

international understandings of piracy." See his "Countering Persistent Contemporary Sea Piracy: Expanding Jurisdictional Regimes," *American University Law Review* 59:5 (2010): 1273.

[11] John Bromley coined the phrase "second hundred years war" to describe this period. See his *Corsairs and Navies, 1660–1760* (London and Ronceverte: Hambledon Press, 1987).

[12] *Encyclopédie*, 12:652.

of their leadership, as much for enrichment as to provide subsistence to those who could not live through their work." Far from being "criminal," they passed for "honourable," and allowed their "nation" to subsist. Other "peoples of the earth" had glorified pillage, Thucydides added. But Jaucourt was quick to point out that valorisation of pirates did not survive. In keeping with his assessment of the practice: "[I]t appears that the profession of pirate was not an honourable profession for long," as it contradicted "all sorts of rights," and, what is more, was "*odious* to all of the people who suffer considerable damages as a result."[13]

Jaucourt's insistence upon the odiousness of the pirate (in contradistinction to the pirate's honour) evokes the famous claim attributed to Cicero (whose concern with piracy we have already noted) that pirates are *hostis humani generis*, or enemies of the human race.[14] The *Encyclopédie's* description is again contrasted with a following account of the Egyptians and Phoenicians – the first civilisations to exercise maritime commerce, which led to their establishment of colonies and cities around the Red Sea and the Mediterranean – who also introduced the practice of "piracy and pillage." These "nomads of the sea," leaderless and without discipline, were scorned at first. But as the Roman Senate was entirely preoccupied with the war against Mithridates, the pirates profited from the occasion to enlarge and enrich themselves by pillaging villages and seizing ships until Pompey was finally sent to "combat them."

Jaucourt's narrative then shifts registers and addresses the reader directly by appealing to the authority of yet another ancient text: "One has to admit that in the manner in which Plutarch describes the life of the corsaires for us, it is not surprising that some wealthy people, even those from famous families, took their share."[15] Jaucourt's easy transition

---

[13] Ibid., 12:652–53. Emphasis added. There appears to be a typographical mistake in the French, and as a result my translation may not be precise. The original reads: "Mais il y apparence que le métier de pirate, n'a pas été long-tems un métier honorable."

[14] In fact, Cicero claimed that the pirate was "*communis hostis omnium*," or the "common enemy of all" in the *De Officiis* (3:107), and in his oration in favour of widening the scope of Pompey's war against the pirates to Asia, the *Pro Lege Manilia* (14), he invoked the "*hostes omnium gentium*," or the "enemy of all peoples." Dan Edelstein has nimbly traced the origins of the expression "*hostis humani generis*" to ninth-century Christian roots, when it was used to refer to the devil, only to be made more general in the eighteenth century to refer to tyrants. See his "Hostis Humani Generis: Devils, Natural Right, and Terror in the French Revolution," *Telos* 141 (2007), 62–63. As Edelstein notes, Cicero is still commonly cited as the source of the phrase, together with English MP and legal codifier Edward Coke (1552–1634). His presence is certainly felt in seventeenth- and eighteenth-century texts on piracy, whether the phrase originated with him or not.

[15] Ibid., 12:653. The text was probably Plutarch's *Life of Pompey*. Françoise Douay has shown that most grammar school-level students in eighteenth- and early-nineteenth-century

from the term *pirate* to the term *corsaire* here is striking, but by no means unusual: The elision manifested itself in most eighteenth-century French texts that dealt with pirates, including what might be considered the most consistent of genres, dictionaries of jurisprudence. These corsaires, Jaucourt explains, were extravagant in their display of wealth, with "gold and crimson bursting from all parts" and "silver-plated oars." Resenting the proximity of these pirates (here the text reverts to the original term without comment), the Romans resolved to war against them, sending General Pompey to the charge. Rather than killing them, Pompey destroyed the pirates "easily" with nothing less than "sweetness" (*douceur*). By relegating them to distant lands, and "by giving [the pirates] the means of living without piracy," Pompey "prevented them from pirating."[16]

So, depending on the *Encyclopédie* for a portrait of the pirate yields peculiar results: They are historical figures, also called corsaires, defeatable by sweetness and alternative means of obtaining wealth. On one hand the article cites ancient texts praising pirates and on the other portrays pirates as odious bandits. Through the veil of the assumed authority of the ancient texts, we find a not-so-hidden revelation of the currency of piratical practices among colonising empires. In other words, "piracy" – though well documented and fictionalised at the time – is conspicuous by its absence.[17]

If we turn again to the *Encyclopédie* for more help with our understanding of piracy in eighteenth-century France, we discover a maze of definitions within its semantic field, far more complex than Jaucourt's historicisation admitted. If his narrative could so easily slide from *pirate* to *corsaire* then we must next ask: What is a *corsaire*? Only a brief entry is

France knew the work by heart. Theirs was the Latin translation by Amelot, not the Greek version learned in England and other Protestant countries. Students of rhetoric deliberated whether the pirates who had entered Pompeii should be left to die. See Françoise Douay, "Valorisation/dévalorisation des corsaires, forbans et pirates dans la rhétorique du 18e siècle (pratiques et théorie)." Paper delivered at the 13ᵉ Colloque International du CRLV, "L'Aventure maritime: Pirates, corsaires et flibustiers." (Château de La Napoule, May 2000).

16 The following brief entry defines *pirating* (*pirater*) as, simply, "doing the pirate's trade." *Encyclopédie*, 12:653. To simplify this discussion, I have opted for the English translation, "corsair," although, as we shall see, "privateer" was a common eighteenth-century rendition of the term as well.

17 Madeleine Dobie offers a nuanced assessment of this kind of "displacement" and "silencing" in eighteenth-century French texts. While her focus is slavery and its transposition onto orientalist discourses, here we can also recognise that her insight is applicable to other key elements of imperial practice. Madeleine Dobie, *Trading Places: Colonization and Slavery in Eighteenth-Century French Culture* (Ithaca, NY: Cornell University Press, 2010), 12.

offered. Like pirate, corsaire falls into the "Marine" category, but, unlike pirate, the article for corsaire is associated with a semantic trio, "corsairs, rogues [*forbans*], pirates" – a rare instance in the *Encyclopédie* where, within a single article title, a term is accompanied by two synonyms. In a gesture that is more representative than exceptional, the article confuses more than clarifies the distinctions among these terms by conflating some with others rather unsystematically.

The author of this brief entry was Jacques-Nicolas Bellin (1703–72), a member of the Royal Academy of London and the French Maritime Academy and recognised as one of the foremost cartographers in France, a profession he practiced from the time he was named chief cartographer, or *hydrographe*, for the French navy in 1721.[18] For corsaire, Bellin drew almost verbatim on the *Dictionnaire universel de commerce* (1723), the standard reference for eighteenth-century French merchants and commercial policymakers. Writing that pirates, corsaires, and rogues were "sea-rovers," Bellin specified outright that the three terms were "synonymous names."[19] All three designated one who "arms" a war vessel without any government commission (that is to say, without license or official sanction) to "steal indifferently" from merchant ships. Bellin then described their legal status. The article informed readers that "corsairs" and "rogues" were treated as "public thieves" who could be hanged without any form of trial. Those who *font la course* (cruise the seas) with several commissions from different powers were treated as "rogues."[20] Finally, the article warned that "one must not confuse the corsairs with the ship owner," as the latter only "cruises the seas" against the enemies of the state with a "particular commission from his prince."

Far from simplifying or clarifying terms and boundaries, Bellin's description complicates the semantic field for the reader. Not only is the term "pirate" never explicitly mentioned in the article, the term "corsair"

---

[18] In the "Discours préliminaire" of the *Encyclopédie*, d'Alembert identified Bellin ("Z") as the principal contributor for maritime articles. Both a royal censor and the "ordinary" engineer of the marine, he also produced maps "eagerly welcomed" by "Wisemen and Navigators." Ibid., xlii.

[19] Bellin uses the term "*écumeurs de mer*," which might be translated more literally as "scourers of the sea." I have opted for "sea-rover", closer to the eighteenth-century English equivalent. See also Abel Boyer, *The Royal Dictionary*, (London : n.p., 1755).

[20] The eighteenth-century French term *course* poses several translation problems. Placing it in the category of "nautical history," the *Hachette-Oxford French-English/English-French Dictionary* renders *course* as "privateering." This translation is unsatisfactory, as it evokes the action of privateers, agents of the British crown. "Corsaire" is certainly the French version of "privateer," but within the discourse of piracy in eighteenth-century France we find *armateurs* (ship owners) who "*font la course*" as often as pirates do.

is given a meaning that is surprising in the light of contemporary legal definitions and practices. In contrast to Bellin's definition, the accepted meaning of "corsair" at the time was a seaman possessing "letters of endorsement" and therefore licensed by the king to capture enemy vessels. The English equivalent tended to be called a "privateer." The *Encyclopédie* here explicitly conflated "corsair" with "rogue" and "pirate," distinguishing it only from "ship owner" (*armateur*). This confusion is notable in that it also perplexed lexicographers across the Channel. We need only to turn to William Falconer's bilingual *Universal Dictionary of the Marine* (London, 1769) to find that the entry for *corsaire* reads: "a privateer, also a pirate!"[21]

As for the second synonym, "rogues" (*forbans*), an article by jurist Antoine-Gaspard Boucher d'Argis[22] offered the loose suggestion that in "certain customs" the term *forban* meant banishment.[23] A second article by Bellin designated the plural *forbans* a "Maritime" category and more explicitly connected rogues to those who cruised the seas without any commission and indiscriminately attacked and pillaged all those they met, friends or enemies. They flew no particular flag, but rather used "those of all the nations indifferently, to better disguise themselves." Employing precisely the same words as the "corsair" article, Bellin ended the piece with a statement of their fate: "[O]nce we take them they are treated as public thieves and are hanged right away."[24]

---

[21] See William Falconer, *An [sic] Universal Dictionary of the Marine: or, A Copious Explanation of the Technical Terms and Phrases Employed in the Construction, Equipment, Furniture, Machinery, Movements, and Military Operations of A Ship ... To which is annexed, A Translation of the French Sea-Terms and Phrases* (London: T. Cadell, 1769).

[22] Antoine-Gaspard Boucher d'Argis (1708–91) was a jurist and councillor at the Châtelet of Paris in 1767, and the principal contributor of articles on jurisprudence, replacing Toussaint as the *Encyclopédie*'s authority on all legal matters in 1753. He was the author of a *Treatise on Nuptial Gains and Survival* (1738), followed by a work on the *Rural Code, or Xamis and Regulations Concerning Country Goods* (1749). See Frank A. Kafker and Serena L. Kafker, *The Encyclopedists as Individuals* (Oxford: Voltaire Foundation, 1988), 51–52.

[23] The French term *forban* derived from the old French *forbannir*, literally, "outside the ban." Alain Rey et al., *Dictionnaire historique de la langue française* (Paris: Dictionnaires Le Robert, 1998), 2:1457. The first usage is here deemed to be 1247, followed by 1273 and 1505. In feudal law, it also designated a sailor who "practiced piracy on his own behalf." Only later did the term migrate from the maritime domain and come to mean an unscrupulous man. The term *forban littéraire*, or literary rogue, emerged in the eighteenth century. The *Trésor de la langue française* (*TLF*) offers a source for the 1247 meaning: the *Coutumes d'Anjou et du Maine*, I, 82. See 8:1063.

[24] *Encyclopédie*, 7:109.

Another example of this synonymy within the semantic field for *pirate* becomes evident when we turn to learn about the ship-owner (*armateur*). The *Encyclopédie*'s entry "Armateur ou Capre," also penned by Bellin and categorised as "Maritime," offered a predictable definition: "commander of a vessel armed to patrol their opponents' ships." But, the article continued, the term *armateur* was also the "specious name taken by pirates to soften/sweeten [*adoucir*] that of *corsaire*."[25] Here the *Encyclopédie*'s maritime specialist offers a glimpse of the convoluted patterns of obfuscation at work in the *pirate* semantic field. To add more confusion to the mix, *armateur* also signified merchants who chartered or equipped vessels either for "cruising" or for commerce. The *armateur* with "vessels armed for war" were called *capres* (not *corsaires*, as one might predict based on the earlier definition), according to the article under that name. At this point, the reader finds herself at the end of the first circuit of terms in the semantic field.

Yet obvious elements of the vocabulary of pirates are clearly missing. Thus far, none of the definitions or references made in the *Encyclopédie* pointed to the famed *filibusterer* (*flibustier*). By all accounts, especially that provided by the *Histoire des deux Indes*, pirates and filibusterers were professional cousins. An independent entry for *filibusterer* did in fact exist in the *Encyclopédie*, although a reader would have had to search specifically for the term to discover that it was considered part of the category of "maritime history" and designated the *corsaires* or *adventurers* from the American islands who had joined forces to cruise the seas and the American coasts and to "war against the Spanish."[26] The

[25] *Encyclopédie*, 1:686. According to Françoise Douay, this passage evokes Aristotle's example of the pirate to illustrate definitions of metaphor. See Aristotle, *Rhetoric*, 3, 1405a, para. 25.

[26] *Encyclopédie*, 7:875. The etymology and origins of the term *flibustier* reveal the international character of the figure and practice. The first appearance of the French term *flibustier* in a publication can be traced to the French translation of Exquemelin's *Bucaniers of America* (1686), according to the OED. The TLF offers 1666 as the date of its first appearance, in a manuscript at the Archives Nationales by J. Clodoré, *Mémoire sur la ville de Saint Domingue*, MS des Archives nationales, Colonies, C9B. The English term probably derives from the Dutch *vrij-bueter*, passing through a more literal transliteration, "freebooter." According to the OED, the French form, *flibustier*, was adopted in England and used until about 1850–54, when the form "filibuster" appeared, probably from the Spanish *filibustero*. In the eighteenth-century English usage of the term, however, "freebooter" was evidenced by, for example, Adam Smith's *Wealth of Nations* (1776), where in book 4, chapter 7, he wrote, "St Domingo was established by pirates and freebooters." As the OED notes, "the mutual relation of the forms is involved in obscurity," and many possible influences can be imagined. One might trace a path to the English *flyboat* from the Dutch *vieboot* (which might explain the Savary brothers'

Encyclopédie thus distanced the filibusterer from the reader's present, but muddied the field again by linking these to privateers and to yet another term, *adventurer*.

While adventurers also did not figure in the *Encyclopédie*'s system of *renvois* related to pirates, a separate article was devoted to them. The author, rather unexpectedly, was a theologian: the abbé Mallet. Appointed to the chair in theology at the University of Paris in 1751, Mallet remained an avid contributor to the *Encyclopédie* when other Catholic theologians had abandoned it for fear of persecution.[27] His article "Aventuriers," or "Adventurers," was also largely drawn from Ephraim Chambers's *Cyclopaedia*, like the more than two thousand others he contributed to the enterprise, and also from the Savary brothers' *Dictionnaire universel de commerce*. Ever concerned to highlight the commercial significance of his writings, Mallet began his article on adventurers he called a "type of pirate" by stipulating that "in commerce," the term *aventuriers* refers to men "without character and without home" who "meddle brazenly in the affairs of others, and whom we cannot distrust enough."[28] An "adventurer" is also "the name given in America" to the "bold and enterprising pirates" who "unite against the Spaniards and seize from them," also known as "buccaneers."[29] The article then refers the reader to the entry "Buccaneers," to which I turn later in this chapter. It is only in the third and fourth parts of the *Encyclopédie*'s definition of the term *adventurer* that we encounter the usage that would prevail in the nineteenth century in which its connection to piracy was obscured. In this version, it was the English who apparently gave the name "adventurers" to those who bought shares in companies formed to establish colonies in America. This distinguished them from those called "planters," who were inhabitants with plantations.[30] Finally, an *adventurer vessel* was a merchant ship that

---

reference to the *flibot* in their definition), or a reverse causality might be surmised, with Du Tertre's use of "*fribustier*" in his *Histoire des Ant-Isles* (1667), 3:151, perhaps a corruption of the English *freebooter*. See the *OED*, 2nd ed., 5:906.

[27] These articles are attributed to "G," which, according to the *Discours préliminaire* written by d'Alembert, referred to the abbé Mallet. D'Alembert offered *Encyclopédie* readers an unusually lengthy biography of Mallet. From it, we learn that the abbé Edme-François Mallet (1713–55) was a Catholic theologian. See also Kafker and Kafker, *Encyclopedists as Individuals*.

[28] *Encyclopédie*, 1:869. As we shall see, this definition is repeated, with a minor variation, in the second, post-Seven Years War edition of Savary des Bruslons's *Dictionnaire universel de commerce* (1765).

[29] *Encyclopédie*, 1:869.

[30] Whereas planters planted and cultivated their lands, adventurers lent their money and "so to speak, venture it in the hope of profits which they should withdraw through dividends." In France, these were, "strictly speaking," called "shareholders."

operated within the limits of a commercial company without permission. These latter definitions more closely parallel the understanding of the term in the nineteenth century, when it came to mean speculator and its initial connections to piracy were submerged.[31]

The cross-referenced article "*Boucanier*," or "Buccaneer," was also attributed to the abbé Mallet. "*Boucanier*" first suggested a geographic distinction between the buccaneer and the adventurer: It was "the name given in the West Indies to certain savages who smoke their meat on a Brazilian wood grill placed at a certain height from the fire which is called '*boucan*.'"[32] Mallet cited "Oexmelin" (Exquemelin) as the source for this "fact," as did the Savary brothers.[33] Exquemelin's famous and widely read history of the "adventurers-filibusterers," as he referred to them, was first published in 1684 in English as *Bucaniers of America*.[34] Given the wide circulation of his text, surprisingly little is known about Exquemelin other than that his origins were Flemish, that he was also referred to as "Oexmelin" (1645?–1717), and that he served the French Company of the East Indies in the 1660s before writing the history. Mallet then

---

[31] See Sylvain Venayre, "Le pirate dans 'l'aventure coloniale', 1850–1940" *L'Ull critic* 11 (2007), 157–68.

[32] *Encyclopédie*, 2:348.

[33] Variations in the spelling of "Oexemelin" or "Exquemelin" persist in literature on piracy today. The first appears to be the Dutch spelling, whereas the second is the Gallicized version.

[34] The work had a complex publishing history. It was first published in Dutch: *De Americaensche Zee-Rovers. Behelsende een … Beschrijving van alle de voornaemste roveryen, en onmenschelijke wreedheden, die de Engelse en Franse Rovers tegens de Spanjaerden in America gepleeght hebben … Hier achter is bygevoeght een korte verhandeling van de macht en rijk dommen die de Koninck van Spaine … in America heeft, etc.* (Amsterdam: J. ten Hoorn, 1678). It was next published in Spanish. The English translation was made from the Spanish version and it first appeared in 1684: Alexander-Olivier Exquemelin, *Bucaniers of America: or, a true account of the … assaults committed … upon the coasts of the West Indies by the Bucaniers of Jamaica and Tortuga … especially, the … exploits of Sir H. Morgan … written originally in Dutch, by J. [or rather A. O.] Esquemelin … now … rendred into English. (The second volume. Containing the … voyage … of Captain B. Sharp … from the original journal … written by … B. Ringrose,* etc.). 2 vols. (London: W. Crooke, 1684–85). The first French translation appeared in 1686. Alexandre Olivier Exquemelin, "known as" Oexmelin, *Histoire des avanturiers qui se sont signalez dans les Indes, contenant ce qu'ils ont fait de plus remarquable depuis vingt années, avec la vie, les mœurs … des habitans de St-Domingue et de la Tortue et une description exacte de ces lieux, où l'on voit l'établissement d'une chambre des comptes dans les Indes et un état … des offices où … le roy d'Espagne pourvoit, les revenus qu'il tire de l'Amérique et ce que les plus grands princes de l'Europe y possèdent … par Alexandre Olivier Oexmelin…* Translated by M. de Frontignières. 2 vols. (Paris: J. Le Febvre, 1686). A new edition was published in the eighteenth century under the auspices of the French Company of the Indies. *Histoire des avanturiers flibustiers qui se sont signalez dans les Indes …* 4 vols. (Trévoux: par la Cie, 1744).

acknowledged Savary: "Savary says that the Spanish, who have large settlements in the island of Saint-Domingue, also have their own 'buccaneers,' which they call '*matadores*' or '*monteros*'; that is to say, '*chasseurs*' (hunters): the English call theirs 'cow-killers.'" This acknowledgement points once again to the connections between the *Encyclopédie* and the *Dictionnaire universel*. Both sources informed readers that these hunters earned their name from the manner in which they prepared their meat, usually boar or wild bull. But they were also distinguished by a "crew" consisting of a pack of thirty dogs and a "special gun" with "special powder" from Cherbourg. On some occasions, the article continued, these buccaneers joined the regimented troops in the colonies and served on military expeditions. Useful to the imperial powers in need of labour, they had come to "exist among all of the European nations who have settlements in America."[35] Thus, according to the *Encyclopédie*, even the "bold and enterprising pirates" in America, as the article on "Adventurers" referred to the buccaneers, were also agents of the colonising powers in the New World.

As represented in the *Reasoned Dictionary*, the category "pirate" is a capacious one containing many overlapping variants – from bandits, corsaires, rogues, sea-rovers, ship-owners, filibusterers, adventurers, to buccaneers. The ease of synonymy among these terms connected through the system of cross references reflects the *Encyclopédie*'s project to create "cultural momentum" and resist the potential for linguistic inertia.[36] But more is at stake here than an example of the still labyrinthine quality of the *Encyclopédie*, despite its editors' aims.[37] This jumbled semantic field also points to a broader political and cultural force at work with implications for our understanding of imperial strategies of control and definition: the elusive pirate.

---

[35] *Encyclopédie*, 2:348.

[36] Wilda Anderson, *Diderot's Dream* (Baltimore: Johns Hopkins University Press, 1990), 96. As David W. Bates has argued, Diderot and d'Alembert conceived of the *Encyclopédie* as "a tool for provoking knowledge, not fixing it in one place." See "Cartographic Aberrations: Epistemology and Order in the Encyclopedic Map," in *Using the "Encyclopédie": Ways of Knowing, Ways of Reading*, ed. Daniel Brewer and Julie Candler Hayes, SVEC 2002:5, 19. Also cited in Joanna Stalnaker, *The Unfinished Enlightenment Description in the Age of the Encyclopédie* (Ithaca, NY: Cornell University Press, 2010), 103.

[37] David W. Bates discusses how d'Alembert's *Discours préliminaire* explained that the *Encyclopédie* was meant to organise the labyrinth of human knowledge into a coherent map in his *Enlightenment Aberrations: Error and Revolution in France* (Ithaca, NY: Cornell University Press, 2002), 30.

Piracies

To develop this notion more fully, let us now turn to examine how these various pirates' actions or practices were represented, moving from categories of pirates to piracies. We have already seen that "piracy" does not figure in the *Reasoned Dictionary*. So the reader is left to puzzle over the meaning of the "cruise" that all of these ship-owners, corsairs, rogues, filibusterers, and pirates were undertaking. We find the meaning of *course*, or cruise, under a subheading of an article entitled "*Courses du cirque*," or "Circus Races." Within the category of "ancient history," these "circus races" comprised the principal event of the games celebrated at the time. The first subheading, "*Course, Faire la Course, Aller en Course*," is deemed part of the "Maritime" category and thus attributed to Bellin. The term describes a ship armed in a "time of war" in order to seize goods from the enemy (*faire des prises*). But there is one caveat: No one, Bellin claimed, could "cruise," or go *en course*, without a commission from the admiral, at the risk of being treated as a "rogue."[38] Written by the hydrographer royal, the *Encyclopédie* article here appears to confirm a sense that "cruising" without official orders was criminal activity.

A second action mentioned in the definition of *course* is the *prise*, or seizure. Here again, two definitions are offered – a first, deemed a term of "Jurisprudence," and a second, "Marine." Probably written by Boucher d'Argis, the first article describes a medieval royal right of seizure of goods from individuals for the use and service of the court. As a term of jurisprudence, this right of "seizure of possessions" extended through a number of authorisations and rulings, papal bulls, and royal edicts. The marine term, "maritime seizure," was regulated by the Ordonnance of 1681. In this latter case, prior knowledge of some sort is clearly assumed by the very general and ambiguous opening definition offered: "This is what is said of a vessel that has been taken from the enemy." Next, the reader is taught how to use the term seizure in speech, for example: "During our cruise which lasted three months, we made four seizures, that is to say, we took four vessels."[39]

The characteristics of a good seizure are then presented as a legal distinction: A ship could be declared by the courts to be a good seizure.

---

[38] The original French read: "COURSES, FAIRE LA COURSE, ALLER EN COURSE, (Marine.) se dit d'un vaisseau armé en tems de guerre pour aller faire des prises sur l'ennemi." *Encyclopédie*, 4:397.

[39] *Encyclopédie*, 4:397.

Here, the reader is referred to the Ordonnance de 1681, book 3, title 9, which describes an elaborate formula for distributing the funds resulting from the property seized by licensed individuals (with commissions) upon ships armed for war. After one-fifth is awarded to the state and one-tenth of the remainder to the admiral, the article explained, the rest is divided among the ship-owners, captains, officers, and sailors according to the charter made among them. On the other hand, for seizures made by warships *of the state*, predictably, a much larger portion of funds went to the state: five-sixths, with one-tenth of the remaining sixth going to the admiral and the rest distributed in the form of a free gift to the captains, officers, and sailors who undertook the seizures and brought them in. In either case, whether individually armed or armed by the state, warships engaging in seizure paid the state a portion of the prize and rewarded the agents of the seizure. The article specifies that these seizures were time-sensitive and also nation-sensitive. Ships seized by enemies of the United Provinces that were then retaken, for example, involved a payment of one-third of their value if they were in enemy possession for more than forty-eight hours. Finally, the article reinforces the definition of a good seizure as a ship that could be stopped as an enemy or that carried contraband merchandise to the enemy.[40]

Written in the present tense, this article on seizure reveals next to no distinction as to the agent – among pirates, ship-owners, corsaires, and rogues, and the undertakings of state-licensed individuals. What is more, the present tense suggests a currency to the practice that other articles in the field obscured.

SAVARY DES BRUSLONS'S PIRACIES

How did this map of definitions offered in the *Encyclopédie* compare with those provided by the famous lexicon for merchants, Savary des Bruslons's *Dictionnaire universel de commerce* (1723, 1748)? As we have seen, the abbé Mallet and other contributors to the *Encyclopédie* drew liberally on the *Dictionnaire* for their articles on commerce and other terms related to piracy. But did the same blurring occur? The *Dictionnaire* defined its subjects within a framework that construed commerce as a branch of natural history, the mechanical arts (*arts et métiers*), and so forth, creating, in effect, a how-to book for the "*ars mercatoria.*"[41] In

---

[40] *Encyclopédie*, 13:383. Emphasis added.
[41] Savary des Bruslons, *Dictionnaire universel de commerce* (hereafter *DUC*). For a more detailed study of the *DUC*, see Rosario Patalano, "Il Dictionnaire universel de

turn, the new (second) edition of the *Dictionnaire* (1748) drew on the *Encyclopédie* to expand its own definitions. Published by his brother, Philémon Louis Savary, after Savary's death, the title page of the second edition stated as much, announcing that it was "revised exactly, corrected and expanded considerably, principally from the *Encyclopédie*." The two texts thus shared a dialectical relationship, and they reveal transformations in understandings of commerce and piracy, as well as instances of their stability. Although they did not share the same constituencies at the outset, the *Dictionnaire* and the *Encyclopédie* eventually presented virtually the same image of the pirate.

That piracies, and the concepts related to them, figured in the *Dictionnaire* at all certainly confirms their centrality to the discourse of commerce in eighteenth-century France. There was no mistaking the *Dictionnaire*'s aim. Immediately upon opening its cover, the reader was presented with an etching of Mercury donning a winged helmet, holding the *caduceus*, or herald's staff, and sporting *telarii*, or winged sandals. He stands in the middle of a market with a city wall and doorway behind him. On his left sits a closed chest and a scale with weights. Little cherubs busy making packages, piling moneybags, and guiding a horse-drawn cart flutter about. Here stood, unmistakably, the god of commerce and communication.[42] The idealised marketplace depicted on the *Dictionnaire*'s first page did not, however, set the tone for its depiction of commerce. Rather it was the underbelly of commerce and its abuses that figured alongside the idealised Mercury.

We learn from Savary des Bruslons's preface that the *Dictionnaire universel de commerce* was originally intended to serve as a reference tool for merchants, or *négociants*.[43] Savary was appointed inspector general of the customs house in Paris in 1686, and he told the reader that the project began at that time as a simple compilation of an alphabetical list of all items subject to duties. Not until later did he expand it to include all

commerce dei Savary e la fondazione dell' autonomia del discorso economico," in *Storia del pensiero economico* (Florence: Florence University Press, 2001) and Deryck W. Holdworth, "The Country-House Library: Creating Mercantile Knowledge in the Age of Sail" in Miles Ogborn and Charles Withers, eds., *Geographies of the Book* (Farnham: Ashgate), 141.

[42] *Lexicon Iconographicum Mythologiae Classicae*, 5, 1 (Munich: Artemis Verlag, 1990), 384–85. See also Walter Burkert, *Greek Religion*, trans. John Raffan (Cambridge, MA: Harvard University Press, 1985).

[43] The first edition of the work was published posthumously in 1723 by Jacques Savary des Bruslons's brother, Philémon Louis Savary, canon of the Royal Church of Saint Maur. The second edition, or "new edition" as it was labelled, first appeared in 1748. I cite from the five-volume, in-folio, 1765 printing of this second edition, published in Copenhagen.

DICTIONNAIRE
UNIVERSEL
DE
COMMERCE.

C   CAA   CAB

Troifiéme Let-   CAABLE'. Terme de commerce de bois. On ap-
tre de l'Alpha-   pellé Bois caablé, les arbres que les vents abbat-
bet. Cette Let-   tent dans les forêts. On dit auffi, pour fignifier
tre, ou feule,   la même chofe, *Bois Verfé*, & *Bois Chablis. Voyez*
ou fuivie, ou   CHABLIS.
précédée de
quelques autres,   C A B
fert aux Mar-   CABALISTE. Terme de Commerce, qui eft en
chands, Négo-   ufage à Touloufe, & dans toute la Province de
cians, Ban-   Languedoc.
quiers, & Te-   C'eft un Marchand qui ne fait pas le commer-
neurs de livres,   ce fous fon nom, mais qui eft intereffé dans le
pour abréger   négoce d'un Marchand en chef.
certains termes,   L'article 24 du Réglement général de la Bour-
qu'ils font obli-   fe commune de Touloufe de l'année 1701, pour
gés de répeter fouvent dans les écritures qu'ils   l'élection du Prieur & des Confuls de ladite
portent fur leurs Journaux, ou Regiftres. C.   Bourfe, porte : Que tout Marchand, ou Fils de
fignifie Compte : C. O. Compte Ouvert : C. C.   Marchand, faifant actuellement la marchandife,
Compte Courant : M. C. Mon Compte : S. C.   fera obligé d'accepter la Charge de Baille, ou
Son Compte : L. C. Leur Compte : N. C. No-   Adminiftrateur de la Confrérie, s'il y eft nommé,
tre Compte.   & que les Cabaliftes, & intéreffés au commerce
Tome II.   A

FIGURE 4. Savary's Mercury in the Market-place. Mercury at work in a
Market-place opens the entries beginning with "C" in vol. 2 of Savary des
Bruslons's *Dictionnaire universel de commerce* (Paris: Chez la Veuve
Etienne et fils, 1748, 3 vols, in-folio).
*Courtesy of the Rare Books and Special Collections Division of the
Library of Congress, Washington, DC.*

terms relating to commerce and industry, so that it finally evolved into a catalogue that included all the rulings and laws regulating commerce and industry, as well as a model of best practices.

The Savary brothers did not include an entry for "pirate" in their "universal dictionary." This might suggest that, as in the *Encyclopédie*, the pirate was here deemed a historical figure and not of immediate concern to eighteenth-century French merchants.[44] Yet, as we shall see, this absence is conspicuous – especially in light of the cross-references to "pirate" within the text. We do again find an entry for "corsair." Here the inquiring merchant would first encounter a string of terms implied to be synonymous: The corsaire was at once a pirate, a rogue (*forban*), and a sea-rover (*écumeur*) who "cruised the seas" with a vessel armed for war without license in order to "steal and pillage" from merchant ships.[45] This grouping of "corsair" with "pirate" points to a perception among writers outside of the royal administration that there was no distinction between a corsair and a pirate. To the merchants' lexicographer, the corsair's practice was indistinguishable from that of the pirate, and the actions of corsairs and pirates had the same deleterious repercussions for merchants' ships. When the article then contrasts the corsair to the *armateur*, or ship-owner, who exercised the same profession but *with* a license (and who attacked only enemy vessels at war with the princes and states from which he had his license), the parallel between the corsair and the pirate is brought into relief; so too, when the *Dictionnaire* specified that the corsair was hanged when he was caught, whereas the ship-owner was treated as a prisoner of war.

The ship-owner also merited an article; it begins semiotically by listing "other" definitions of the term, almost as though the Savary brothers had anticipated that the reader would have read the "Corsair" article first.[46] Thus, the reader learns that "we also call *Ship-owner*" those "merchants, traders, and others, who make armaments, or who are interested

---

[44] This might be also be explained by the currency of the term *pirate* within a "common language," causing it to be disregarded within more "technical" contexts, as Isabelle Turcan has suggested. Isabelle Turcan, "Les flibustiers de la lexicographie française des 17ᵉ et 18ᵉ siècles." Paper delivered at the Colloque du CRLV, May 2000.

[45] *DUC*, 1533.

[46] In addition, one had to register with the clerk of the admiralty from the site where the armament was made and pay a deposit of fifteen thousand livres, which, in turn, was to be received by the lieutenant of the admiralty in the presence of the king's prosecutor, no less. These legal restrictions for *armateurs* were drawn from articles 1 and 2 of book 3, title 9, of the 1681 Ordonnances de la Marine, specifically the long section concerned with the right to seizure. Ibid., 147.

in them," for example (here again the reader is taught how to use the term in speech), "Messieurs N. Traders of S. Malo who are the *Ship-owners* of the vessel *le Pontchartrain*." It is then plainly stated that one cannot arm a vessel for war without a license from the admiral.[47] Finally, the *Dictionnaire* adds that a ship-owner is also, simply, a merchant who equipped a vessel to traffic goods.

The second part of the "Corsair" article makes the connection with piracy explicit: A corsaire is "he who exercises piracy, who attacks and takes friendly and enemy ships." This entry then refers readers to the entry for pirate – but, of course, as we have seen, there was no entry for pirate in this edition! The reader is then referred to the entry for ship-owner. Thus, the corsaire, the rogue, and the sea-rover are all equated with the ship-owner and the pirate.

As if to compound the synonymy, the *Dictionnaire*'s entry for "rogue" (*forban*) begins by listing the terms "pirate, corsair, sea-rover." Furthermore, here a rogue is one who "troubles maritime commerce by cruising merchant vessels, friend and foe, at any time and without a license; and who takes them and ransoms them."[48] While maintaining its focus on commerce, the *Dictionnaire* once again conflates and subsumes the agents who seize ships into the piracy idiom. Citing the Ordonnance of 1681, the article specifies that rogues were to be "punished with death," as was the case for pirates. What is more, this second reference to allies and enemies continues to connect the acts of seizure with the international imperial system. The various subsections of the article "*Navire*" (ship) continue the trend. Whereas a *navire marchand* (merchant ship) was one that went to sea "only to engage in commerce," a *navire en course* (cruiser) was a ship armed for war by individuals who took a license to cruise upon enemies of the state and interrupt their commerce.

Not until the second edition of the *Dictionnaire* (1748) do we find an entry for "filibuster." It states, rather curiously, that a filibuster is one who commands a *flibot* for herring fishing.[49] Only the second sentence

---

[47] The French reads: "Celui qui a obtenu cette Commission est tenu de la faire enregistrer au Greffe de l'Amirauté, du lieu ou il fait son armement & doit donner caution de la somme de 15000 liv. laquelle doit être reçue par le Lieutenant de l'Amirauté, en présence du Procureur de Sa Majesté." Ibid.

[48] Ibid.

[49] Here I draw on the 1765 printing of the second edition, published in Copenhagen. Both the *Encyclopédie* and the *DUC* carry entries on the *flibot*. The *Encyclopédie*'s article (written by Bellin) tells us that it is "a little 'flûte' under 100 tons, which normally has a rounded back [*sic*]. This ship is hollow and wide in the hull, and has neither a mizzen

recalls part of the *Encyclopédie*'s definition: "This is what is said of 'Rogues,' or 'Adventurers' of all Nations who unite in America to make war against the Spaniards."[50] Compare this to the *Encyclopédie*, which cites corsaire, as opposed to rogue, as the first synonym for filibusterer and makes no reference to herring fishing. Still, the essence of both articles is the same and reveals the easy exchange of terms in this blurred semantic field.

The term "adventurer" is one of the synonyms of pirate that also appeared in the *Encyclopédie*. In the first edition of the *Dictionnaire*, however, we find but one small entry for an "adventurer-ship": a merchant ship that "traffics" within the expanse of a commercial company's concession without having received permission to do so.[51] The second edition, thirty years later, included four separate headings for the term, each offering a different meaning within two broad categories. Here the *Dictionnaire* drew almost verbatim from the *Encyclopédie*, with some variations. It first offered a word of caution to its readers against adventurers: These were "little-known or unknown men, with neither hearth nor home, who meddle brazenly in the affairs of others, and whom we cannot distrust enough."[52] The adventurer was also a variety of the "hearty and entrepreneurial *pirates* who unite against the Spaniards in the West Indies and who cruise them on the seas and operate against them on land." The pirate is here yet again invoked (but not defined). A cross-reference to "buccaneer" suggests that it is the name "more ordinarily given" to adventurers, even if "it was less honourable."[53]

In the first edition of the *Dictionnaire*, the less honourable buccaneer was "one who grilled meat and/or fish." The term referred mainly to the French of Saint-Domingue who hunted bulls and boars to trade the skin of one and the flesh of the other.[54] In this second edition, thirty-two

---

mast nor a top gallant sail." *Encyclopédie*, 6:875. The *DUC*, on the other hand, informs readers that the *flibot* is "a small sea-ship, also called a 'Log,' used in Holland for herring fishing." *DUC* (1723), 1:71.

50 "Celui qui commande un flibot pour la pêche du hareng. Il se dit aussi de ces Forbans, ou Avanturiers [*sic*] de toutes les Nations, qui s'unissent dans l'Amérique, pour faire la guerre aux Espagnols." *DUC* (1765), 2: 638.

51 See Ibid., 1:189: "AVENTURIER, On appelle vaisseau aventurier, un vaisseau Marchand qui va trafiquer dans l'étendue de la concession d'une compagnie de Commerce, sans en avoir obtenu permission. Voyez INTERLOPRE."

52 "Aventuriers. Signifie un homme peu ou point connu, qui n'a peut-être ni feu ni lieu, qui se mêle hardiment d'affaires, & dont on ne sauroit trop se défier. Tous les bons Négocians doivent bien se garder de telles personnes." *DUC* (1765), 1:263.

53 Ibid.

54 There were four sections covering the "Buccaneers of Saint-Domingue," "the Buccaneers Hunters of Beef," "the Buccaneers Hunters of Boar," and "Spanish Buccaneers." This

years later, we recognise the *Encyclopédie*'s text, verbatim, at first. Yet the account begins to diverge. As the *Dictionnaire* informed its readers, "We also sometimes understand by the name buccaneer those famous adventurers of all of the nations of Europe who unite to war against the Spaniards of America." In this case, a more precise citation is offered: These facts were "given to the Public in 1686 by Alexandre Olivier Exquemelin."[55] Here, Savary emphasised a synonymy between the adventurer and the buccaneer absent from the *Encyclopédie*. For the eighteenth-century merchant, therefore, the buccaneer, the adventurer, and the filibusterer were nearly interchangeable: They were all international figures who pillaged and fought against the Spaniards in the West Indies.

The *Dictionnaire* also specified what these actions comprised. "Cruising" (*faire la course*) was not only the time that a merchant vessel took for a voyage; the term also encompassed the "incursions made by sea upon vessels of state enemies." Here again the reader is taught how to employ the term in speech. "[T]he merchants of S. Malo armed twenty vessels this year to cruise against the English and the Dutch: the cruise was successful; the ship-owners enrich themselves from it."[56] In the meantime, a separate article entitled "Seizure" (*prise*) summarizes the confused state of affairs quite succinctly. Seizure was the term used to describe state enemy or pirate vessels taken at sea by the king's ships or ships commissioned by the admiral, as well as merchant vessels taken by state enemies or by pirates.[57] For good seizure, the seized vessel had to belong to "enemies of the state" *or* to be "commanded by Pirates, Rogues and others cruising the sea without commission from any Prince or Sovereign State."[58] Merchants learned that a good seizure was sanctioned whether or not it constituted an official act of war against a state enemy, or, simply, an individual outside of the imperial system. Following a good seizure, the "ships of the Subjects of the King" could recapture the original ship after twenty-four hours. The technical term for this recapture, we learn, was *recousse*, identified as a term of "maritime commerce." What follows is a significant instance in which all of the synonyms under review so far were made explicit: *Recousse* meant recapturing merchant

article is nearly identical in both the first and second editions of the *Dictionnaire*. In the first edition (1723), we find it on pages 417–22; in the second edition (1765), on pages 592–93.

55 *DUC* (1765), 2:592.
56 *DUC* (1723), 1:1569.
57 Ibid., 2:1217.
58 Ibid.

vessels and other effects stolen and taken on the sea by "corsairs, pirates, rogues, sea-rovers and enemies of the state."[59]

The Savary brothers then explained further: "[W]e ordinarily say such and such a ship-owner or such and such a captain who had recaptured [*recoussé*] such and such a merchant ship in order to say that this ship-owner or captain retook it." The entry ended with a familiar didactic statement instructing merchants of the ways in which one might employ the term in question. "[W]e also use the term 'recousse' in this sense – we saved a few goods from a ship wrecked on the Coast but it is a poor 'recousse' for the merchants who have investments in it."[60] Remarkably, the dictionary article not only provided technical information and details about the term but also, through the use of example sentences, carried out a pedagogical mission, endeavouring to teach the merchant this new universal language of commerce. The core of the article detailed the jurisprudence regarding the conditions for recapture and the parameters for redistribution of the goods aboard.[61]

Though there was a fundamental congruence of terminology between the *Encyclopédie* and the *Dictionnaire universel de commerce*, at moments the *Dictionnaire* offered words of warning to its readers. The actual term pirate was relegated to the background, whereas a slew of other terms, among them corsair, buccaneer, and filibusterer, were used interchangeably at times and at others qualified as specific varieties of pirates. The semantic field for pirate and piracy was thus marked by contingency and flux.

THE *GAZETTE DU COMMERCE*

Another key source for merchants and other eighteenth-century French readers seeking to understand the vocabulary of commerce and its relationship to piracy was the *Gazette du commerce*.[62] Two months after

---

[59] Ibid., 2:1186.

[60] Ibid., 2:1185. It was not until the "Supplement" created for the dictionary and consisting of a third volume that we find an entry on the *Lettres de Marque*, known in English as the letters of reprisal, the letters of endorsement, or, alternatively, the commission. Gosse, *History of Piracy*, 102. This curious piece maintained that these letters of endorsement applied to the Dutch alone. The entry stated that the term *Lettres de Marque* was used in Holland to name the certificates that the "Jurez Maîtres Marqueurs de Mesures" delivered to the captains or owners of ships subject to the "right of Lastgelt."

[61] Here the citation was, once again, to book 3, title 9, articles 8, 9, and 10.

[62] Here I draw on Georges Dulac's article on the *Gazette du commerce* (no. 555) in Jean Sgard, *Dictionnaire des journaux, 1600–1789* (Oxford: Voltaire Foundation; Paris: Université de Paris, 1991).

the periodical was first published, the *Gazette* changed its title to one that gave primacy of place to agriculture – the *Journal de l'agriculture, du commerce et des finances* – pointing unmistakably to its Physiocratic leanings. The journal served as a source of information on prices, agricultural techniques, and imperial affairs.

It is rather curious, therefore, to discover a seemingly randomly placed article on the pirate in the 11 May 1765 issue, published a mere six months before the appearance of the *Encyclopédie* volumes containing the entries for pirate and seizure. Here, as in the *Dictionnaire* and the *Encyclopédie*, the pirate is identified as a figure of the past. This "historical note on the pirates" is not explained in any way, nor is an author named.[63] It begins with a very recent piece of history indeed: The notice reports that, a few days earlier, a Dutch vessel travelling from Nantes to Rotterdam was attacked in the English Channel by a small ship "whose mariners dressed in the English fashion stole three barrels of indigo." The author then introduces an account of the seas of "ancient times, infested by Rogues from whom there was never any respite, and whose very name, by the very terror it spread in the Ports, harmed commerce more than the plundering they committed."[64] The name "pirate," by the *Gazette*'s admission, caused as much harm as the pirate.

The history of pirates, or "international terror-mongers," began in the early Middle Ages, the article continued. First, "Saxon Pirates" and other "sea-rovers" covered the "German Sea." Banned by "Emperors and excommunicated by Popes," their power only grew more formidable. The note then offers a series of parallel accounts of successful movements against the pirates, including one by the "Hamburgers," who dispelled the pirates by force of arms. According to the piece, the pirates in the Baltic Sea were "Gentlemen who had good castles on the coast" and who damaged commerce and the herring fishery on the Scandinavian side.[65] There, too, a "league" was formed against them composed of the Hanseatic towns and the Swedish queen in partnership with the Danish

---

[63] The "Notice" for the first *Gazette du commerce* (1763) pointed the reader to Dufresne for information on the author. This article was probably written by either Bertrand Dufresne or Dufresne de Saint-Léon. The two are often confused. See L. G. Michaud, *Biographie universelle ancienne et moderne ...* Nouvelle édition. 45 vols. (Paris: Madame C. Desplaces et M. Michaud, 1854–1865) and the *Dictionnaire de Biographie française*, 11:1460.

[64] *Gazette du commerce*, 11 May 1765, 303.

[65] This account is far removed from the vilification associated with the *hostis humani generis* constructed in the English imaginary, according to Hans Turley. See his *Rum, Sodomy, and the Lash*, 2.

nobility. The league retained the possessions taken from all of the strong-holds from which the rogues were expelled.

Returning to the present, the *Gazette* explained that contemporary piracy was largely confined to American "sailors who rebelled against their Officers" and left them to perish on the coast. It specified that it was rare for these "rebel crews" to remain active for very long: On parts of the English coast and along the Thames, these scoundrels paid for their crimes on the gallows.[66]

This representation of pirates in a text targeting a merchant audience reveals a casual attitude towards the figure of the pirate while at the same time acknowledging that pirates caused serious damage to commercial relations. It is because of the perceived harm they did to commerce that pirates were targeted by French jurisprudence.

If we turn to the juridical context in which pirates and piracies were understood and represented, we can test whether this semantic blurring was as prevalent in the discourse of commerce, and further consider how it figured in the institutions of sovereignty. At the core of this investigation has to be the category *prise*, or seizure, characterised as either good or bad by the courts of the royal administration. As we have seen, the concept of a good seizure had already permeated the language of enlightened readers of the *Encyclopédie* and merchants consulting the *Dictionnaire universel de commerce*. But where did it come from? The following suggests one response.

A JURIDICAL BACKDROP

Underlying this confused semantic field for piracy in eighteenth-century France was a pervasive and influential juridical foundation. To understand it, we must first address the most influential original source of international jurisprudence on the rights of seizure: Hugo Grotius's *De iure praedae commentarius* (*Commentary on the Right of Prize and Seizure* (1604–06). This foundational document developed the first theoretical premises that would later guide international law, and at its heart lay a concern with redefining piracy as a justifiable form of *prise*.

Hugo Grotius is still referred to as the "founding father of international law," but his influence extended to the foundations of Western moral and political thought as well.[67] He is remembered by his Latin

[66] *Gazette du commerce*, 11 May 1765, 304.
[67] See, for example, Martha Nussbaum, "Rules for the World Stage," *Newsday* (New York), 20 April 2003; David A. Ackerman, "International Law and the Preemptive Use of

name (the Dutch version being "De Groot") in part because he wrote and spoke to his peers in Latin.[68] A precocious humanist, Grotius was hired at a young age as the assistant to the Dutch Republic's leading politician, Johan van Oldenbarnevelt, who, in turn, arranged a commission from the influential United Dutch East India Company, known by its Dutch acronym, VOC.[69] It was in response to the VOC's 1603 seizure of a Portuguese carrack laden with valuable goods, the *Santa Catharina*, that Grotius penned his earliest treatise, a defence of that act by the Dutch Republic's monopoly trading company.[70] The stakes were high: This seizure launched a war between the Dutch and the Portuguese that would eventually lead to Dutch dominance in the East Indies trade. Though this manuscript was never published in his lifetime, we know that Grotius extracted his famous *Mare Liberum (Free Seas)* (1609) from it, and seems to have drawn from it as he began to compose his influential *De iure belli ac pacis (The Rights of War and Peace)*, first published in 1625.[71] The *De iure praedae commentarius* (which he may have

Force against Iraq," CRS Report for Congress, Order Code RS 21314, updated 11 April 2003; or a *Bulletin of the International Criminal Tribunal for the former Yugoslavia.* ICTV-Bulletin No 15/16. On Grotius's influence on moral and political thought, see Knud Haakonssen, *Natural and Moral Philosophy: From Grotius to the Scottish Enlightenment* (Cambridge: Cambridge University Press, 1996).

[68] Richard Tuck, Introduction to *The Rights of War and Peace* by Hugo Grotius (Indianapolis: Liberty Fund, 2005), xii.

[69] We now know that Grotius was in fact assisting the directors of the Amsterdam VOC with all ranges of policymaking.

[70] Martine Julia Van Ittersum's several and expert analyses of the *De iure praedae* set the standard for study of this text. On the South Asian context in which the capture of the *Santa Catarina* occurred, see her "Hugo Grotius in Context: Van Heemskerck's Capture of the Santa Catarina and its Justification in De Jure Praedae (1604–1606)" *Asian Journal of Social Science* 31, no. 3 (2003): 511–48. Cf. Peter Borschberg, "Hugo Grotius, East India Trade and the King of Johor" *Journal of Southeast Asian Studies* 30, no.2 (1999): 225–48.

[71] Martine Julia van Ittersum has shown meticulously how the arguments of the *De iure praedae* were "at the foremost of his mind" when Grotius prepared the *Mare liberum* for publication. See her "Preparing *Mare Liberum* for the Press: Hugo Grotius' Rewriting of Chapter 12 of *De Iure Praedae* in November-December 1608" in Hans W. Bolm, ed., *Property, Piracy and Punishment: Hugo Grotius on War and Booty in De iure praedae – Concepts and Context*, Leiden: Brill, 2009 246. On the influence of the *De iure praedae* on the *De iure belli ac pacis* see Richard Tuck's introduction to Hugo Grotius's *The Rights of War and Peace*, where he first suggests that Grotius "must have turned" to the *De iure praedae* manuscript while imprisoned in the Dutch castle of Loevestein (after the execution of his patron, Oldenbarnevelt), and next provides several examples of how the text of the *De iure belli ac pacis* drew directly from the *De iure praedae*, xvii, xix, xxi, xxiii, xxv, and xxix. (Grotius later escaped from the castle in a trunk of books, and spent the rest of his exile in Paris, where the *De iure belli ac pacis* was published in 1625 and dedicated to Louis XIII.)

also referred to as the *De Indis*) addressed the differences between the rights of individuals and the rights of states, but Grotius's primary goal in the text was to distinguish between legitimate and illegitimate seizure, justifying the former.[72] He did so by redefining the terms surrounding seizure itself. Much attention has focused upon the work's *Prolegomena* and chapters 3, 6, and 7 through 11, which sought, respectively, to define whether war was just, whether it was Christian, whether the seizure of prize or booty was ever just, and what distinguished a public war from a private war. Chapter 12 has received the most attention since it formed the basis of the *Mare Liberum*, which laid the foundations for the international law of the sea by claiming, essentially, that the sea belongs to all, and all – states, private individuals, and "particular parties" – have the right to trade upon it.

But what has been overlooked is Grotius's attention to the question of the justice of seizure in the work's last three chapters.[73] Two central elements of the work's argument depend on definitions: first, the way in which Grotius defined seizure and prize; and second, the way in which he distinguished prize and booty from piracy. At the outset of the *Commentary*, Grotius made clear that the stakes of his defence were high: "[I]f the Dutch cease to harass the Spanish [and Portuguese] blockaders of the sea ... the savage insolence of the Iberian peoples will swell to immeasurable proportions, the shores of the whole world will soon be blocked off, and all commerce [*negotiatio*] with Asia will collapse."[74] In short, all of Holland's commercially derived wealth lay in the balance.

The first attention to the definitions of key terms in the treatise appears in chapter 10. Grotius begins by asking: "[B]y whom may prize or booty

---

[72] This text, consisting of 163 manuscript pages, was not widely available until its discovery in 1864 and its later publication in 1868. The manuscript, available at the Leiden University Library, is entitled *De Iure Praedae Commentarius*, BPL 917. See Peter Haggenmacher, "Genèse et signification du concept de 'ius gentium' chez Grotius," *Grotiana*, 2 (1981): 44–102.

[73] The work is most easily understood when broken down into four sections: Chapter 1 is followed by the *Dogmatica*, Grotius's own term for the fundamental principles or dogmas governing war in general and the acquisition of spoils in particular (chapters 2–10); the *Historica*, a factual account of the circumstances preceding and attending the seizure of a Portuguese ship, the *Santa Catharina* (chapter 11); and a final section on the application of the abstract principles expounded in the *Dogmatica* (chapters 12–15). Division of the work in this way was first suggested by George A. Finch's preface to the first modern English translation of the *De iure praedae*. See Hugo Grotius, *De iure praedae commentarius. Commentary on the Law of Prize and Booty.* 1604. Vol. 1. Translation of the original 1604 manuscript by Glwadys Williams. Vol. 2. Collotype reproduction of the original MSS of 1604 (Oxford: Clarendon, 1950).

[74] Ibid., chap. 1, 1.

be acquired?"[75] He replies: "[W]e have satisfactorily demonstrated, so I believe, the truth of the proposition that enemy property [*res hostiles*] can be rightfully seized and acquired." Up to this point, he had conflated *praeda* (prize) and *res* (thing or property). Only when Grotius asked, "By whom may prize or booty be acquired in private wars?" did he provide the reader with specific meanings for these central terms, and he did so by means of sophisticated semantic gymnastics that would smooth the way for his case. A notation in the margin reads "*PARADOXON*."[76] Grotius's "paradoxical contention" affirmed that "a great many interpreters of canon or civil law and writers on the laws of war appear to repudiate the supposition that "body of law governing seizure and prize, '*praeda*' [could be] derived from 'private warfare.'"[77]

Grotius challenged this interpretation with the claim that its proponents had "neglected to acquaint themselves with the precepts based upon the fundamental truths of the law of nations [*juris gentium*]." His argument was founded on the then radical claim that the "law of nations" trumped all other jurisprudence, including canon and civil law.[78] He offered a historical form of reasoning, explaining that Roman law did not adequately address the question at hand, that is, the right of acquiring prize or booty in private wars, because the "majesty and power of the Roman Empire were such that Rome was hardly ever troubled by a lack of judicial recourse [*penuria iudici*], an especially weighty factor in the development of private wars."[79]

At this point, Grotius explicitly equated enemy property (*rem hostilem*) with "[what we call the] acquisition of prize or booty" (*quod praedam vocamus*).[80] Through this overt association of the two concepts of enemy property and prize, Grotius reconfigured prize as a category of hostile relations. He admitted the possibility that "some objection may be advanced against designating the person who attacks us privately

[75] Ibid., chap. 10, 130.
[76] Ibid., 53. Although there are several different numbering schemes in the collotype, I am using the page numbers written on the top left-hand corner of the manuscript.
[77] Glwadys Williams, the first modern translator of Grotius's treatise, used the terms *prize and booty* to designate the Latin *praeda*. She justified this usage by stating that both terms are necessary to convey the double meaning of *praeda*, which, like the French term *prise*, evokes both the action of seizing and the thing seized. I have opted for the term *seizure.*
[78] On the radicalness of Grotius's thought here, see Benjamin Straumann, "Is Modern Liberty Ancient?" *Law and History Review* 27:1 (2009): 69.
[79] Grotius, *De iure praedae commentarius*, 57 (mss.), 132 (Williams trans.).
[80] Ibid., 132–33.

as an enemy [*hostem*] and the property seized in such circumstances as prize or booty [*praeda*]." Yet, he persisted, it was "extremely important for the clarification of the whole question" that enemy property (*res hostilem*) and "prize or booty" (*praeda*) be considered one and the same. He emphasised that "different terms should not be employed in the discussion of a single right." Thus, in a mere three paragraphs, Grotius connected two jurisprudential traditions and, with his characteristic rhetorical agility, evaded the potential objection that his was a loose, though convenient, definition of terms. The most outstanding claim made here was that the acquisition of enemy property or possessions of adversaries and the acquisition of booty constituted one right.

Grotius substantiated these arguments with the lengthy *Historica*, which, not surprisingly, trumpeted Dutch glory and innocence. Richard Tuck provides one of the reasons for this celebration.[81] The value of the *Santa Catharina*'s goods (copper, silk, porcelain, bullion, and the lucrative musk oil) was over three million guilders. This sum amounted to almost half the total capitalisation of the VOC and may have led to its formation. Indeed, the value of the prize approached the total annual expenditure of the English government at the time.[82]

Grotius ended the *Historica* with the assertion that it is "not without reason" that we doubt "whether that seizure was a rightful act."[83] The reader had yet to be shown a link between the maligned Dutch of the *Historica* and the Dutch East India Company. This was addressed in the "analytical discussion" of chapter 12, wherein Grotius famously argued in a third thesis that "neither the sea itself nor the right of navigation thereon can become the exclusive possession of a particular party, whether through seizure, through a papal grant, or through prescription (that is to say, custom)." Nevertheless, he maintained that "even if the war were a private war, the prize would be justly acquired by the Dutch East India Company."[84]

---

[81] Tuck, *Rights of War and Peace*, 79–80. Tuck cites Masselman, *Cradle of Colonialism* (New Haven: Yale University Press, 1963), 131. His figures for England draw upon the totals of government expenditure from 1598 to 1608 in Frederick C. Dietz, *English Public Finance, 1485–1641*. 2nd ed. (London: F. Cass, 1964), 113: they average £470,000 p.a. The pound in this period was worth ten guilders, according to the table in E. E. Rich and C. H. Wilson, eds. *The Cambridge Economic History of Europe* Vol. 4. *The Economy of Expanding Europe in the Sixteenth and Seventeenth Centuries* (Cambridge: Cambridge University Press, 1967), 4:458.

[82] Ibid., 180.

[83] Tuck, *Rights of War and Peace*, 214–15.

[84] Grotius, *De iure praedae commentarius*, 216.

At the heart of Grotius's case for the Dutch seizure of Portuguese booty lay a concern with establishing that commerce should be open and free for all and that it should be conducted in a spirit of fellowship and good faith. But what of exchanges conducted in bad faith? Would these retain the status of commerce, or would the discourse and practice of commerce be bifurcated into two variants, one sweet and the other odious? Grotius considered in succession whether the seizure of the prize was "honourable" and whether it was "useful," drawing quite transparently on the model of Cicero's *De Officiis*. These were themes and language that would remain central to the jurisprudence of seizure in eighteenth-century France.[85] Within this model, he distinguished the definition of the right of prize and booty from the action of pirates, freebooters, and robbers. These latter were agents of "dishonourable gain." By reframing the terms of the case in an obviously Ciceronian language, Grotius lodged his argument firmly within the terms of classical republicanism and consequently grounded it in a familiar and respected tradition. He thereby conferred upon it a greater legitimacy than it possessed as an innovative appeal to a new jurisprudence: the natural law.[86]

After determining that what was "just" (*justem*) was honourable, Grotius examined how the "necessary distinction" between honourable and dishonourable seizure could be drawn. He listed four types of dishonourable gain.[87] Gain by "individuals" who "despoil others through privately exercised force and without urgent reasons for so doing" was deemed dishonourable. Those who carried out such dishonourable acts at sea were known as pirates – the first definition of *pirate* in the document. Grotius also classified as dishonourable those "persons who, without any legitimate cause, usurp authority to wage public war."[88] These "despoilers" he called "freebooters." A third group "deserving of blame" were those who "snatched away property prior to the execution of the

---

[85] The Ordonnance elaborated the conditions for a good seizure in articles 4, 5, and 6 of title 9, and these were later discussed in the *Encyclopédie*, the *Dictionnaire du commerce*, and, as we shall see, in Valin's *Nouveau commentaire* and Guyot's *Répertoire universel*, among other texts.

[86] For an authoritative analysis of the ways in which Grotian natural right theory structured French imperial sovereignty and jurisprudence, see Dan Edelstein, "War and Terror: The Law of Nation as from Grotius to the French Revolution," *FHS* 31:2 (2008), especially 235.

[87] This discussion is reminiscent of Aristotle's discussion of the honourable and dishonourable forms of "wealth-getting" in the *Politics*.

[88] Grotius cited "whole peoples" such as the Cretans, Cilicians, Germans, Normans, and, according to Homer, the Greeks, who "engaged openly and publicly in the practice of despoliation" without having "so much as an appropriate pretext."

measures required in order that war may be lawfully undertaken." He called their attacks upon property "acts of 'robbery.'" The description of the fourth and final type of dishonourable seizure is remarkable for the ways in which it reveals seventeenth-century mores: "In the course of a just war or a war believed to be just," there were those who grasped at profit "for profit alone, and profit for its own sake, and not for the true objective of war, namely, the attainment of rights." Theirs was a "course of conduct clearly incompatible not only with Justice but also with fortitude."[89]

The Portuguese were then singled out as members of the "uncouth class" of despoilers. Indeed, Grotius's configuration of the Portuguese owners of the *Santa Catharina* as pirates was based upon this modification of the Ciceronian and Aristotelian notions of dishonourable gain.[90] This rendering of the Portuguese as pirates was doubly significant: It revealed the extent to which Grotius was concerned with limiting that right and justifying the action of his employer, the Dutch East India Company. But it also suggests how arbitrary the denomination *pirate* was in the seventeenth century, just as it would be in the eighteenth century and perhaps still is today.[91] Grotius wrote, "[F]or if the name 'pirate' is appropriately bestowed upon them who blockade the seas and impede the progress of international commerce, shall we not include under the same head those persons who forcibly bar all European nations (even nations that have given them no cause for war) from the ocean and from access to India?" Such persons were "worthy objects of universal hatred" in Grotius's account, because they harmed "mankind."

For Grotius, as for Cicero, that which was beneficial was tied to that which was just and honourable. In addition, Grotius argued, "[T]hat which befits the circumstances in which the state is situated is especially beneficial," as is "doing good" to allies, doing harm to enemies, and ease of accomplishment.[92] Drawing on an overtly Ciceronian vocabulary that

[89] Grotius, De iure praedae commentarius, 327. As the translator notes, these are the two important virtues included in the concept of what is honourable, discussed earlier by Grotius and of course established by Cicero.

[90] Aristotle, Politics, book 1, 12, lines 29–32.

[91] Anne Pérotin-Dumon, "The Pirate and the Emperor: Power and the Law on the Seas, 1450–1850," in C. R. Pennell, ed., *Bandits at Sea: A Pirates Reader* (New York: New York University Press, 2001), 27. Pérotin-Dumon argues similarly that "Iberians declared pirates other Western Europeans with whom they came into conflict in regions where they had asserted initial imperial dominion."

[92] Together, these form the six theses presented in chapter 15, wherein the seizure of the prize is said to have been beneficial as is "retention of possession of the said prize."

distinguished between honourable and dishonourable gain, Grotius contrived an intricate argument justifying the right of prize for the Dutch East India Company. This argument, which drew on the "right of peoples" [*ius gentium*], would come to influence maritime jurisprudence in France. The spirit of the natural law he sought to bolster – the "Grotian moment" as Erik Thomson has referred to it – persisted in French imperial practice.[93] We saw it in the reasoning behind the declaration of the Seven Years War which opened this chapter. But it becomes readily apparent when we turn to an influential eighteenth-century legal commentary and note how Grotius's process of redefinition permeated prerevolutionary French jurisprudence and manifested the semantic blurriness of the politics of definition at work in the idiom of piracy.

VALIN'S *COMMENTAIRE*

Probably the most influential reflection of French maritime jurisprudence in the eighteenth century was René-Josué Valin's little studied but, as evidenced by its number of editions and publishing history, well-read commentary on Jean-Baptiste Colbert's comprehensive Ordonnance de 1681. The *Commentaire sur l'ordonnance de 1681* first appeared in 1759, pioneering the genre in this period.[94] The second edition, a "new commentary" (the *Nouveau commentaire*), appeared in 1766 amid a cluster of works defining piracy in France. Born into a family of Dutch refugees in La Rochelle, Valin studied law in Poitiers and later worked as a lawyer in the appellate court of La Rochelle and then as the king's prosecutor for the same city's admiralty.[95] A vibrant port in the eighteenth century, La Rochelle shared the bulk of France's colonial traffic, including its slave ships, with Nantes and Bordeaux. The admiralty court at which Valin worked was among the most active in the country, so it is perhaps natural

---

[93] Erik Thomson, "France's Grotian moment? Hugo Grotius and Cardinal Richelieu's commercial statecraft," *French History* 21, no.4 (2007): 377–94.

[94] Other commentators on maritime jurisprudence included the work of a lawyer from Marseille, Balthazard-Marie Emerigon (1716–84), author of a *Treatise on Maritime Insurance and Bottomry Bonds*, whom Valin thanks in his introduction for assistance. Robert Joseph Pothier, another eminent "commentator," wrote his own treatise on maritime insurance contracts, the *Traité du contrat d'assurance*. See Émerigon, *Traité des assurances*. Emerigon collaborated with Valin on his *Nouveau commentaire* and even published a draft of it with the title *Nouveau Commentaire sur l'ordonnance de la Marine de 1681. Par M ... Avocat en parlement*.

[95] He also served as a member of the Academy of La Rochelle. Michaud, *Biographie universelle* (1827), 47:343.

that one of its lawyers should examine the jurisprudential foundations of the maritime law.

Valin's commentaries were, predictably, premised on the view that Colbert's ordinance was "the cradle of nautical jurisprudence."[96] But in the second edition, published in the wake of the Seven Years War, Valin turned his focus to the right of prize. The aims of this commentary are unmistakable. Valin positioned himself firmly as the defender of the state's interests. His remark on title 9, "On Seizures," begins by stating that it is within the right, as well as the interest, of the state to weaken its enemy as much as it can by disrupting its possessions and its commerce.[97] This right derived from the right of war and originated with the admiralty that held sole authority over the granting of commissions for war and for leave to arm for "the cruise." Valin minced no words in chiding the "alleged Philosophers" who disapproved of this right. In their view, the right of prize was "not the way to serve the State and the Prince," and the profit to individuals that may have resulted was "illicit, or at least shameful." Valin responded categorically that these philosophers were in this case acting as "bad Citizens" who, operating under the mask of a "false wisdom or a deceitfully delicate conscience," sought to hide their "indifference for the good and the benefit of the State."[98] He sought to reinforce the jurisprudence that bolstered that right by way of a claim that its opponents were essentially unpatriotic, and at the same time he also attempted to ensure that his state did not abuse it.

In the light of the above, Valin's next comment appears naïve: He noted that the first article of title 9 stated that the admiral alone could grant a commission.[99] The only exception to this rule was afforded to the king: The admiral's commission was not needed for ships that the king armed at his own cost and for which he granted command to some of his officers so that they might "cruise" [*faire la course*]. Thus, in no uncertain terms, the Ordonnance, and consequently Valin's commentary, plainly acknowledged the practice of royal cruising. The practice did not

---

[96] Ibid., préface, viii. He also claimed that the *Ordonnance* became "in an instant the universal law of maritime commerce between nations." (Cf. Valin, *Nouveau commentaire*, iv). Writing during the Seven Years War, Valin joined a choir of publicists keen to revive a national glory lost in defeats by the British. Ibid., xi, xiii. Cf. David A. Bell, *The Cult of the Nation in France: Inventing Nationalism, 1680–1800* (Cambridge, MA: Harvard University Press, 2001), chap. 3.

[97] "Il est du droit de la guerre d'affoiblir son ennemi autant qu'il se peut, en le troublant dans ses possessions & dans son commerce." Valin, *Nouveau commentaire*, 2:213.

[98] Ibid., 67.

[99] Valin, *Nouveau commentaire*, vol. 2, book 3, title 9, article 1, 215.

trouble Valin. What did preoccupy him was the absence of any article in the Ordonnance stating what punishment would be incurred by a ship owner who went to sea without a commission from the admiral. Valin had a severe punishment in mind: "[A]fter all, whether a king's subject, without his permission, cruise with a commission of a foreign prince, and under his banner, or whether he do so without any commission whatsoever, it is the same thing; he must, in one and in the other case, be treated as a pirate."[100]

This passage is striking for two reasons. First, it reveals the extent to which Valin sought to improve the existing jurisprudence by clarifying confusions and eliminating conspicuous silences. Second, it introduces definitions of *piracy* and *pirate* that, for Valin at least, described persons and activities at once illegal and reprehensible. In seeking to rectify an apparent imbalance in the jurisprudence, Valin's commentary bolstered the Grotian technique of redefinition, and he made it applicable to French international maritime law.

DICTIONARIES OF JURISPRUDENCE

The principal dictionaries of jurisprudence in eighteenth-century France also contribute to our understanding of the terms and the "notions relative to actual jurisprudence" with respect to piracy in France.[101] Whether we look at Jean-Baptiste Denisart's *Collection of Decisions and Notions Relative to Current Jurisprudence* (1763–87); Claude-Joseph de Ferrière's *Dictionary of Law and Practice* (1778), or Joseph-Nicholas Guyot's edition of the *Universal and Reasoned Directory of Civil, Criminal, Canonic and Beneficial Jurisprudence* (1784), we find that no clear consensus about the usage of the pirate vocabulary existed in a juridical context. Whereas Denisart's *Collection of New Decisions and Notions Relating to Current Jurisprudence*, published in 1763, contained no entry for *pirate*, *seizure*, or *cruising*, it did provide a brief article on *corsaires*.[102] Denisart explained that *corsaires* were people who "cruised the seas without a commission, to steal and pillage all that they could take." He reflected that "these types of people" were also called "pirates." The article distinguished between "corsairs" and "enemy corsairs," implying but never stating explicitly that *corsaires* might be agents of the state. The "enemy

---

[100] Ibid.
[101] See the title page for Jean-Baptiste Denisart, *Collection de décisions nouvelles et de notions relatives à la jurisprudence actuelle.* 3 vols. (Paris: Vve Desaint, 1763–87).
[102] Ibid., 3:615.

corsairs who commit disorders in the bays and big rivers of the Kingdom" Denisart called "little corsairs." They were treated as prisoners of war if captured. Here, he cited the entire text of the *Edict of the Month of July 1691*, which condemned "enemy corsairs entering the Kingdom's rivers" to "perpetual gallows."[103] In Denisart, then, the pirate was not allotted a separate entry but was conflated with the *corsaire* and deemed an outlaw, a destructive agent lacking state endorsement. Attention to the subtle implication of the discussion of the "enemy corsair," however, offers a sense that the categories blurred across a much wider spectrum: Enemy looters, conceivably commissioned by their state, are elided with the pirate and the *corsaire*.

In contrast, Claude-Joseph de Ferrière offered no entry for *corsaire* in his *Dictionnaire de droit et de pratique, contenant l'explication des termes de droit, d'Ordonnances, de Coutumes et de Pratique* (*Dictionary of Law and Practice, Containing the Explanation of Terms of Law, Rulings, Customs and Practice*).[104] Nor did he have entries for *cruising* or *seizure*. Instead, the pirate is described with a short paragraph that provides a series of synonyms, echoing the *Encyclopédie's* take: "Pirates are corsairs, sea-rovers who cruise the seas, without the admission or the authority of the prince or the Sovereign." Their crime was punished by death – that is, de Ferrière added, when they could be caught.

Jean-Nicholas Guyot's "universal and reasoned" index of civil, criminal, canonical, and beneficial jurisprudence, the *Répertoire universel et raisonné de Jurispruence civile, criminelle, canonique et bénéficiale* (1784), in turn, referred the reader of the entry for *corsaire* to the entry for *pirate*.[105] Yet again, the pirate was described as a sea-rover. But in contrast to his colleagues, Guyot was more attentive to nuances. He explained that a pirate is one who "cruises the seas with a ship armed for war," but he added that the pirate's aim is "to steal from enemy *or* friendly vessels, without distinction." Guyot contrasted the pirate to the *armateur*, who

---

[103] The full text of the edict, *Edit du mois de Juillet 1691, registré le 21 Novembre suivant*, was reprinted in Valin's *Nouveau commentaire*, 2:326.

[104] Claude-Joseph de Ferrière, formerly an *avocat en parlement*, or lawyer in the French high court, wrote his dictionary as dean of the doctors-regent of the Law Faculty of Paris. See *Dictionnaire de droit et de pratique*.

[105] Joseph-Nicholas Guyot, ed., *Répertoire universel et raisonné de Jurispruence civile, criminelle, canonique et bénéficiale; ouvrage de plusieurs juisconsultes...* Nouvelle édition corrigée, et augmentée tant des loix nouvelles que des arrêts rendus en matière importante pour les parlemens et les autres cours du royaume, depuis l'édition précédente. 17 vols. (Paris: 1784), 5:95.

combatted "as an honest man, only attacking enemy vessels, for which he is authorised by a commission from the Admiral."[106]

Among all of the dictionaries of jurisprudence in eighteenth-century France, only Guyot's contained information about the right to seizure. The article on *prise* is imposing and one of the lengthiest in the entire work.[107] It begins by describing the royal right to seizure of goods on land – an account that reproduces the *Encyclopédie*'s text nearly verbatim. In the second half of the article, Guyot states simply that *prise* referred "in maritime jurisprudence [to] a ship taken from enemies."[108] He then delineated the articles of book 3, title 9 of the Ordonnance, beginning with the stipulation that "no one can arm a vessel for war without a commission from the Admiral" and including article 4, which defined good seizure. Guyot pointed out that later articles in the Ordonnance forbade all "chiefs, soldiers and sailors to sink seized vessels" at the "risk of death."[109] It was not until 28 March 1778 that the royal administration saw fit to amend the distribution formula. Guyot incorporated this ordinance which gave the king permission to turn over captured enemy ships to those who had captured them, reserving a third of their value for himself, "to be applied to the fund for the invalids of the Navy."[110]

In the same year, Louis XVI created a Conseil des Prises, a council responsible for adjudicating whether or not a seizure was in fact good. At its founding, Richelieu presided over the institution then deemed the Conseil de Marine, making most of the decisions himself.[111] As an institution animated by war alone, the Conseil des Prises reflected the degree to which the royal power took the definitions of good prize, as opposed to piracy, into its own hands. As Goethe reminded us at the opening of this chapter, piracy, commerce, and war were indeed intertwined. The Conseil des Prises was originally composed of three counsellors from the Royal Council on Finances, three counsellors of state, the secretary of state for the navy – another position originally created by Colbert – and three *maîtres de requêtes*; it remained relatively unchanged during the eighteenth century. During the Seven Years War, the duc de Penthièvre presided as the admiral. The 1778 ruling, recopied by Guyot, confirmed

---

[106] "Il diffère d'un armateur, en ce que celui-ci fait la guerre en honnête homme, n'attaquant que les vaisseaux ennemis, à quoi il est autorisé par une commission de l'amiral." Ibid., 14:125–26.
[107] It takes up twenty-three pages of text. Ibid., 13:631–54.
[108] Ibid., 13:632.
[109] Guyot, *Répertoire universel*, 13:641. This was stipulated in article 8.
[110] Ibid., 13:645.
[111] Cf. Villiers, *Les corsaires du littoral*, 182–83.

that seizures would continue to be judged by rulings given by the admiral and commissioners named by the king, without having to rely on prosecutors.[112] Louis XV also sought to attend to the needs of the agents of his "good cruising." The first article declared that "ships armed for cruising" would now enjoy duty exemptions for "food supplies, wines, brandies and other beverages serving as their provisions," as well as for their ships' supplies.[113] Finally, seizures made in the French colonies "and in other dependent establishments" were to be administered in the same manner as in the kingdom: Officers of the various admiralties were to send their documentation to the admiral so that the "validity or invalidity of the seizure" could be decided in Paris.[114]

Guyot's attention to the colonies did not end there. The entry for "colonies" in the *Répertoire universel* revealed the deep-rooted connection between piracy and the imperial enterprise. Guyot reported, "[T]he first colonizers of the American islands were adventurers exiled from their homeland because of the anxiety born of ambition and misery: first happy soldiers and navigators, they soon became formidable destructive forces." After having sacked the "huts of the savages," they divided themselves into bands and called themselves "Filibusterers." They "knew no restraint" other than the "subordination inspired by the fearlessness of their leader." The only law observed among them was "the equal sharing of booty."[115] This section illustrates how embedded the terms and deeds of piracy were within the imperial system, as well as the slippages between terms in the vocabulary of piracy.

PIRACIES VERSUS PIRATES IN THE *HISTOIRE*

In the *Histoire*'s account, as in many of the others, pirates are often set in opposition to the action of piracy. But the *Histoire des deux Indes* does so with a twist, foregrounding the figure of the noble brigand, the virtuous bandit most famously rendered a modern historical subject by E. J. Hobsbawm, while moralising the act of piracy and attributing it to the major European powers.[116] This double manoeuvre is exceptional, as we shall see.[117]

[112] Guyot, *Répertoire universel*, 13:646–47.
[113] Ibid., 13:649.
[114] Ibid., 13:648.
[115] Emphasis added. Ibid., 3:699.
[116] E. J. Hobsbawm, *Bandits* (London: Weidenfeld and Nicolson, 1969).
[117] To my knowledge, only one secondary source has specifically addressed the relationship between the perceived and pronounced threat of pirates and the piratical acts of

The *Histoire*'s account of European imperial commerce is replete with references to pirates. The first books tell the story of the European imperial and commercial experience in the East Indies, and we meet our first pirate here: "A pirate named Tchang-Si-Lao, having become powerful through his banditry, had taken hold of the little island of Macao, and blockaded the ports of China."[118] Tchang-Si-Lao had also placed Canton under siege, we are told. The Chinese "mandarins" sought the help of the Portuguese, who won a total victory over the pirate. In the end, Tchang-Si-Lao killed himself and, in thanks to the Portuguese, the Chinese emperor made a gift of the island of Macao. We meet our second pirate in book 2 amid an account of the Dutch experience in the East Indies. Coxinga, son of the captured pirate Fquam, resister of the Tartar invaders in China, took Formosa in 1683. Coxinga defeated the Dutch, who sought to appropriate this island. In consequence, the Dutch lost their privileged access to Formosa and were forced to resume trading through Canton, with all of its restrictions. We learn nothing more of Coxinga's personality.

A third pirate engaged in a battle against England. Conagi Angria became leader of the Angrias in Goa after overturning the despot in charge. The *Histoire* explains that he was a "good leader," the antithesis of the despot he overturned. Conagi became a pirate after taking possession of the island of Severndtroog. He attacked Moorish and Indian ships, and soon his "experience, courage, and generosity attracted adventurers by his side and enabled him to engage in great things, including the foundation of a state." In cooperation with the rival "Marates," the English eventually overturned Goa and defeated this pirate after several attempts by the Dutch failed. Later, the Marates took control of the area through their own banditry. The Indian Sea then became "infected with pirates" who intercepted navigation and prevented devout Muslims from making the voyage to Mecca. In order to put an end to the "banditry" of the English, the Mogul chief invited Conagi to serve as admiral of his camp. This pirate is not the "enemy of the human race" (*hostis humani*

European governments at the time. Long the dean of the field of pirate history in an English context, Robert Ritchie has examined this subject in part. The source base for this reflection is English, however. See Robert Ritchie, "Government Measures against Piracy and Privateering in the Atlantic Area, 1750–1850," in David J. Starkey, E. S. van Eyck van Heslinga, and J. A. de Moor, eds., *Pirates and Privateers: New Perspectives on the War on Trade in the Eighteenth and Nineteenth Centuries* (Exeter: University of Exeter Press, 1997), 10–28.

118 "Un pirate, nommé Tchang-Si-Lao, devenu puissant par ses brigandages, s'étoit emparé de la petite isle de Macao, d'où il tenoit bloqués les ports de la Chine."

generis) of Coke's *Laws* or of the legend of Black Beard. He is not a shifty character, but a model leader. Nor is he a brigand, though his piracy does pose a threat to imperial commerce.

In these accounts of European experience in the East Indies, pirates are named, but, with the exception of Conagi, they have little personality. They overturn despots and they take islands. They intercept navigation and prevent pilgrimages to Mecca. The only hint of a possible menace comes with the reference to their presence on the sea as a form of infection. Tchang Si-Lao is described as a powerful bandit. By contrast, Conagi Angria was promoted to admiral in order to put an end to the banditry of the English.

Pirates do not begin to have voices until book 10 of the *Histoire*, which tells the story of European settlements "in the Grand Archipelagos of America."[119] The title of chapter 10 displays the multiple piracy idiom – it reads: "The Filibusterers desolate the American seas. Origins, mores, expeditions and decadence of these corsairs." From the outset, the reader is exposed to the now familiar string of synonyms. Largely a compilation of narratives borrowed from travel literature and the most famous and infamous histories and pirate accounts, those of Exquemelin, Charlevoix, and Raveneau de Lussan, book 10 introduces some of the most vivacious piratical characters in the *Histoire*. We find Montbars the Exterminator, whose "hatred ... led to frenzy" after reading Las Casas's account of the Spanish treatment of the Indians. Montbars's "enthusiasm for humanity developed into a furore crueller than the thirst for gold or the religious fanaticism that had sacrificed so many victims."[120] In one instance, he is constantly "furious" and "ferocious," massacring and pillaging; in another, he contemplates a pile of corpses with a "sanguine voluptuousness" and swears an insatiable hatred of carnage, ultimately leaving all of the joy of the rich booty to his companions. Similar accounts of the "feroce l'Olonois," "Le Basque," and "Morgan, the most accredited of the Filibusters" give a voice to romantic heroes.[121]

[119] Jenny Mander's introduction and commentary in the forthcoming critical edition of book 10, "Livre X. *Établissement des nations Européennes dans le grand Archipel de l'Amérique*" offers the definitive account of the sources and compositional methods for this book. See Guillaume-Thomas Raynal, *Histoire philosophique et politique des établissements et du commerce des Européens dans les deux Indes, Édition critique.* Vol. 3, ed. Anthony Strugnell et al. Ferney-Voltaire: Centre international d'étude du XVIIIe siècle, forthcoming.

[120] *HDI* (1780), book 10, 285.

[121] Ibid., 288.

But the filibusterers in the *Histoire*'s account were more organised than their flamboyant leaders. Book 10 describes how they also formed that new contentious eighteenth-century category, a "society." It is a special society indeed: "Without a system, without laws, without subordination, without means, the *society* of filibusterers became the surprise of the century, as she would be in posterity." This society would have subjugated all of America had its "spirit of conquest matched its spirit of banditry."[122] The filibusterers of America formed a virtuous society, but also a finite one. They were ultimately powerless in the history of imperialism, because their community of banditry was less powerful than the spirit of conquest. Thus, filibusterers were bandits, filibusterers were pirates, and pirates were bandits in the *Histoire*.

They were all of these things, but were they "enemies of the human race"? In book 10, the descriptions of individual filibusterers are followed by a break in the narrative, and then a new voice with a new tone states: "The principle which put into action these extraordinary and Romanesque men is too easy to untangle."[123] The new voice delineates the implausible explanations:

We cannot say that it was need: they trampled over land that offered them immense riches, gathered before their eyes, by people less skilful than they. Was it avarice? They would not have squandered in one day the booty of a campaign. Since they had no homeland properly speaking, it was not for its defence, aggrandizement, or vengeance that they devoted themselves. The love of glory, if they had known it, would have preserved them from the mass of atrocities and crimes that offended the splendour of their greatest actions. The hope for rest never grew within continuous labours, and inexpressible dangers.

From matching passages in the *Fragments politiques*, we know that it was Diderot who asked what *moral* causes gave the filibusterers such a particular collective existence. He concluded that the cause was the desire for freedom.[124] If we go back to the sources of "this revolution," we see that the filibusterers had, in the *Histoire*'s account, lived under the shackles of European governments. Soon, the "spring of liberty compressed in souls for centuries began to agitate incredibly," and "anxious and enthusiastic men of all nations joined these adventurers at the first news of their successes." They were, Diderot told readers, "attracted by novelty, the idea

---

[122] "Elle auroit subjugué l'Amérique entière, si elle avoit eu l'esprit de conquête comme elle avoit celui de brigandage." Ibid., 312.

[123] Ibid., 313.

[124] See Gianluigi Goggi, ed. *Denis Diderot, Fragments politiques échappés du portefeuille d'un philosophe* (Paris: Hermann, 2011).

and desire for distant things, the need for a change in situation, the hope of a greater fortune, and instinct which yields the imagination to great enterprises, the admiration which leads promptly to imitation, and the necessity to surmount the obstacles where imprudence has precipitated, the encouragement of example, the equality of goods and ills between free companions." He concluded: "In a word, this passing fermentation that the sky, the sea, the earth, nature, and fortune had excited within men by turns covered in gold and rags, plunged in blood and voluptuousness, rendered the Filibusterers a people isolated in history, though an ephemeral people who shone but a moment."[125]

Thus the filibusters are conveyed as social, freedom-seeking yet ephemeral. Diderot claimed that it was customary to view these bandits with abhorrence. This outlook was fair, he explained, because the loyalty, probity, disinterestedness, and generosity that they practiced among themselves did not prevent the affronts they committed every day against humanity. But, Diderot asked, "How can we not admire in the midst of these hideous crimes a mass of heroic actions which would have honoured the most virtuous of peoples?" Despite their heinous acts, the filibusters are comparable to the most virtuous of peoples. Their actions are judged distinctly from their persons. The act of transgressing commerce, violently disrupting the transport of goods from the New World to the Old, is held reproachable, but the transgressors are not. Besides, Diderot added at the end, "If they had not been the scourge of the New World, they would have scourged the Old."

Elsewhere in the *Histoire*, we learn that groups of pirates were indeed the scourge of the New World. Indeed, as we saw in Chapter 2, the *Histoire*'s book 11 explains that before founding their new society, pirates incited the trade in slaves: Before the arrival of the Europeans, a beneficent and not yet commercialised slavery existed in Africa. In time, however, a number of piracies were "committed upon the eastern coasts of Africa." This was the *Histoire des deux Indes*' principal explanation for the rise of the European commerce in slaves. The "civilised nations" then adopted this commerce without hesitation.[126] It was this adoption by the so-called civilised nations of a practice instigated by pirates to which I would now like to turn. The central point is that in the *Histoire*'s pirate economy, the make-up of individuals was irrelevant. It was instead the set

---

[125] Ibid., 316.
[126] These citations are drawn directly from the three sections in book 11 where the pirates, or "*Flibustiers*," are discussed: *HDI* (1780), book 11, 157–59, 188–93, and 276–77.

of practices they perpetuated that were menacing and morally reprehensible. The *Histoire* viewed the act of piracy as conceptually distinct from the category of persons called, variably, pirates, filibusterers, buccaneers, and so forth. The act of "Brigandage," or banditry, was a capital crime, but if a pirate was sometimes a bandit, the *Histoire* did not prevaricate about who the real bandits in the world system were.

Let us now return to the opening three books of the *Histoire* and recall that in book 1, when the Portuguese helped defeat Tchang-Si-Lao, the Chinese emperor awarded them the island of Macao, site of his blockades and banditry. Though Tchang-Si-Lao ended his own life, Portugal, the *Histoire* tells us, soon "changed its commercial projects into plans of conquest, [and] the nation, which never possessed the spirit of commerce, appropriated the spirit of banditry."[127] After losing Formosa to Coxinga, the pirate in book 2, the Dutch eventually obtained an exclusive trading privilege for their company. They subsequently "became more belligerent" and sought to protect their commercial exclusivity in Sumatra and Malacca by hiring pirates to intercept Sumatran and Malaccan commerce. Indeed, according to the *Histoire*, Holland established its maritime power by offering asylum to pirates of every nation in order to use them against the Spanish. This savvy policy, combined with "wise laws, an admirable order, a constitution preserving equality, an excellent *police*[,] and tolerance," was responsible for making the Netherlands "a powerful state."

But agents designated as pirates did not carry out the most odious piracy of all, according to the *Histoire*. Rather, it was the English East India Company, a tool of imperial commerce, that did so. Book 3 of the *Histoire* notes that by 1682, the company had made such massive profits that English merchants had begun to petition Charles II for access to the East Indian market. A "voluptuous and squandering" individual, Charles II granted this access to the merchants, sparking a form of competition. In the logic of the *Histoire*, this competition was by its very nature "bound to degenerate," as it did, into a form of brigandage. Although James II, a despot who nevertheless understood commerce, put an end to the disorder, the members of the company had nevertheless been "won over by this plundering spirit" and continued to intercept English merchant ships coming from Surat. It was this odious piracy – the sanctioned seizure of merchant ships by the company – that led to a doubly ruinous war, a war that incurred greater expense and completely interrupted business in the rich and vast state of Indostan. English members of the company then

127 *HDI* (1780), book 1, 290.

committed the most odious piracy of all – even more odious as it was committed upon their own nation, in the *Histoire*'s account. An already heinous monopoly transgressed good commerce doubly, and this act was called a piracy, a form of banditry.

The filibusterers were the models for a truly new world – a world of freedom, an egalitarian republic liberated from the shackles of the Old World. This utopian potential existed despite the banditry upon which it was founded. But lacking a spirit of conquest, the filibusterers were unable to perpetuate their society. This "surprise" of the century was not renewable as a social system. And yet the representation of the filibusterers as a society was but one image of pirates proffered by the *Histoire des deux Indes*. For pirates were also individuals. They had names and voices. It turns out that a pirate in eighteenth-century France was rarely an enemy of the human race (*hostis humani generis*), as Diderot reminds us. More remarkable, however, is that the *Histoire*'s portrayal of the eighteenth-century pirate distinguishes the individual from the practice. Indeed, it was the practice of piracy that was dubious, transgressing the moral codes of commerce. Piracy was equated with banditry, an odious capital crime. In effect, this portrayal had a powerful consequence: it exposed the hypocrisy of the European powers in condemning individuals, called variously pirates, rogues, *corsaires*, and so on, while at the same time justifying a right of seizure – piracy – through the newly formed jurisprudence of international law.

In the end, the *Histoire* informed its readers that European monopolists were more piratical than any pirate. It was not pirates but rather the monopolistic agents of imperial commerce who committed *cette odieuse piraterie*, the most odious commerce of all. The piracy idiom in eighteenth-century France, characterised by a blurry semantic field of agents, was mobilised by the imperial authority and its jurisprudence to justify acts of violence, in the name of commerce, committed by a single-sanctioned "author," the sovereign state. The *Histoire* understood this manoeuvre, and displayed it for the discerning reader. This stance is all the more striking when we consider how few texts actually made this connection.[128] It appears that the *Histoire* was ahead of its time with

---

[128] The French translation of John Milton's *Eikonoklastes* (1652), for example, deplored that "piracy has become an avowed monopoly." Yet it appears that it is not until the nineteenth century that the connection between piracy and monopoly is made in France, as evident, most famously, in Charles Fourier's *Égarement de la raison démontré par les ridicules des sciences* (1848), or Pierre-Joseph Proudhon's *Système des contradictions économiques, ou philosophie de la misère (1846)*.

this position correlating piracy and monopoly. The chapter that follows develops this theme further by tracing another limit to the ideal of *doux commerce*, the evolution of the monopoly trading system. We will see that this system was the object of another piercing critique of established authority by the authors of the *Histoire des deux Indes*.

4

Indigne atelier

Monopoly and Monopolists

Amid a collection of manuscript notes on the history of France collected by Fevret de Fontette, we find a pair of anagrams.[1] The first, "Anagram of the Indies Company in the year 1727," reads: "East Indies Company / Shameful shop made up of asses" ["*Compagnie des indes orientales / Indigne atelier composé d'anes.*"][2] This quip not incidentally likened the

[1] These range from a note on the "history and legend" of "Leskinka [*sic*], daughter to the Polish king," to a list of remonstrances by the Parlement of Rouen addressed to Louis XV. Charles Marie Fevret de Fontette (1710–72) was a director of the Académie de Dijon and a councillor in the Parlement of Burgundy who completed Père Lelong's *Bibliothèque historique de la France*, first published in 1719. Part of his research notes now form an important part of the collections at the Bibliothèque de l'Arsenal in Paris, and another section contributes to the Prints (Estampes) collections at the Bibliothèque nationale.

[2] Arsenal MS 3724, Recueil de Fevret de Fontette, "Pièces concernant l'histoire de France," MS. B. Tome II, Fol. 119. The date on the anagram indicates that it was written – or at least it referred to a moment – two years after the French Indies Company's monopoly had been redefined and confirmed in 1725. See Phillipe Haudrère, "L'État et les négociants: Deux mémoires sur la situation de la compagnie française des Indes en 1730," in Martine Acerra, Jean-Pierre Pousson, Michel Vergé-Franceschi, and André Zysberg, eds., *État, Marine et Société: Hommage à Jean Meyer* (Paris: Presses de l'Université de Paris-Sorbonne, 1995), 1:135. A second anagram of Pelletier, the controller general of the time, read: "Pelletier Pille le reste" (Pelletier pillages the rest). The author, probably Fevret de Fontette, noted that the letter "s" was added to arrive at "Pille le reste" from "Pelletier." Ibid. Claude Le Pelletier (1630–1711) succeeded Colbert as controller general of finances from 1683 until 1689. See France, *Les Archives Nationales*, 45, for a description of Le Pelletier in the list of items in Série G7 1–62. As Philippe Haudrère notes, when Philibert Orry became controller general of finances in early 1730, his first item of business was to repair the mediocre situation of the Compagnie des Indes. The implication is of course that Pelletier had not addressed the problem adequately. Haudrère, "L'État et les négociants," 135. See also Michel Morineau, *Les Grandes compagnies des Indes orientales (XVIe-XIXe siècles)* (Paris: Presses universitaires de France, 1994).

French East Indies Company to an *atelier*, or trade workshop, as it signalled the growing hostility towards the company in the early eighteenth century. In doing so, it foreshadowed the terms of a debate that would eventually lead to the company's dissolution, but also to a broadened, moralised, and politicised recasting of monopoly within the discourse of commerce. Fontette's anagram also prefigured a strategic conflation made by the *Histoire*. Companies of artisans (or *corps*) and companies of international traders were likened to those who abused power and privilege in prerevolutionary France. As we shall see, these two types of monopoly were conjoined by a single powerful critique of monopoly, and through this to a critique of despotism as well. Thus, the *Histoire* condemned the abuse of commerce for privileged gain, whether at home or abroad, and paired the abuse of commerce with the abuse of political power.

Founded in 1664 by Colbert, the Compagnie française des Indes orientales, or French East Indies Company, represented the French state's first and longest-standing international monopoly over colonial trade for nearly two centuries. Enmity towards the company such as that expressed in Fontette's notes existed since its inception, but during the eighteenth century it developed into two animated polemics: a "debate over the Exclusif" and a debate over the suspension of the company's privileges. Historians of imperial commerce have tended to focus on the debate over the Exclusif, so-called since Jean Tarrade entitled and published his massive thesis on the subject.[3] As we have seen, the Exclusif – literally, the Exclusive – was a policy first formulated by the Bureau des colonies, or Colonial Office, in 1728 forbidding the colonies to purchase goods that were not French in origin or brought by French merchants while simultaneously forcing all colonial productions to be taken to French ports. Its notoriety was such that it was deemed a "regime" by contemporaries. While the debate over the Exclusif was an important one, the historiographical focus on it has meant that one important context for the *Histoire*'s portrayal of monopoly has received less attention: an equally important 1769 polemic over the very survival of the French Company of the Indies, often called the "affair of the Indies Company."[4]

---

[3] Jean Tarrade, *Le commerce colonial de la France à la fin de l'Ancien Régime: L'évolution du régime de l'"Exclusif" de 1763 à 1789*. 2 vols. (Paris: Presses universitaires de France, 1972). Paul Cheney offers fresh perspectives on the Exclusif in his *Revolutionary Commerce: Globalization and the French Monarchy* (Cambridge, MA: Harvard University Press, 2010), 168–70, 179–87, 208–10. The Company of the East Indies is analysed separately from these, however.

[4] One exception is John Shovlin, *The Political Economy of Virtue: Luxury, Patriotism, and the Origins of the French Revolution* (Ithaca, NY: Cornell University Press, 2006),

The "affair" lends a new perspective on certain connections in the eighteenth-century discussion about monopoly. On one hand, writing on the colonial experience in the eighteenth century has tended to isolate colonial concerns from the equally passionate national debates over domestic monopolies that occurred almost contemporaneously: the "quarrel" about whether or not the state ought to maintain a monopoly on the grain trade in France and about reforms calling for an end to the guilds. On the other hand, literature on the debate over the "liberalisation" of the grain trade and on the guilds has shied away from taking issues surrounding colonial trade into account, issues that equally preoccupied the royal administration.[5] Yet, as I will suggest, these processes were intertwined, with the abbé André Morellet (1727–1819) serving as the pivotal figure linking both strands.

To expose this connection, I consider 1769 as a crystallising moment in the formulation of a broadened concept of monopoly among eighteenth-century French writers, polemicists, and politicians. In that year, the abbé Ferdinando Galiani (1727–87) published his *Dialogues sur le commerce des blés*, a work critical of the recent edicts of 1763–64 liberalising the grain trade and the Physiocratic principles which informed them. Galiani's text hit Paris like a "bomb," by his own account, and set in motion the "flour war," though this was far from his intention.[6] The

---

123–24. Madeleine Dobie alludes to it as well in *Trading Places: Colonization and Slavery in Eighteenth-Century French Culture* (Ithaca, NY: Cornell University Press, 2010), 219. Paul Cheney uncovers a 1746 defence of the company which foreshadows one side of the 1769 debate, but does not discuss the controversy in *Revolutionary Commerce*, 42–43.

[5] Steven L. Kaplan conceptualised this term in his *Bread, Politics, and Political Economy* (1976). As Louis Cullen notes, historians have "postulated a dual economy in which the two sectors (internal and external) evolved (in the words of Jean Tarrade) *'parallèlement mais indépendamment l'une de l'autre.'*" Louis M. Cullen, "History, Economic Crises, and Revolution: Understanding Eighteenth-Century France," *Economic History Review* 46, no. 4 (1993): 651. Here I would like to suggest that a similar phenomenon has marked the history of ideas. Jean Claude Perrot's *Une Historie intellectuelle de l'économie politique* discusses Morellet's *Prospectus for a Dictionary of Commerce* (published in 1769) at length, but not Morellet's involvement in the polemic over the suspension of the Compagnie des Indes Orientale's privileges. Catherine Larrère addresses the connection between internal and external trade concerns, but does not mention the polemic either. Emma Rothschild points to this same connection in Adam Smith's work but sidesteps the 1769 suspension of the Compagnie's privilege. See her *Economic Sentiments: Adam Smith, Condorcet and the Enlightenment* (Cambridge, MA: Harvard University Press, 2001), 16, 27, 30, 32, 73. Cynthia A. Bouton refers briefly to Morellet in the conclusion to *The Flour War*, but not the Compagnie; the same is true of Judith Miller's *Mastering the Market*.

[6] Although Galiani appeared to boast in his letter of 18 November 1769 to Louise Épinay (author, *salonnière*, and his confidante) when he wrote: "J'attend les nouvelles du bruit que ma bombe aura fait, en crevant à Paris," his intention was also to model a more amicable form of disagreement about policy within the Republic of Letters, as Dena Goodman

year 1769 also marked the date when Galiani's dear friend Diderot first engaged seriously with the politics of international trade. For 1769 further marked a threshold in the history of monopoly in France. As we shall see, the French Company of the Indies's exclusive trading privilege was suspended in 1769 following a far-reaching public debate. This debate about France's *external* trade intersected, in turn, with those contemporaneous debates over whether the state should maintain its monopoly over the *internal* grain trade. Both Diderot and the authors of the *Histoire* approached domestic and international monopolies as one and the same problem; in conflating the issues in their analyses, they rendered their critique more comprehensive, but also brought into relief their ambivalence about these questions. And as with the other categories that I have suggested were central to the discourse of commerce in eighteenth-century France, the very definition of monopoly proved to be at the core of the contest as well.

DEFINING MONOPOLY

"This hideous monster," wrote lawyer Guy-Jean-Baptiste Target (1733–1807) in his *Observations on the Commerce of Grain*, "causes such an automatic fear that one does not dare look it in the face." Yet his subject, monopoly, was one which "almost no one knows what it is."[7] Though Target's text was published in 1775, he could still pronounce on the instability of the term several years after the debates over the monopoly of international and national commerce crowded French printing presses.[8] To be sure, in dictionaries then, as today, there was at least agreement on the word's etymology: the terms *monopole* and *monopoly* both derived from the Greek *monopolion, -polia,* itself an aggregate of *monos,* alone, and the verb *polein,* to sell.[9]

has shown. See *The Republic of Letters: A Cultural History of the French Enlightenment* (Ithaca: Cornell University Press, 1994), 186–97.

[7] "Mais ce monstre hideux cause une peur si machinale qu'on n'ose pas le regarder en face; presque personne ne sait même ce que c'est." Guy-Jean-Baptiste Target, *Observations sur le commerce des grains* (Amsterdam and Paris: L. Cellot, 1775), quoted in Philippe Steiner, *Sociologie de la connaissance économique* (Paris: PUF, 1998), 99.

[8] Target also participated in the debate over the Company of the Indies, as the pen for one of its shareholders. See *Mémoire pour le comte de Landivisiau contre la Compagnie des Indes* (Paris: L. Cellot, 1769).

[9] See Alain Rey and Josette Rey-Debove, *Le Nouveau Petit Robert* (Paris: Dictionnaires Le Robert, 1994), 1432. Cf. *Shorter Oxford English Dictionary,* s.v. "monopoly," 1822.

MONOPOLY IN THE *ENCYCLOPÉDIE*

The *Encyclopédie* article "Monopole," published in 1765, maintained an identical etymology. Its author, Boucher d'Argis, was the same specialist in jurisprudence selected for the articles "Prise" ("Seizure") and "Jouissance" ("Enjoyment"). The choice of Boucher d'Argis suggests an editorial assumption about the connections among these various commercial categories, including their status as legal problems.

The reader first learns that monopoly is "the illicit and odious traffic" by "one who renders himself the sole master of a type of merchandise." The use of the term *odious* recalls odious piracy in the *Histoire des deux Indes*; the term foreshadows the dominant adjective also used to describe monopoly in that work. As Boucher d'Argis continues, this "master of a good" sought "to be its sole vendor, and to put [it at] a price which seems to authorise him alone to engage in the trade of a certain kind of merchandise." And finally, a monopoly occurs "once all of the merchants of the same corps have enough intelligence to raise the merchandise price or alter it somewhat."[10]

Following an etymology from the Greek which aligns with the etymologies noted earlier, Boucher d'Argis listed several classical references that confirmed the view that monopoly was an abhorrent practice. The Romans, for example, had deemed monopoly so odious that Tiberius dared ask for permission from the Senate to engage in monopoly only by arguing that the term was borrowed from the Greek. Boucher d'Argis then invoked Aristotle's *Politics* to illustrate the even longer history of monopolies. In it, Aristotle made an example of Thales the Milesian, who had used astrology one summer to predict an abundance of olives, which he promptly bought and then "sold alone" at great profit.[11]

---

[10] *Encyclopédie*, 10:668.

[11] The *Encyclopédie* cites book 1, chap. 7. In twentieth-century editions of the work, this section appeared later, in chapter 12. Cf. Aristotle, *Politics*, 26–27. This same section of the *Politics* contains Aristotle's discussion of wealth. Aristotle divided the "practical part" of obtaining wealth into three. "The true and proper art of wealth-getting," or the "first or more natural mode," was knowledge of livestock and husbandry. Exchange also consisted of knowledge of commerce, usury, and "service for hire." Finally, the "intermediate" mode, which combined the first two, was "partly natural, but is also concerned with exchange" and consisted of "the industries that make their profit from the earth," such as timber and mining. This was a revealing example: Aristotle's section on the practical arts of achieving wealth concluded by suggesting that the "statesman as well ought to know these things; for a state is often as much in want of money and of such schemes for obtaining it as a household."

Historical examples of the prohibition of monopoly in France provided next in the article referred to a monopoly of hedgehog skins in Pliny's *Natural History* – apparently useful for napping cloth – and to monopoly's status as a crime in ancient Rome punishable "by the confiscation of all goods and perpetual exile."[12] Emperor Charles V decreed the same in 1548. Finally, the article identifies François I as the first French king to prohibit the monopoly of workers.[13]

The article ends with an attack on monopoly – and not just any attack. For Boucher d'Argis, there was no more "glaring" monopoly [*"il n'y a point de monopole plus criant"*] than the monopoly on wheat. The cross-reference to "Wheat, Commerce, Grains" is especially telling as it points to another key context in which monopoly was understood in this period and suggests that Boucher d'Argis and the editors' views on monopoly had significant political stakes. The article, published in 1765, appeared contemporaneously with the 1764 Edict of Compiègne, the first of three instances in the prerevolutionary period in which the king proclaimed the liberty of commerce in grains and authorised both their import and export.

This proclamation soon unleashed a debate that Dena Goodman has shown to be as much about defining the rules of the Republic of Letters as it was about grain. The 1775 *guerre des farines*, or "flour war," for the violent polemics it generated, emerged from these attempts by the French crown to liberalise the commerce of grains in some instances and to control it in others.[14] The "war" was a pamphlet war, but agitation was also expressed in the streets. Massive protests, riots even, incited

---

[12] Indeed, chap. 56 "On Hedgehogs" in book 8 of Pliny the Elder's *Natural History*, on hedgehogs, makes just this reference. See 8:56, Pliny the Elder, *Natural History*, Vol. 3, trans. Harris Rackham (Cambridge: Harvard University Press, 1967).

[13] The reader is referred to a certain *Ruling of 1539*, article 191. The reference is to François I's so-called *Ordinance of Villers-Cotterets of 1539*, a foundational document of France's civil registry, which reappears as a reference in other works analysing monopoly in the period, including Joseph-Nicolas Guyot's dictionary of jurisprudence discussed later in this chapter. This example stands out because it invokes a ban on an early form of workers' union and not, as the other examples attest, a more standard form of monopoly on a commodity. See *Ordonnance de Villers-Cotterets, du mois d'août 1539, avec les dispositions spéciales à la Bretagne* (Rennes: Jacques Berthelot, 1539).

[14] On the "flour war" and its repercussions, see Steven Laurence Kaplan's magisterial *Bread, Politics and Political Economy in the Reign of Louis XV*. 2 vols. (The Hague: Martinus Nijhoff, 1976); Florence Gauthier, *La Guerre du blé au XVIIIe siècle* (Paris: Editions de la Passion, 1989); Cynthia Bouton, *The Flour War: Gender, Class, and Community in Late Ancien Régime French Society* (University Park, PA: Pennsylvania State University Press, 1993); and Judith A. Miller, *Mastering the Market: The State and the Grain Trade in Northern France, 1700–1860* (Cambridge: Cambridge University Press, 1999).

by the return of state controls over grain prices erupted across the French countryside.[15] For nearly two decades, this issue divided French farmers, intellectuals, and pamphleteers. But it also eventually drove a wedge between the *parlements* and the king in the mid-1770s, marking a period of overt squabbling between the two powers, for in this period the *parlements* stood firmly on the side of those opposing restrictions on manufacturing.[16]

For all of these reasons, the "reasoning" about wheat (about which Voltaire had quipped) has long been considered one of the primary forces acting to create a newly defined notion of public opinion in the prerevolutionary period.[17] Catherine Larrère has identified and analysed the range of political debates which preceded this "flour war," wherein different conceptions of commerce "asserted and affronted" each other. These included the so-called affair of the painted calicos (*toiles peintes*) and the quarrel over whether the nobility should be permitted to trade (*noblesse commerçante*). But as she concludes, the debate over the liberty of the grain trade surpassed the others in reach and effect.[18]

Most significant for our present purposes are the terms that the *Encyclopédie* entry used to qualify monopoly. The use of *illicit* and *odious* by Boucher d'Argis is important for two reasons. First, it points to the existence of a moral judgement of monopoly. The term *illicite* in French meant then, as it does now, that an action was contrary to both morality and the law. Second, it is significant that the editors of the *Encyclopédie* limited their concern with monopoly to internal trade. Conspicuous by its absence is any reference to the country's most powerful, and indeed lucrative, monopolies: those companies that controlled colonial commerce

---

[15] A pamphlet commenting on these riots was attributed to the future controller general of finances, Anne Robert Jacques Turgot. See the *Lettres sur les émeutes populaires que causent la cherté des bleds et sur les precautions du moment* (n.p., 1768).

[16] For one of the earliest discussions of this tension in an English monograph, see Paul A. Beik, *A Judgement of the Old Regime: Being a Survey by the Parlement of Provence of French Economic and Fiscal Policies at the Close of the Seven Years War* (New York: Columbia University Press, 1944), 141–47, 161–84.

[17] See Keith Michael Baker, "Politics and Public Opinion under the Old Regime: Some Reflections," in Jack R. Censer and Jeremy D. Popkin, eds., *Press and Politics in Pre-revolutionary France* (Berkeley: University of California Press, 1987) and Roger Chartier *Les origines culturelles de la Révolution française* (Paris: Éditions du Seuil, 1990), chap. 2.

[18] On the *toiles peintes*, see Catherine Larrère, *L'Invention de l'économie au XVIIIe siècle: Du droit naturel à la physiocratie* (Paris: Presses universitaires de France, 1992), 7. On the "trading nobility" debate, see Jay Smith, "Social Categories, the Language of Patriotism, and the Origins of the French Revolution: The Debate over *noblesse comerçante*," *JMH* 72 (2000): 339–74.

with the sanction of the king. Yet the two types of commerce were deeply connected, as Diderot and the *Histoire* made clear, raising the stakes for their resolution.

BEYOND MORALS: MONOPOLY AND JURISPRUDENCE

We can verify the stability of the *Encyclopédie* definition by comparing it to the definitions appearing in dictionaries compiled in the eighteenth century. Though jurisprudence was far from the sole focus of Boucher d'Argis's "Monopole" entry, it emphasised the existence of a strong legal tradition opposed to monopoly.[19] Dictionaries of jurisprudence allow us to test the *Enyclopédie*'s representation of monopoly against the formal legal one in the principal sources of the period: Jean-Baptiste Denisart's *Collection of Decisions and Notions Relative to Current Jurisprudence* (1763–87); Claude-Joseph de Ferrière's *Dictionary of Law and Practice* (1778), and Joseph-Nicholas Guyot's edition of the *Universal and Reasoned Directory of Civil, Criminal, Canonic and Beneficial Jurisprudence* (1784). Although the encyclopedists' influence on these juridical sources is evident, their definitions also bear out the deeper sense that monopoly was a moral problem.

Thus, in Denisart's *Collection de decisions nouvelles* (1763) "Monopole et monopoleurs," anyone who "amass[ed] merchandise of whatever type excessively, with the aim of making it rare and being the sole possessors, in order to sell at an exorbitant price" met the definition.[20] Denisart invoked the emperor Zenon's "most ancient law" against monopoly and rehearsed French jurisprudence from King John's Ordinance to the *arrêt* (judgement) of 12 July 1721 that condemned the "named Orient, Merchant Grocer," for hoarding "prodigious piles of merchandise at the Augustins [market] of Paris." In 1763, then, monopoly also included the notion of excessive hoarding described two years later in the *Encyclopédie*, but added additional blame onto the oriental merchant.[21]

---

[19] This despite the fact that the sole focus of his entry was not jurisprudence. We recall that Boucher d'Argis's use of the term "odious" also introduced a moral, in addition to a legal, condemnation of monopoly.

[20] Jean-Baptist Denisart, *Collection de décisions nouvelles et de notions relatives à la jurisprudence actuelle*. 3 vols (Paris: Vve Desaint, 1763–87), 204.

[21] Here we can detect traces of the orientalist bias prevalent in eighteenth-century France, and studied by Madeleine Dobie in *Trading Places* and by Thomas Kaiser in "The Evil Empire? The Debate on Turkish Despotism in Eighteenth-Century French Political Culture." *JMH* 72, no. 1 (2000): 6–34.

When Ferrière's dictionary appeared in 1778, the entry on monopoly essentially reproduced the article by Boucher d'Argis.[22] Ferrière defined *monopoly* as an "illicit and odious traffic" by one who rendered himself the "sole master" of merchandise. The dictionary added one caveat, however: "Today," monopoly was "understood to mean a tax placed on the People: something that could not be done without the authority of the Sovereign." Here arose the implication that the sovereign was exempt from the laws, or else complicit in the "illicit and odious traffic." This comment reflected an important difference from the views on monopoly that appeared in the work of Denisart: Writing in post-1769 France, Ferrière – and later Guyot and the *Histoire* in its third edition – reflected a newfound sensitivity to the arguments put forward during the animated polemic over the liberalisation of the grain trade. They perpetuated the moral reprimand of the *Encyclopédie* by construing monopoly as both odious and illicit.

In Guyot's *Répertoire* (1784), monopoly remained an abuse of the power procured to sell merchandise, but was not always illegal. Guyot also construed monopoly as an extra-state phenomenon: "[I]t is also said of all of the iniquitous conventions which merchants undertake with one another in commerce, to 'tamper or augment the prices' of certain merchandise, in concert."[23] We are here not far removed in both tone and content from Adam Smith's famous claim, "People of the same trade seldom meet together, even for merriment and diversion, but the conversation ends in a conspiracy against the public, or in some contrivance to raise prices."[24] This is not surprising, given the immediate and widespread reception of Adam Smith in France. Smith's *Wealth of Nations*

---

[22] Ferrière stated that all who needed this merchandise "must necessarily pass by his hands, and pay the price he wants to set." *Dictionnaire de droit et de pratique, contenant l'explication des termes de droit, d'Ordonnances, de Coutumes & de Pratique. Avec les jurisdictions de France ...* Nouvelle édition, revue, corrigée & augmentée (Paris: Veuve Brunet, 1778–79), 2:213.

[23] Joseph-Nicholas Guyot, ed., *Répertoire universel et raisonné de Jurispruence civile, criminelle, canonique et bénéficiale; ouvrage de plusieurs juisconsultes ...* Nouvelle édition corrigée, et augmentée tant des loix nouvelles que des arrêts rendus en matière importante pour les parlemens et les autres cours du royaume, depuis l'édition précédente. 17 vols. (Paris: 1784).

[24] Adam Smith, *An Inquiry into the Nature and Causes of the Wealth of Nations.* 1776. 2 vols. R. H. Campbell and A. S. Skinner, eds. (Oxford: Oxford University Press, 1976), 1:130. For Smith, although enlarged monopolies prevented free trade, it was possible for competition to take place among the smaller number of men. Smith stated, however, that this possibility was never fully realised because of a "spirit of monopoly," which prevails among traders and artisans of all kinds (1:127–29, 427; 2:77, 225).

was translated immediately upon its first publication in Edinburgh.[25] The earliest and most complete translation was anonymous and appeared as serialised extracts in the *Journal de l'agriculture, du commerce, des arts et des finances* in 1779–80.[26] By 1784, the work had been disseminated so widely that we can safely assume that readers of the *Répertoire* would have recognised the reference.[27]

Guyot also offered a historical account of the laws prohibiting monopolies, beginning with the emperor Zenon's prohibition of the "crime of monopoly" pertaining to "dress, fish, combs, scallops, sea urchins, or of any species of matter whatsoever" under pain of "confiscation of goods, and perpetual banishment."[28] A detailed legal history of French judicial positions against monopoly followed.[29] The effect was to confirm that monopoly had been illegal historically and to apply moral condemnation to monopoly throughout French history.

[25] The fullest account we have of the history of translations of Smith into French is Kenneth E. Carpenter's *The Dissemination of "The Wealth of Nations" in French and in France, 1776–1843* (New York: Bibliographical Society of America, 2002). This section is highly indebted to it. While the first translations we know of are those fragments undertaken by the abbé Morellet in February 1776, Morellet's translations never found a publisher, nor did any of his successive attempts up to 1802. The first translated extract, "On the colonies in general, and on the English ones in particular," was published anonymously in 1778 in Switzerland, followed by a second anonymous translation in 1778–79 in The Hague. *Fragment sur les colonies en général, et sur celles des anglois en particulier. Traduit de l'anglois. A Basle, Chez Jean-Jacques Flick, libraire* (1778). Drawing on Barbier's *Dictionnaire des ouvrages anonymes* (Paris, 1964), Carpenter identifies the author as Élie Salomon François Reverdil, tutor to Christian VII of Denmark and translator of Adam Ferguson. *Recherches sur la nature et les causes de la richesse des nations … Traduit de l'anglois de M. Adam Smith, par M***. A La Haye*. 4 vols. 1778–79. The publisher is unknown. See Carpenter, *Dissemination*, 16–17, 20–24.

[26] These extracts turned out to be the work of Jean-Louis Blavet, who publicly acknowledged his work in a letter to the *Journal de Paris* in November 1788. Carpenter, *Dissemination*, 24–25. Carpenter's version contrasts with Jean-Claude Perrot's, who writes that Blavet's translation "was contemporary with" Morellet's and appeared "in fragments" in the *Journal du commerce*. See Jean-Claude Perrot, *Une histoire intellectuelle de l'économie politique, XVIIe – XVIIIe siècle* (Paris: Éditions de l'École des Hautes Études en Sciences Sociales, 1992), 105.

[27] Carpenter notes that translated extracts of the *Wealth of Nations* appeared in the *Encyclopédie méthodique*, the famous and widespread "manual for the businessman, statesman and even the philosopher." Volume 1 (1784) referred to these, and volume 2 (1786) contained several economic articles "almost always drawn from *Wealth of Nations* (usually with added introductory and concluding material)." See Carpenter, *Dissemination*, 40.

[28] Guyot, *Répertoire universel*, 11:604.

[29] The passage began with François I's *Ordinance of Villers-Cotterets of 1539*, the foundational document of France's civil registry (also invoked by Boucher d'Argis in his *Encyclopédie* article), and ended with a discussion of the various actions taken by different *parlements*, from Flanders to Metz, against individuals engaging in the monopolistic sale of commodities necessary to the public.

The major dictionaries of jurisprudence in eighteenth-century France, then, emphasised the association of monopoly with domestic trade. In addition, they pointed to a broader discursive field for the term, one that emphasised the connection between monopolies, moral judgement, and a history of illegality.

THE AFFAIR OF THE INDIES COMPANY

These lexicographical definitions provide a backdrop against which we can assess that animated moment of the cultural and political definition of monopoly in France called the "Affair of the Indies Company." The very first French Company of the Indies, as it was called, was chartered by the king in 1604, but never organised any expeditions. A series of other companies were founded in turn, when in 1664, an edict of Colbert's chartered the Compagnie Royale des Indes Orientales (CIO), the Royal Company of the East Indies, and endowed it with a fifty-year monopoly on trade east of the Cape of Good Hope. In 1719, John Law merged the French East Indies Company with the newly established French West Indies Company and China Company by way of a Reunion Edict (*Édit de reunion*). Together, they formed the Perpetual Company of the Indies (Compagnie perpétuelle des Indes), by far the largest company in the history of France to that point.

After the crash of Law's so-called *Système*, however, the financial basis of the company was redefined and its monopoly confirmed in 1725.[30] By all accounts the monopoly over maritime commerce of the French state then reached its peak, and the company enjoyed tremendous success. Its sphere of influence was extended to India under the energetic direction of Joseph François Dupleix (1697–1763), though, in contrast to its English competitor, it failed to garner enough support from the state.[31] From its

[30] In 1723, Law had even persuaded the king to concede the revenues from the tobacco taxes (*ferme du tabac*) to the company, ensuring thereby an annuity of three million *livres*. The revenues from the sale of tobacco had increased to eight million *livres* by mid-century. Georges Dulac, "Introduction au 'Dossier de la Compagnie des Indes,'" *DPV*, 20: 20:223n29. Cf. Edgar Faure, *La Banqueroute de Law* (Paris: Gallimard, 1977), 187, and Philippe Haudrère, *La compagnie française des Indes au XVIIIe siècle (1719–1795)*. Vol. 1. (Paris: Librairie de l'Inde, 1989), 1:78–82. For more on the Law imbroglio, see Thomas E. Kaiser, "Money, Despotism and Public Opinion in Early Eighteenth-Century France: John Law and the Debate on Royal Credit," *Journal of Modern History* 63, no. 1 (1991): 1–28.

[31] On the comparisons between the English and French companies and their "familial states," see Julia Adams, *The Familial State: Ruling Families and Merchant Capitalism in Early Modern Europe* (Ithaca and London: Cornell University Press, 2005), 188.

headquarters in the newly created port city of Lorient, and its Paris office in the Hôtel de Tubeuf, the company was transformed into the flagship enterprise of France's international commerce and colonisation, as well as a major hope for national economic growth and financial recovery.[32] This phase in the company's history lasted nearly forty-five years, until its privilege was suspended in 1769.

The suspension was the result of the convergence of several vectors of resentment, in evidence as early as Fontette's anagrams in 1727. Pressure came, on one hand, from independent traders and merchants who organised themselves into groups – in Marseille, Bordeaux, Le Havre, and, especially Nantes – to protest the reign of privilege.[33] As Pierre Boulle has shown, the Nantais slave traders, in particular, were among the most vocal critics of the Compagnie des Indes's monopoly.[34] Equally influential, however, was the set of printed contestations of the company's merits that came from the networks of power in Paris and exploded into the "affair of the Indies Company." We can trace the launching of this polemic to 1755, when the *intendant général du commerce* himself, Vincent de Gournay, attacked the company.[35] By this time, Gournay had assembled his circle of administrators and intellectuals, all of whom shared an ambition to reform France's economy through liberalising markets and trade – an ideology for which, as we have seen, Gournay allegedly provided the catchphrase: "*laissez faire, laissez passer.*" In a report to the *contrôleur général* of finances, Étienne de Silhouette (1709–67), Gournay argued that the company's "management does not conform to the spirit of commerce, and its spending is foreign to its goal."[36] Also at fault, he argued, were the company's incessant borrowing and the directors' negligence and attention to their own interests. Gournay's accusations were largely accurate. Further, it is now understood that the wars of the Austrian Succession

---

[32] See André Garrigues, *Musée de la compagnie des Indes: Guide du visiteur* (Morbihan: Citadelle de Port-Louis, 1993). See also Georges Dulac, "Dossier de la Compagnie des Indes (été 1769)," *DPV*, 20: 212. Cf. Henry Weber, *La compagnie française des Indes* (Paris: A. Rousseau, 1904), 329–30.

[33] Adams, *The Familial State*, 188.

[34] Pierre Boulle, "Slave Trade, Commercial Organization and Industrial Growth in Eighteenth-Century Nantes." *Revue française d'histoire d'outre-mer* 59 (1972): 70–112.

[35] See the *Observations sur le rapport fait à M. le contrôleur général par M. de S*** le 26 juin 1755, sur l'état de la Compagnie des Indes, par feu M. de Gournay*, printed in the same volume as Morellet's *Mémoire* of 1769.

[36] Vincent de Gournay, *Observations sur le rapport fait à M. le contrôleur général par M. de S*** le 26 juin 1755, sur l'état de la Compagnie des Indes, par feu M. de Gournay, Intendant du Commerce*, in l'abbé Morellet, *Mémoire sur la situation actuelle de la Compagnie des Indes, juin 1769* (Paris: Desaint, 1769).

(1740–48) and the Seven Years War had affected the company's ability to trade and seriously decreased its profits.[37]

Enter Swiss banker Jacques Necker (1732–1804), who at this stage was only beginning his transition from the world of banking to the world of court politics. Joined by Jean-Baptiste Dubucq (1717–95), the first clerk of the Colonial Bureau, and Charles de La Croix, marquis de Castries (1727–1801), who represented the company at court, Necker was given a quasi-official role as its financial counsellor.[38] From 1765 to 1767, however, his continuing policy of borrowing only worsened the company's finances.[39] In an opposing camp, several successive controllers general of finances openly expressed their hostility to the company's continued commercial activity, ending with Étienne Maynon d'Invau (1721–1801) and the faction of economic reformers surrounding the duc de Choiseul.

This "affair" erupted into a crisis in the spring of 1769. In the assembly of shareholders on 29 March, a Genevan banker, Isaac Panchaud, accused Necker and the company's administration of falsifying the company's financial status. Panchaud introduced a plan whereby its monopoly would be abolished; the company was to renounce commerce in the Indies and become a *caisse d'escompte*, or discount bank.[40] Panchaud's

---

[37] After 1756, the company was used by the government to lead the French struggle against the English in India, and by 1763, in the aftermath of the Seven Years War, it found itself having lost most of its possessions and funds. Dulac, "Introduction au 'Dossier de la Compagnie des Indes,'" 202.

[38] In a very brief section on the history of the Company of the Indies during this period, Tarrade highlights Lüthy's erroneous claim that Necker was in fact the company's syndic at the time. This mistake is reproduced by Dulac in his introduction to Diderot's writings on the company. Cf. Tarrade, *Le commerce colonial*, 1:59; Lüthy, *La Banque protestante en France*. 2 vols. (Paris: SEVPEN: J. Touzot, 1959–70), 2:381, and Dulac, "Introduction au 'Dossier de la Compagnie des Indes,'" 203. The archives of the Company of the Indies have famously disappeared; Tarrade drew on correspondence and other documents in the National Archives to understand the details of this crisis. These include summaries of the company's shareholders' assemblies. See A. N., Col., C²47, ff.201–2, Assembly of 24 June 1764.

[39] Herbert Lüthy famously argued that Necker's "medications killed the patient." *La Banque protestante*, 2:394, cited in Dulac, "Introduction au 'Dossier de la Compagnie des Indes,'" 203. See also Gilbert Faccarello, "Galiani, Necker and Turgot: A Debate on Economic Reform and Policy in Eighteenth-Century France." In Gilbert Faccarello, ed., *Studies in the History of French Political Economy* (London: Routledge, 1998).

[40] Panchaud's plan was later realised under the ministry of Turgot in 1776. See François Crouzet, "Politics and Banking in Revolutionary and Napoleonic France" in Richard Eugene Sylla, Richard H. Tilly, and Gabriel Tortella Casares, eds., *The State, the Financial System, and Economic Modernization* (Cambridge: Cambridge University Press, 1999), 27–29.

plan was opposed, however, by a single outspoken adversary, Jean-Jacques Duval d'Eprémesnil (1745–94), who convinced the assembly to refuse the motion. In the aftermath of this session, Maynon d'Invau, a friend of Gournay's supported by Choiseul, commissioned the abbé André Morellet (1727–1819) to write a *mémoire*. The assignment called on him to push Gournay's earlier observations further and reveal the poor state of the company's finances in order to ultimately argue that commerce with the Indies should be opened to all. Considered a student of Gournay's school and therefore a proponent of freed commerce, in 1758 Morellet published an intervention in the earlier debate about freeing the commerce of the *toiles peintes*, painted calicos from India.[41] A translator of Cesare Beccaria's theory on style, Morellet was apparently nicknamed the "abbé Mords-les" ("abbot Bite-them") by Voltaire for his sharp tongue and a pen which he did not hesitate to use.[42] He is a pivotal figure in this moment of debate about liberalisation in France, both domestic and international.

The *Mémoire sur la situation actuelle de la Compagnie des Indes* appeared in June 1769, not long after Morellet had published his plan for a new dictionary of commerce, the *Prospectus d'un nouveau dictionnaire de commerce*.[43] We know that it caused quite a splash – *un effet prodigieux*, according to the notorious *Mémoires secrets pour servir à l'histoire de la République des Lettres*, attributed to Louis Petit de Bachaumont. The press paid special attention to the ensuing polemic. For instance, the *Courrier du Bas-Rhin* printed several long analyses of the different publications beginning almost immediately on 2 August 1769. The slew of satirical writings that appeared are yet another indication that Morellet's *Mémoire* reached an audience far vaster than the company's

---

[41] *Reflexions sur les avantages de la libre fabrication et de l'usage des toiles peintes en France pour servir de réponse aux divers mémoires des fabriquans de Paris, Lyon, Tours, Rouen, &c. sur cette matiere* (Paris and Geneva: 1758).

[42] L. G. Michaud, *Biographie universelle ancienne et moderne* ... Nouvelle édition. 45 vols. (Paris: Madame C. Desplaces et M. Michaud, 1854–1865).

[43] André Morellet's *Mémoire sur la situation actuelle de la Compagnie des Indes* (Paris: Desaint, 1769) was first dated June 1769. This second edition, published in the same year, included a copy of Gournay's 1755 remarks on the company, *Observations sur le rapport fait à M. le contrôleur général par M. de S*** le 26 juin 1755, sur l'état de la Compagnie des Indes, par feu M. de Gournay*. This was followed by the brief, anonymous, *Éclaircissemens sur le Mémoire de M. l'abbé Morelet* [sic], *concernant la partie historique de la Compagnie des Indes et l'origine du bien des actionnaires* (n.p., 1769). According to Jean-Claude Perrot, the *Prospectus* was commissioned by the Estienne brothers, owners of the privilege for Savary's *Dictionnaire universel de commerce*. See Perrot, *Une histoire intellectuelle*, 104.

shareholders.[44] All of this despite its girth – the essay was over 200 pages in length, in-4 – leading historian and politician Ambroise-Marie Arnould (1757–1812) to comment, "[T]here does not exist any issue related to commerce that has been examined in such depth in France."[45]

Necker's response to the charges against the company came at an assembly of shareholders held shortly thereafter, on 8 August. His speech there was published a week later under the title "Reply to M. l'abbé Morellet's Report."[46] It took a month for Morellet to refute Necker again.[47] In the meantime, the Physiocrats entered the fray in support of the abbé with Dupont de Nemours's publication of *Du Commerce et de la Compagnie des Indes*.[48] Dupont compared the company's condition with its condition under John Law, fifty years before, when it operated under a ferment of speculation. Dupont despaired at the result in which abstract values, like paper money, became the fashion and overwhelmed trust in the stable asset that was land.[49] Then soon enough, on 13 August 1769, a ruling from the King's Council officially suspended the company's privileges. Morellet, the mouthpiece for Maynon d'Invau and his anti-company clique, had won. More important, so had the Choiseuliste policy. The once-crucial cog of France's colonial machine was liquidated

[44] Georges Dulac has identified several of these in Bachaumont's *Mémoires secrets* (London, 1777–89). They include a "Prospectus for the funeral march of the most high and most powerful, most excellent Princess, Madam Company of the Indies" (3 April 1769, *Mémoires secrets*, 4:248) and the "Account of Doctor Bawdy, confessor of […] Madam the Company of the Indies" (19 June 1769, *Mémoires secrets*, 19:104). See Dulac, "Dossier de la Compagnie des Indes," 20:21 ff. See also, Lüthy, *La Banque protestante*, 376–97, and Georges Dulac, "Pour reconsidérer l'histoire des *Observations sur le Nakaz* (à partir des réflexions de 1775 sur la physiocratie)." In *Éditer Diderot: Études recueillies par Georges Dulac*, 467–514 (Oxford: Voltaire Foundation, 1988), 179n7. The following discussion of Diderot is clearly indebted to Dulac's careful research.

[45] Ambroise-Marie Arnould, *De la balance du commerce* (Paris: Buisson, 1791), 1:289, cited in Tarrade, *Le commerce colonial*, 59. It is notable that despite Arnould's comment, Tarrade devoted no more than a total of three non-consecutive pages to this debate in his 800-page study.

[46] Jacques Necker's reply, *Réponse au mémoire de M. l'abbé Morellet sur la Compagnie des Indes, imprimée en exécution de la délibération de Mrs les actionnaires, prise dans l'assemblée générale du 8 août 1769* (Paris: Imprimerie royale, 1769), was a quarter of the length of Morellet's *mémoire* at fifty pages, in-4.

[47] This time, André Morellet's *Examen de la Réponse au mémoire de M. N.** au Mémoire de M. l'abbé Morellet, sur la Compagnie des Indes* (Paris: Desaint, 1769), dated September 1769, comprised only 150 pages.

[48] There were two editions in quick succession. I cite from the second, in-8, at 288 pages. Dupont de Nemours, *Du Commerce et de la Compagnie des Indes. Second edition. Revue, corrigée, et augmentée de l'Histoire du Système de Law.* (Amsterdam and Paris: Delalain, 1769).

[49] On Dupont's intervention, see John Shovlin, *The Political Economy of Virtue*, 124–25.

and the way paved – if only momentarily – for free commerce with the East Indies. But this would be short lived. By December, Choiseul was removed and a new *contrôleur general* was appointed – Joseph-Marie Terray (1715–78) – whose views more closely resembled Necker's. The Exclusif was revived, though in mitigated form, in 1784. The company was reinstated, named after its newest defender, yet another controller general, Charles-Alexandre de Calonne (1734–1802), only to be shut down for good in the anti-corporatist fervour of the Assemblée nationale in 1790. For most of the *Histoire*'s publishing life, then, no state monopoly existed over international trade.

DIDEROT AND ALCIBIADES'S DOG

The suspension of the company's privilege was an important moment in the history of French colonialism and monopoly. But it also marked a key period in the evolution of Diderot's thoughts and writings on commerce. Georges Dulac has confirmed that a dossier of five manuscript articles joined in a bundle within the Vandeul collection in the Bibliothèque nationale are definitely the written reactions of Diderot to each stage of the affair.[50] We know that Diderot had entered a phase of seclusion at this time, following the publication of the last volumes of the *Encyclopédie*. But this did not mean his manuscripts were not circulated or discussed. A study of this dossier composed in 1769 reveals that far from taking any clear position in support of one or the other debater, Diderot argued both sides in a posture best understood as ambivalent. He was certain about one thing: that political and economic issues were, in his words, "complicated," and therefore important questions such as the role of monopoly in society had to be addressed with attention to issues broader than those considered by Morellet or Necker. Diderot's opinions on the Compagnie complemented the view expressed in the *Histoire* that monopoly was a moral problem and warranted critique when it promoted a society of privilege and inequality. The analysis of the economic and financial question was incomplete without incorporating the political and moral problems of monopoly derived directly from its economic implications.

Diderot's dossier has an added significance: It bridges the gap between the quarrels over the company and the quarrels over grain and establishes the framework that made the *Histoire*'s later critique possible. As Georges Dulac has argued, Diderot's writings on the company reveal

---

[50] Dulac, "Introduction au 'Dossier de la Compagnie.'"

a paradox in his thinking. Whereas Diderot remained conscious of the excessive complexity of economic problems and hesitated to assert any single truth on the subject, he drew attention to the ways in which others ignored important questions.[51] Political economy, he argued, was best studied within literary and philosophical frameworks.[52] But if we consider Diderot's writings in tandem with the *Histoire*'s arguments, an additional explanation suggests itself. At the core of the issue for both Diderot and, as we shall see later for Raynal, were the moral problems caused by the existence of monopolies.

The first account in Diderot's dossier responded to Morellet's *Mémoire*, which Diderot acknowledged as a text that deserved the attention of "public men."[53] Diderot classified Morellet's proofs into one type that pertained to the principle of exclusive commerce in general, while the other challenged the company's exclusive commerce in particular.[54] Part of the essay is couched in the form of an invented dialogue; following literary theorist Mikhail Bakhtin, Dena Goodman has called this form a "dialogic imagination" and has suggested that Diderot learned it from his friend, the Neapolitan Galiani, who began composing his "dialogues" on the commerce of wheat as early as 1768.[55] Of interest here is the way in which Diderot appropriated this form for *both* of his reflections on commerce – national and international, internal and external. To be sure,

---

[51] Georges Dulac, "Les Gens de lettres, le banquier, et l'opinion: Diderot et la polémique sur la Compagnie des Indes," *Dix-huitième siècle* 26 (1994): 194–99.

[52] Ibid., 198.

[53] Ibid., 214. In 1769 Diderot boasted of having read "all of the Correspondence of the Isle of France to the French Court." Why would he do such a thing? A plausible suggestion is that the *philosophe* was in fact preparing to contribute to the *Histoire* at this time. Or could Diderot also have been anxious about a promised life annuity from the company? Although the specific reasons behind his participation have yet to be clarified, a simple reminder of his nearly constant involvement in the major issues of his day, as his complete works and correspondence attest, may suffice for the purposes of this chapter. Three letters to Sophie Volland demonstrate Diderot's immediate concern with the suspension of the company's privileges: the first written on the eve of the company's shareholders' assembly, 9 August; the next written on 23 August, shortly after its privileges were suspended; and the last, dated 11 September, that, fifteen days later, indicated that Morellet was busy preparing his reply to Necker. In tandem with this correspondence, Diderot produced five accounts that made up the dossier.

[54] Ibid.

[55] Goodman, *Republic of Letters*, 221. Goodman has elsewhere argued that the increasingly "inabsolute" power of princes following Louis XIV's reign caused a fundamental shift in the focus and shape of criticism. At this point, the reading public became the focus of social and political criticism and consequently began to be constituted as a political agent. See Dena Goodman, *Criticism in Action: Enlightenment Experiments in Political Writing* (Ithaca, NY: Cornell University Press, 1989), 6.

Diderot certainly appropriated the form and drew on it thereafter for most of his political and economic writings.

Let us look closely at how Diderot proceeds in his examination. To a first question asking no one in particular what an "exclusive" was, the reply is simple: "a title which restricts to a number of citizens commerce that is prohibited to others." And what reason, the questioner continues, did the privileged one have for maintaining his exclusive? Here, the reply is "His own interest." The terms next shift slightly but potently into another register: a father's obligations. "Why would the common father listen to *this* interest to the prejudice of the other children?" asks the questioner. The "privilege" (that is, the company) replies in turn that the "unlimited concession would become ruinous for most of them." The interrogator's sarcasm betrays Diderot's position: "I hear you! It is not your private interest that guides you, but your concern for your co-citizen's ruin. This is truly noble, beautiful, heroic, and charitable of you." The dialogue finishes with the "privileged" one consoled by the interrogator: "[Y]ou will not suffer long and soon you will receive eternal sanction for your privilege." Diderot's voice returns at this point to intervene: "Frankly, I don't know what one can reply to this."[56]

Diderot chose not to reply. Instead, his text turned to Morellet's *mémoire*. He began by making a "little reproach," that the abbé Morellet had attacked a friend, "M. Necker."[57] This was surely meant to be understood as sarcasm. In a letter to Sophie Volland, dated 23 August 1769, Diderot wrote that with his *mémoire*, Morellet

has been shown to be a mercenary villain who sells his pen to the government against his fellow citizens. Mr Necker has responded with a gravity, a haughtiness, and a disdain that ought to desolate him. The abbé proposes to respond, to say that after having stabbed a man with his sword, he wishes to have the pleasure of trampling the corpse underfoot. The abbé sees things better than all of us. A year from now, nobody will remember the dishonourable deed, and he will enjoy the pension he has been promised.[58]

Diderot appears to concede that this "small and vain consideration" carried "no weight" when set against the interests of commerce and the

---

[56] Diderot in *DPV*, 20:214.

[57] Ibid., 20:215.

[58] Diderot to Volland, quoted in Dena Goodman, *The Republic of Letters*, 226–27. This, and what follows, clearly owes much to Dena Goodman's exhaustive and lively account of the acrimony and critique of acrimony in the Republic of Letters which developed around the abbé Galiani's *Dialogues sur le commerce des blés* (1769) and the "disputatious" reply by his former "best friend," the abbé Morellet in "Into Print: Discord in the Republic of Letters," chapter 5 of her *Republic of Letters*.

shareholders. The "beautiful guarantee" of the ministry rested only on the manoeuvres of "administrators eager to maintain the Company's credit" by way of a "dissimulation." As a result, shareholders "received larger dividends than was their due." The restitution of this excess could legitimately be demanded. What is more, the "commentator" then alleges that "the Comptroller General (Maynon d'Invau) is at the bottom of the bag" and that "the goal of this entire manoeuvre is to relieve the State of the assistance the King granted the Company."[59]

Neither the abbé nor Gournay, Diderot next claims, called for the company's dissolution.[60] Rather, "[L]et her last if she can last" by drawing the greatest advantage from existing settlements, by earning the confidence of the private interests (*particuliers*), and by having these private interests pay for its care and needs through a steady interest on their commerce.[61] Both "Morellet" and "Gournay" agreed, but for one last and essential condition: that no exclusive exist and that every Frenchman be allowed to spread productions along the shores of India, to "penetrate" its lands, "money in hand," and to order works and to load his ship with them. This the company had "no right to refuse," especially since several examples of success in this domain existed both before and during the company's "reign."[62]

In a second dialogue, a speaker voices attacks on Morellet, and a second replies in a more muted and measured defence. Whereas the first questions Morellet's "calculation," the second replies that "he could only calculate based on the figures he was provided." The first suggests that the abbé's chosen time frame overrepresented the period after the war, when the company's losses were greater, and the second answers soberly, "[T]his is something to examine." Finally, the first character persists in claiming that the "defenders of the Company were given too little time to respond," obtaining here the acquiescence of the second: "[T]hat is not good." It had happened even "against the opinion of the Abbé," one of the more violent apologists for the liberty of the press.[63] The essay ends with a final cheeky remark: "[A]midst all of this, one could not refuse the advantage Morellet gained from having been attacked by the Count

[59] Ibid., 20:216.

[60] This claim that neither Gournay nor Morellet were of the opinion that the company should be dissolved contradicts a later statement by Diderot that the count of Lauraguais and Morellet believed that the company's dissolution was "necessary." Diderot in *DPV*, 20:218.

[61] Ibid., 20:216–17.

[62] Ibid., 217.

[63] Diderot in *DPV*, 20:218.

of Lauraguais." Louis-Léon-Félicité de Brancas, the count of Lauraguais (1733–1824), a well-known playwright and socialite, had published an essay on the company in early 1769.[64] An early contributor to the burgeoning polemic, Lauraguais had not so much disagreed with the arguments against the exclusive privilege as he took issue with certain premises in Morellet's *Mémoire,* in particular the central claim that the company should be dissolved.

Diderot turned to Lauraguais's *Mémoire* next, spelling out these premises: The count objected to the assertions that the king owed a great deal to the company in import and export subsidies (*les droits de tonneau*), that administrators profited from "illegitimate gain," and that it was an advantage for the ministry to be able to arm the company's vessels for war, an advantage the government could not have with merchant vessels.[65] Expressing an as yet uncommon perspective, Lauraguais suggested that if the "competition from the nations of Europe" had "diminished the benefits" of the commerce from India, "competition between individuals must produce the same effect." The influence of other European nations also came to bear on another rebuttal: Lauraguais claimed that, given the Dutch and the English "wish" to see the dissolution of the French company, it was unfortunate that the project was "pleasing to our enemies."[66] Ultimately, Diderot reported, the count finished by mocking the "laughable" Morellet, who postured as the "author" of his report when he clearly was serving as the voice for others.[67]

All of this leads Diderot to conclude of these duellers that a "fool" can "hold forth well" and that a "modest man" can "go out of character"; a "great lord" can "insult an individual" and that all that is left for this individual to do is to "shut up."[68] This drawing of the problem into the realm of psychological motivations and attributes hints at Diderot's later conclusion that the situation of the company ought not be considered separately from broader concerns or without attention to human factors. The economic arrangements of the company did not exist in isolation

---

[64] See L. L. F. Lauraguais, *Mémoire sur la Compagnie des Indes, précédé d'un discours sur le commerce en général* (Paris: Lacombe, 1769). Louis-Léon-Félicité, count of Lauraguais and later duke of Brancas, was famously saved during the Terror by "Gracchus" Babeuf, who told revolutionaries sacking his castle that he was a good noble. He eventually became a member of the Club des Cordeliers.

[65] See Diderot in *DPV,* 20:218n21.

[66] Ibid., 20:219.

[67] Ibid. "D'ou il conclut que l'Abbé Morellet fait rire, quand il dit, j'entreprends, j'établis, j'avance, je crie, je décide, je combats, je dissipe, je renverse."

[68] Ibid.

from the political space in which it was situated. The injunction also extended, as we have seen, to his understanding of political economy in general.

In his third contribution to the dossier, Diderot composed a commentary on a shareholders' meeting that occurred immediately after Lauraguais published his letter to Morellet. We do not know the source of Diderot's information. The commentary resembles a report and was possibly destined for the abbé Galiani, whom Diderot would defend against Morellet's harsh "refutation" of the Neapolitan's *Dialogues sur le commerce des blés*, also published in 1769.[69] Diderot wrote that Necker had sought to depict Morellet as ignorant of commerce, accusing him of making "considerable errors" in his calculations and of delivering his comments on the administration of the company in "bad faith." Subsequently Necker proposed various measures through which the company could be saved. In a gesture Diderot deemed "mortifying" for the abbé Morellet, Controller-General d'Invau, who it was widely presumed had commissioned Morellet to write the refutation, announced that he would have Necker's two speeches published by the Royal Printer. D'Invau proceeded to read from a letter by which he sought to "disabuse" people from "calumny" against the company. He claimed that he had neither asked Morellet to attack the company nor forbidden the company to defend itself.[70] A vote was then held, and "not a single arm was raised" in favour of the company's dissolution, in Diderot's account. Diderot's essay ends with the following prediction: "[I]t appears that the Company will subsist."[71]

The "great risk," our *philosophe* warned in his fourth essay, was that the affair would end in *libelles* that would amuse the "idle" and lead the public to miss the substance of this "very important affair." Necker's defence of the company turned on an argument about the benefits the company brought to the state. As Diderot reported, Necker allowed that exclusive trading privileges could be regarded as generally "harmful." But "when the State is at a loss for resources," however, the privilege was the "sole means of encouragement and reward."[72] To bolster his argument, Necker asked rhetorically: "[I]f, as you claim, all 'exclusives' violate social laws [*droit de la société*], why are there exclusives among those people

[69] Galiani's *Dialogues*, Morellet's *Réfutation de l'ouvrage qui a pour titre "Dialogues sur le commerce des blés."*
[70] Ibid., 20:220.
[71] Ibid.
[72] Ibid., 20:221.

most jealous [*jaloux*] of liberty?"[73] As in Lauraguais's earlier letter, the reference was to the English and Dutch use of exclusive privileges for their trading companies (as well as to their now famous love of liberty, which even Necker conceded here).

In retort to Morellet's charge that the company was formed "for the advantage of a few individuals," Necker maintained that, to the contrary, it had been created "for the utility and general designs of the State." Indeed, it was managed by the king's commissioners and the directors were named by the ministry. He contended further that the abbé's calculations were misguided: Not only did his figures prove nothing, but the data had been selected from a year in which sales were low due to external circumstances.[74] Necker insisted that the "sovereign power" had "always profited" from the company's trade. "Look, reader," he prods, "notice the multitude of establishments [they helped create]." Among other things, the company provided employment for four thousand sailors, a consideration no public figure could ignore. Turning to a more rhetorical line of question, Necker – as penned by Diderot – asks how the enemies of the company could intend to "reverse the fortune of an infinite number of co-citizens?" They had a right to property, was the reply, and to the common good.

Who, Necker asks further, possessed "more legitimacy" than the shareholders? What authority could "rob them" (*les dépouiller*), other than a tyrant? In an attack on the theory of general good then prevalent in "enlightened" thought in France, Necker defended the conservative position of his king. He then launched a vicious attack on the very basis of Morellet's brief. Calling Morellet's arithmetic "laughable," he accuses the abbé not only of bad calculation but of bad faith – unforgivable given that the stakes were the "ruin" of "co-citizens" and their "starvation." No "house of commerce" could defend its capital against Morellet's arithmetic. Morellet's "system of retroactive inquisition is as unjust as it is odious," he claims, and the abbé was "either very hard or very little informed about our rights and our woes." Touching on several of the main philosophical debates of the period, Necker asks: Do you know what type of battle has been raised among us? In his view, it was that

---

[73] The language of jealousy, and other anthropomorphisations of the state, circulated widely in the period. David Hume is remembered for coining the phrase "jealousy of trade," but it was employed quite currently in many languages. See Istvan Hont, *Jealousy of Trade: International Competition and the Nation-State in Historical Perspective* (Cambridge, MA: Harvard University Press, 2005).

[74] Ibid., 20:222.

of "theory against experience" and "possibility against facts." Whereas "good philosophy" might consist in less disdain for ideas of the day in affairs of interest, what followed was praise for the values of experience. He argued that commercial houses were not formed in "the blink of an eye," nor could obstacles be removed by a "quill mark on paper."

In his analysis of Necker's speech Diderot concluded that Necker's "principles and facts" were clearly indicated in his brief (*mémoire*) and that with more reflection Necker believed that the abbé's "vanity" had led him into an "affair" whose most harmful repercussion would be the "end of a friendship."[75] Necker's reply did not "annihilate" Morellet, but rather, Diderot conceded, left "one hundred" possibilities for rebuttal. Diderot here displays the ambivalence we have been detecting in the discourse of commerce, with his positions in favour of Necker's policy following his arguments against him.

By the time the company was suspended, the abbé had become, according to Diderot, the "object of public indignation." Diderot concurred, calling Morellet "Alcibiades' dog."[76] According to Plutarch, Alcibiades had the tail of a magnificent dog cut, saying, "I want the Athenians to chat about this, so that they say nothing of me."[77] Thus, in Diderot's account, d'Invau had unleashed the abbé on the town "with his tail cut" to distract the public from "the atrocity he was poised to commit." Morellet succeeded, Diderot concluded, for "the abbé is more talked about than the Company and next to nothing is said about d'Invau."

It was at this juncture that Diderot saw fit to provide his own reasoning about the lot of the shareholders in a fifth and final essay. Both the past and present administrations of the company were known to be "vicious," he began. Necker had failed to realise one central contradiction: He could not expect to borrow based on confidence in the company. In order for confidence to be established and for credit to be granted, the company's "vices" had to be demonstrated and destroyed. Here Diderot echoed the views of his newfound colleague, the abbé Raynal, who argued the same in the *Histoire*.[78]

Assuming the position and voice of the shareholder, Diderot again displayed his ambivalence when he contradicted his favourable portrait of Necker by dismantling Necker's proposals, of which the first was to

[75] Ibid., 226. Many contemporaries went so far as to imagine that the two had staged the dispute.
[76] This is in a folio describing the "Suppression de la Compagnie des Indes." Ibid., 228.
[77] Cited in Ibid., 228n43.
[78] Ibid., 228n44. Cf. *Histoire des Indes*, vol. 2, book 4.

guarantee a loan by mortgaging the pension (*rente*) of eighty *livres tournois*. Diderot had his imagined shareholder respond, "I have been trading for a hundred years and I have won nothing after I risked losing much over a long period. I no longer want to trade. I prefer the condition of the privileged pensioner [*rentier*] and mortgage holder [*hypothècaire*]."[79] The second proposal was to create a kind of mutual fund drawing on 600 *livres tournois* per share, to which Diderot's shareholder replied, "I do not want to be a banker.... I am tired of running risks. I hold to my invariable pension of eighty *livres tournois* and to the maturity of the life annuities [*rentes viagères*] that would increase it." No doubt, Diderot imagined, Morellet would reply by issuing a threat to reduce the shareholders' pensions. To this, the shareholder would reply in turn, "How, in spite of registered edicts ... ? There is therefore nothing certain with this government."

The final sections of the piece stated that "everything is in the air," and the *Parlement* now had taken an interest and even summoned the company's directors and syndics. As for the abbé, Diderot predicted any reply would make him appear to be the "man who punched another, and who seeks again the pleasure of jumping on his corpse." His awkward boldness and the "cackling" of people around him would not trouble Morellet, Diderot predicted, for in six months he would enjoy his pension peacefully. In the final analysis, however, Diderot's overwhelming impression was that all "honest people" were "stupid."

When Morellet's reply to Necker appeared, Diderot swung back again and noted that his tone had greatly changed, becoming more "honest and moderate" and showing "good faith" regardless of whether he was correct. Although every one of his responses to Necker was filled with "nerve, logic and precision," Diderot had four arguments with the abbé. In the first, Diderot revealed that Morellet had neglected to mention that the king ensured that the company could not claim any indemnities but the king, in turn, could not claim any restitution. Against this synallagmatic agreement, Morellet opposed the contract that held reciprocal obligations to both parties and put forth the law that selling for less than fair value more than once would be grounds for breaking a contract.[80] In Diderot's view this "law of lesion" could not apply when the price was a function of one's industry; moreover, it did not become a king to deal with his subject as an apprentice to his master, except when the subject was in a losing situation.

79 Dulac, "Introduction au 'Dossier de la Compagnie des Indes,'" 20:229.
80 Ibid., 232n54.

In the second argument, Diderot found it ironic that a "defender of liberty" would so easily grant a master the right to rob the company of its privilege and to impose the necessity of keeping its settlements. It was at this stage that Diderot reintroduced the figure of the company shareholder, whom he had converse with a fictional Morellet. The shareholder protested: "I no longer want to trade. I do not care about these settlements. My most pressing goal at the moment is to recover my funds … !" The abbé responded that these settlements were useful to national commerce. Here, Diderot's shareholder reminded Morellet that he himself had called it "absurd" to demand that a merchant "sacrifice his individual interest for the general interest." The shareholder not only accused the abbé of being incoherent, he also chided him for his "tyrannical threats."

Third, Diderot suggested that Morellet was "too severe" about the company's expenses at Pondicherry; instead, Diderot defended the company, stating that these expenses had in fact been demanded by the king's commissioners. The shareholder reiterated: "We have sacrificed our management for you and you then drew on the bad state to which you reduced us in order to justify annihilating us."[81] Again, the timing of the attack was brought to the fore: The shareholder argued that the abbé chose the moment when the shareholders had "little hope of recovering our losses."

In the fourth and final comment, Diderot expressed uncertainty about the abbé's suggestion that the expenses of sovereignty should be removed from the company and redirected to the state. In his view, the "faithful and loyal" servants of the king would also clearly be prone to "unlimited pillage." Finally, Diderot responded to the question: "Is private commerce with the Indies possible or is it not?" Would this private commerce create "a greater advantage for all citizens," he continued, than commerce restricted to a single company? Yet again, his reply to his own question revealed ambivalence about the problem. Finding this question ultimately "too complicated" for anyone to resolve, Diderot offered that he saw no harm in letting the company subsist as a "pure and simple association of merchants" whose vessels would have no right to distance "mine and yours from the shores of India."

What should we make of Diderot's apparent duplicity in these five accounts? In the summer of 1769, two of Diderot's fables on "evidence" appeared in the Physiocratic journal, the *Éphémérides du citoyen*. Whereas

[81] Ibid., 232.

these fables expressed a deep sympathy for the *économistes*, Diderot simultaneously repudiated their abstract dogmatism in his defence of Galiani.[82] In addition, Diderot began to carve out an explicit argument about the necessity of incorporating broader perspectives and less certainty when approaching important economic issues. Here he made an implicit claim that an understanding of internal politics and personalities could lead to a better understanding of the problem. He held to the view that the economy and the polity were interdependent. In Diderot's first foray into the issues surrounding the liberty of commerce, he broadened the concept of monopoly to include the dangerous connection between privilege and trade. These issues would come to the fore in the *Histoire*'s account.

The dossier ended with a call for the "dear Neapolitan's" views, in reference to the abbé Galiani, he who had once been Morellet's dearest friend. Only Necker, Diderot suggested, could shed light on the several issues that the abbé and Morellet "left intact," such as the "true value of an Indian manufacturer's day"; whether "this trade, where a large part of our money would be lost without resource, is necessary for us"; and whether "in India where the people are exposed in every instant to the tyranny's threaten of cutting the cords on their trade, it is possible to have people work without having a territory and the authority of a Protector and Sovereign."[83] The abbé Galiani would indeed pronounce on the problem of monopoly, as Diderot had hoped, but he would do so by focusing on the problems of the internal grain trade in France. Here we appear to come full circle. By invoking Galiani, Diderot reminds the reader of the connection between exclusive commerce with that of grain within France's boundaries.

CONDORCET: MONOPOLY AND THE MONOPOLIST

Shortly after Diderot completed his dossier on the "affair of the Company of the Indies," the *guerre des farines* came to a head. France suffered a poor harvest in 1774, which raised grain prices dramatically. Searching for a way out of the state's growing financial and economic troubles, the monarchy took a risk and named a new comptroller general: Anne Robert Jacques Turgot (1727–81), former intendant of Limoges and a

---

[82] Ibid., 181. Dulac has even suggested that we might imagine Diderot "trying these ideas and the different persona on for size." Ibid., 184.

[83] Ibid., 233–34.

philosophe known as a partisan of the *économistes*, if an unorthodox one. Turgot took up the liberalising torch of the mid-1760s and immediately issued another edict freeing the grain trade on 13 September 1774. In the same period, he released Morellet's refutation of Galiani's *Dialogues*. This provoked his rival, Necker, to prolong the public dispute with a critique of liberalisation, the *Essai sur la législation et le commerce des grains* (1775). The connection between commerce and privilege was raised yet again in 1775 in an essay entitled "Monopole et monopoleur," by mathematician and academician Jean-Antoine Nicolas de Caritat, marquis de Condorcet (1743–94).[84] A loyal friend of Turgot's, Condorcet in turn refuted Necker's work in a satiric "Letter by a farmer in Picardy, to Mr N***" ("Lettre d'un laboureur de Picardie, à M. N***") (1775), later adding an essay in the same vein, on "Monopoly and the monopolist," to the Supplement to the *Encyclopédie*.[85]

This essay, which also circulated as a pamphlet in 1775, provided a variation on the prevailing definition of monopoly: "the exclusive sale of a commodity done either by a single man or a company." Condorcet added a caveat and a distinction. First, monopoly exists when a "certain class of men" or a number of vendors smaller than would have existed "in the case of a perfectly free circulation" controls the sale of a good. Condorcet warned against confusing two kinds of monopoly: monopoly by right and monopoly of fact. The law established monopoly by right, such as the exclusive sale of salt and tobacco by the tax collection agencies, the General Farms (Fermiers Généraux). But the corps, or guilds of merchants, the masters, and so forth, were also monopolies, "because all of these establishments tend to diminish the number of vendors, the ease of sale, and in consequence augment the price of commodities."[86] Condorcet's amalgamation of the legal and practical forms of exclusive sale within the same conceptual category of "monopoly" reflected a conceptual transformation that would be fully completed by the *Histoire*, which incorporated the exclusive rights for export that structured colonial trade within the category as well.

Condorcet continued by arguing that exclusive sales for government profit were a "form of indirect taxation" arising from "the weakness, the

---

[84] On Condorcet, see Keith Michael Baker, *Condorcet: from Natural Philosophy to Social Mathematics* (Chicago: University of Chicago Press, 1975). On Condorcet's economic thought, see Emma Rothschild, *Economic Sentiments*.

[85] See Louis-François Métra, *Corrrespondance secrète, politique & littéraire, ou mémoires pour servir à l'histoire des cours* ... (London: John Adamson, 1787), 2:53.

[86] Ibid., 37–38.

corruption and the ignorance of the legislative power." This last point comprised the crux of his argument. By imposing a tax on "the people" for goods they could not live without, such as salt, but also on "artificial needs" (*besoins factices*) consumed primarily by the people, such as tobacco, the government engaged in what Condorcet rather dramatically called the "sublime art of finance," that is, "taxing those who have nothing." The crux of the essay relates a similar view concerning the monopoly over grain, emphasising that "all regulations, all constraint" were an "affront on the property and the liberty of citizens." For Condorcet, the "absurd and oppressive" laws on the commerce of grain were a product not only of "avidity" and "bad reasoning" but also of fear of popular uprisings.[87] Again, Condorcet minced no words to express his contempt: "Fear is at the origin of nearly all human foolishness, and especially political foolishness."[88]

The essay focused mainly on the problem of monopolies in France. Condorcet ended, however, by referring to monopolies in foreign trade. But his subject was the Dutch, not the French. In reference to the Dutch government's monopoly over the spice trade, he remarked that landowners in the Spice Islands "know how onerous this monopoly is."[89] Condorcet then advised the "nations of Europe" to garner the "courage and will" to "remove themselves" from the "tribute" imposed by Holland. Although the Dutch believed this "exclusive and tyrannical commerce" to be the source of their greatness, Condorcet warned, "They will soon cease to believe it."[90]

The entry for *monopolist* (*monopoleur*) that followed synthesised both the tone and content of the article while raising the stakes. A monopolist, Condorcet explained, is "a man who acts or writes against the liberty of commerce." By this definition, even advocates of monopolies were deemed monopolists. Condorcet then revived the sarcasm with which the essay began: "We must not hang these people; and capital punishment for this kind of crime must be ridiculous."[91] This final nod to the existence of monopolies and monopolists in France's international trading system was no more than that – a nod. Not until 1780, when the third version of the *Histoire des deux Indes* appeared, did a comprehensive, politicised synthesis of these two domains emerge.

[87] Ibid., 55.
[88] Ibid., 54.
[89] Ibid., 57.
[90] Ibid.
[91] Ibid., 58.

MONOPOLY IN THE *HISTOIRE*

As we have seen, the *Histoire* was compiled in the wake of the affair of the French Company of the Indies in 1769. Indeed, book 4 of the *Histoire* is devoted to French trade and settlements in the East Indies and includes the question of the viability of the Company of the Indies, even though no international trading company existed from 1769 to 1785, the span of the *Histoire*'s publishing history.[92] Although the Exclusif is mentioned, a more significant portion of the ten-volume *Histoire* is devoted to a discussion of monopolies in general, referring mainly but not solely to the monopoly trading companies that governed France's international trade after the Seven Years War.[93] As we shall see, the *Histoire* paired its discussion of international trading companies with a discussion of monopolies of artisans or workers – that is, of the guilds. It treated both with equal disdain, construing them as forms of *commerce odieux*; this thesis is, however, broken up by defences of privilege, which reflect yet again the ambivalence within the discourse.

"May my hand run dry," the abbé Raynal vowed, "if it happens that, through a very common tendency, I would deceive myself and others about my nation's misdeeds."[94] He also promised to "abandon [himself] to the scorn" of the Portuguese, the Dutch, and the English if they found him lacking in "severity" towards the French. With this vow, he embarked upon a general history of commerce in France from the ancient Gauls to the formation of the Company of the Indies in 1664. The first "company of merchants" to whom "great privileges" had been granted was given the name "Nautes" for their trade in the ports of Arles, Narbonne, and Bordeaux.[95] Then a period of enclosure followed, with

---

[92] It was not until 1785 when, under the direction of Controller-General Calonne, the company was refurbished and revived under a new name, Calonne's Company. This moment is significant since it marks the time when Raynal was finally given authorisation to return to France after a five-year exile following the publication of the third edition of the *Histoire* under his name. Raynal had escaped arrest in 1780 by travelling to Liège, Darmstadt, Gotha, Weimar, to Frederick II's court in Berlin, and, finally, to the Prussian enclave of Neuchâtel. The 1785 authorisation for his return included the condition that he not leave the provinces of Languedoc and Provence. That restriction expired in 1791, when the decree of the Paris Parlement was cancelled.

[93] As Tarrade has noted, the *Histoire*'s position on the Exclusif changed over time: Whereas in 1770 Raynal revealed a fear of losing the colonies by opening the ports to foreign vessels, by 1780, in the third version, the work conformed to the views of first clerk of the Bureau des Colonies, Jean-Baptiste Dubucq: "It is time that the prohibitive laws fold under the imperious law of necessity."

[94] *HDI* (1780), book 4, 271–72.

[95] Ibid., 273–74.

most manufacturing occurring in monasteries, until "Dagobert awakened spirits in the seventh century."[96] A true rebirth of commerce reigned under Charlemagne until it was interrupted by Norman pirates. Their ravages lasted a century, a period during which "there was no communication between peoples and consequently no commerce." It was "impossible" for commerce to "prosper under the chains of slavery" and amid the "continuous troubles generated by the cruellest of anarchies."[97] This indictment of the Capetians thus opened a restatement of the *commerce odieux* thesis: "Industry ... fears servitude. Genius expires without hope [and] emulation, and there is no hope nor emulation where there is no property."[98]

It was not until Saint Louis that French kings were able to understand this, according to Raynal. Saint Louis incorporated commerce, which had previously been the "work of chance and circumstance," into the "system of government" and gave it consistent laws and statutes.[99] Barriers to the transport of commodities outside of the kingdom were "struck down" by this "wise monarch." It would seem that Raynal had transformed Saint Louis into the founder of free trade in France. Yet he next praised Philippe le Bel for introducing privileges that attracted commerce to Nismes from Montpellier. The ministry first developed a growing role in "guiding the hand of the artist and directing works" in this period. This remained for the abbé a "century of ignorance" because of the way in which the ministry fixed the size, quality, and dressing of cloth, as well as prohibiting the export of woollens.[100]

With Catherine de Medici's crossing the Alps, the entire nation was taken by "seductive luxury," such that manufacturing industries had to improve to meet newly created wants.[101] The wars of religion, the government's "ignorance," and a "spirit of finance" (with a focus on banking) slowed the progress of industry from the reign of Henri II to that of Henri IV. The pendulum swung twice again: towards commercial "brilliance" under Sully to "near annihilation" under Richelieu and Mazarin.[102] It was at this moment in history and in the *Histoire* that Raynal introduced the story of France's commerce with India.

[96] Ibid., 275–76.
[97] Ibid., 278.
[98] Ibid., 279.
[99] Ibid., 280.
[100] Ibid., 282.
[101] Ibid., 283.
[102] Ibid., 284.

The story begins with the unsuccessful voyage to India of a few Rouen merchants in 1503 and details further failed voyages in 1601, 1616, and 1619. Not until 1633 did a certain Captain "Reginon" hire several merchants in Dieppe and return to France with goods and a "high opinion" of Madagascar.[103] Conspicuous by its absence is any reference in the *Histoire* to the creation of the Compagnie française in 1604. Instead, the narrative jumps to the 1642 concession granted to the Maréchal de la Meilleraie for the creation of a new company, which ended "in disaster," despite de la Meilleraie's efforts.[104] All of these individual merchants, then, by Raynal's account, failed in their attempts to trade with India. "Finally," Raynal explained, Colbert undertook to "give the commerce of the Indies to France" in 1664.

This decision to connect "Asia" with "France" posed several disadvantages, according to Raynal. In the first instance, it meant that only luxury objects could be procured. Second, this search slowed the progress of the "arts" that had been "happily" established: It did not offer any prospects for French commodities. Finally, it would result in the export of a large amount of metals. Raynal suggested the trade with India was powered by French vanity and pride. The French, according to Raynal, followed the example of the "other peoples of Europe" and demonstrated a "pronounced taste" for the "excesses of the Orient." In addition, they believed it "more useful, more honourable, even" to go and fetch these objects from across the ocean rather than receive them from their "rivals."[105]

Raynal concluded that at this time, an "exclusive privilege" alone could carry such "delicate and complicated operations." But Colbert did not stop with creating companies in the style of the Dutch and the English; he "went further" out of fear that "big commercial businesses" have more confidence in republics than in monarchies. Thus, the exclusive privilege was granted for fifty years, and the state was to pay fifty francs per tonne of merchandise brought to India from France and sixty-

---

[103] Ibid., 285.

[104] Ibid., 286. In fact, Charles de La Porte, maréchal (and later duc) de la Meilleraye (1602–64), a reputed general, was granted the concession for the Île Dauphine (Madagascar) in 1655 by Mazarin, receiving cargo from it until his death in 1664, when Louis XIV joined the concession for the Île Dauphine to that of the new Compagnie des Indes. See Gabriel Marcel, *Mémoire inédit de Grossin sur le Madagascar* (Paris: Institut géographique de Paris, chez Delagrave, 1883), 20. From a renowned Breton family, Jean Eon (1618–81) dedicated his 1646 treatise, *Le Commerce honorable*, to la Meilleraye. Henry C. Clark, *Compass of Society: Commerce and Absolutism in Old Regime France* (Lanham, MD: Lexington, 2007), 66.

[105] Ibid., 287.

five livres per tonne for merchandise that would return. Also, the state committed itself to offering military support for the company's establishments and to escorting its convoys as needed.[106] It promised honours and hereditary titles to all who would "distinguish themselves in the service of the Company." The company soon fascinated the nation and indeed became its "dominant passion." Since "commerce was only just being born in France," it was out of the question that the state alone subsidise the company. The government was able to loan only three million for the company's fund, and all of the "grands, magistrates, citizens of every order" were "invited" to contribute the rest. The "nation" answered the call with "extreme enthusiasm."[107]

The *Histoire* then shifted to the advent of John Law and the consequences of his *Système*, including the merging of a new Compagnie d'Occident with the former privileged companies. It was at this moment that the government accorded the company the sole right to sell tobacco.[108] The *Système*'s failure led to total "confusion and chaos," which fed the ever-increasing bankruptcies and left a deficit in the state's treasury at the time of Louis XV's death.[109]

The narrative then abruptly shifted registers; what followed was a lengthy but feisty exhortation to Louis XVI, addressed, quite subversively, with the familiar *tu*. We know that this section was Diderot's. With this apostrophe, Diderot sustained his efforts to engage the reader who was also, in effect, interpolated by the informal and singular second person. A tirade of several pages implored the "young Sovereign" to recognise "what is gold, what is blood in comparison to honour!" In this post-Seven Years War argument, the *Histoire* stated that the "forces and treasures of the nation" had for too long been given to "interests that were foreign and perhaps opposed to our own."[110] There was a very sentimental plea for the king to recognise the "two classes of citizens" in his empire – the first "gorged with riches, spreading luxury," the second "plunged into indigence" – and to take action against their inequality. Not only did Raynal call for a "return to primitive liberty," the "respectable enterprise of the first acts of natural justice," but forebodingly, he also demanded the "assembly of all the Estates of the great nation."[111]

[106] Ibid., 288–89.
[107] Ibid., 289.
[108] Ibid., book 4, chap. 12, 399.
[109] Ibid., 407.
[110] Ibid., 409.
[111] Ibid., 418.

When the narrative returned to the fall of Law's *Système*, the reader learned that at that time the government had abandoned its tobacco monopoly to the company. In return for the loan, the state granted the company an exclusive privilege on all the lotteries in the kingdom and allowed it to convert some of its shares into annuities.[112] "Unfortunately," Raynal wrote, the company had also preserved the privileges from the other companies from which it had been formed, leaving it with a prerogative that gave it "neither power nor wisdom." These privileges authorised "odious monopolies" and led the company to "burden the Negro trade" and "stop progress in the sugar colonies." Here, Raynal stood in clear contradiction to the primary thrust of book 11, the central book concerned with the trade in African slaves, by speaking of the trade in slaves as one burdened by monopolies. What is more, the narrative continued, the newly constituted company neglected to populate or cultivate the most fertile countries of the earth, and it became "entrapped" by a "spirit of finance," one that "narrows views" in the same way that the "spirit of commerce widens them." The company had evolved into "a society of collectors [*fermiers-généraux*] rather than of traders [*négocians*]."[113] This marked the beginning of the company's perversion, which the *Histoire* traced through the rest of its narrative.

By 15 January 1761, the growing, impressive, and oppressive presence of the French on the Indian subcontinent had come to an end. The French squadron finally capitulated before the English navy, but Lally, the French commander, sent a note to the English general to inform him that he did not want to surrender "because the English were not people to keep [their word]."[114] When the English took possession of Pondicherry, they not only destroyed and burned the town but sent all of the defending troops and all of the French attached to the company's service away. The outcries of the deported led to Lally's arrest and eventual beheading on the charge of betraying "the King's interests, estate and the Company of the Indies."[115] To Raynal, the punishment seemed excessive and the charge obscure. "What does it mean to betray interests?" he asked. This "vague

---

[112] Ibid., 419.

[113] The *fermiers*, or *fermiers généraux*, collected taxes on behalf of the king. They took a share, and for that reason their office was much coveted. See Mousnier, *Institutions of France*, chap. 7. See also Bély, *Dictionnaire de l'Ancien régime*.

[114] "[A]uquel il marquoit qu'il ne vouloit point capitulation, parce que les anglois étaient gens à ne pas la tenir." *HDI* (1780), book 4, chap. 23, 477.

[115] Ibid., 478. Thomas Arthur comte de Lally-Tollendal (1702–66) appears to have been taken to England as a prisoner of war before his return to France, as the title of a "memoir" he authored while there attests. See Thomas Arthur comte de Lally-Tollendal,

and undefined" crime was listed under no law, he protested. Yet the affair "tormented" citizens, for Lally was also justly accused of "vexations, extortions, [and] abuses of authority."

The French "disgrace" in Asia was predictable to all observers, Raynal argued.[116] The nation had been "corrupted" and its *moeurs* "degenerated" in the "voluptuous climate of the Indies." Prices were grossly inflated, the quality of goods diminished, and people's fortunes bloated. By way of its "blindness or by its weakness," the government ignored these excesses, becoming an accomplice in "the ruin of the nation's affairs in India."[117] Indeed, Raynal now argued that the government could justly be accused of having been the "principal cause" of this ruin because of the "weak or disloyal" instruments it employed to run and defend an important colony.

But the company was not only weakened by corruption: It had been foiled in Europe as well. This "double" portrait had to be drawn for the shareholder.[118] The "storms" this information caused soon calmed, and the enemies of the exclusive privilege who sought the company's abolishment opened their hearts to "hope" and reform. Thus, in 1730, reforms allowed greater freedom in deliberations and in relationships between administrators and owners, and they severed the immediate connection between the administrators and the government. This attempt at reform failed, however. In 1764, shareholders asked again that the company be "given its liberty" and returned to "its essence."[119] "Great activity" ensued for five years, with sales rising annually to eighteen million livres from around fourteen million annually from 1726 to 1756. According to the account books, however, these apparent successes barely covered several "abysses," for the company was "more indebted than was believed," and, following several "harmful errors," "miscalculations," and "late payments," the government asked for a report on its situation.[120] When

Memoirs of Count Lally from his embarking for the East Indies, as commander in chief of the French forces in that country, to his being sent prisoner of war to England, after the surrender of Pondichery, consisting of pieces written by himself and addressed to his judges in answer to the charges brought against him by the attorney general of his M. C. M. . . . to which are added accounts of the prior part of his life, his condemnation and execution. (No translator specified). (London: F. Newbery, 1766). Raynal seems to have quoted directly from the court's verdict dated 6 May 1766, available at the BNF: Factum (Affaire). Cf. France, *Arrêt qui prive de Lally.*

[116] *HDI* (1780), book 4, chap. 24, 480.
[117] Ibid., 482.
[118] Ibid., book 4, chap. 25, 483.
[119] Ibid., 485.
[120] Ibid., 488–90.

the company appeared not to know its own financial status, Raynal recounted, the government "judged that it had to suspend the exclusive privilege for commerce with the Indies."

Although the company was unable to provide an account of its state of affairs, Raynal next proposed to do just that for the reader. In his discussion of the changing value of the company's dividends and shares, he was careful to note that these were "necessarily subject to the risks of commerce and the flux and reflux of public opinion."[121] The company had possessed many assets, both moveable and fixed, including privileges for the exclusive trade in tobacco, coffee, and the transportation of slaves to the American colonies. These were all revoked, the first in 1747 and the last two in 1767. A few sources of revenue were kept intact, such as the company's exclusive privilege to trade in the isles of France and Bourbon, though the government had taken over the obligation to fortify and defend these territories in 1764.[122]

As Raynal told it, the story of the company was one of failed opportunities. Even with "so many apparent means for prosperity," the company became more indebted every day and could no longer subsist if not for the government's assistance. Passing over the polemic to which Diderot had devoted so much energy, Raynal stated simply that Louis XV seemed "indifferent" to the "existence of this great corps." With his ruling on 13 August 1769, the king not only suspended the exclusive privilege of the Company of the Indies but, Raynal noted, he had granted "all of his subjects the liberty to sale and trade beyond the Cape of Good Hope." Still, this liberty was not unlimited. Private ship owners were now subject to different conditions: They still required passports from the administrators of the Company of the Indies, they were obligated to make Lorient their only port of return, and an entry tax was posed on all merchandise coming from the Indies. Though the ruling of 13 August seemed to grant shareholders the right to take control of the company once again, they chose instead to liquidate, a move Raynal deemed wise.[123]

Describing the various negotiations with the king that determined a value for the shares and the debts of the shareholders," the abbé concluded, "[I]t is difficult based on these details to get a precise idea of the Company's actual state of being." Indeed. This concession on the part of Raynal must have been in some way ironic, even if it did echo Diderot's

---

[121] Ibid., book 4, chap. 26, 492.
[122] Ibid., 502.
[123] Ibid., 504.

final conclusion that the affair was too "complicated." But as the abbé noted, the company had the potential to be reconstituted yet again, for it had not been "absolutely destroyed." The possibility of rebirth remained alive, given that shareholders reserved in common the mortgage capital for their shares, maintained a private bank and deputies to care for their interests, and kept the power to grant vessels permission to sail to India for commerce. This proved to Raynal that the liberty of commerce granted to private individuals in 1769 was a "precarious" one. As for the company's chances for resuscitation, the abbé judged them poor, due not only to the shareholders' "impotence" in enforcing their right to grant permissions but also to the fact that "all of their other rights, properties, trading posts have passed into the hands of the government."[124]

In the end, the abbé recounted, navigation to India continued, even if policy had not prepared in advance the course for the free commerce meant to replace the exclusive privilege. Undertaken without any preparation and with "faulty forethought," this abrupt transition not only made free commerce difficult, it stopped it from being "lucrative once it had spread." The abbé bemoaned that a more incremental approach had not been taken, whereby the company's private traders would have been "substituted, indiscernibly and by degrees." These traders ought to have been allowed to acquire "positive knowledge about the different branches of a commerce heretofore unknown to them." They needed time to "build relationships" in the trading posts, and they needed careful guidance and supervision for their "first expeditions." These operations were undertaken in the trading posts once occupied by the monopoly, Raynal reflected.[125]

Up to this point, the *Histoire* had focused on commerce and privilege. The first explicit discussion of monopoly in the work is not found until the account of the Dutch presence in Goa and Java. We learn that the Dutch East India Company was granted an "exclusive privilege" that included the Magellan Straits. Isaac Lemaire, "one of those rich and entrepreneurial traders [*négociants*]" whom, the *Histoire* instructs, "we should all regard as the benefactors of their fatherland," is then introduced.[126] Lemaire conceived the idea to enter the South Sea by way

---

[124] Ibid., 509.
[125] Ibid.
[126] Le Maire, a disgruntled shareholder of the VOC, organised the first episode in history of futures trading on its stock. See Jan de Vries and A. M. Van der Woude, *The First Modern Economy: Success, Failure, and Perseverance of the Dutch Economy, 1500–1885* (Cambridge: Cambridge University Press, 1997), 151, and J. G. Van Dillen,

of the lands of the south because the only known path was prohibited. He sent two ships that were eventually confiscated in Java, their mariners sent to Europe as prisoners.[127] The commentary began: "[T]his act of tyranny disgusted those minds already warned against all exclusive commerce." It "appeared absurd" that a state that was "purely commercial" would "shackle" industry instead of offering the incentives deserved by those who "attempt discoveries."

The *Histoire* here equated monopoly with exclusive commerce and exclusive privileges. Thus, monopoly, the product of "the greed of individuals," became more odious when the company extended its concessions beyond what had been granted. Here, the *Histoire* attributed human characteristics to the monopoly company, literally anthropomorphising the corporation. Its pride increased with its power and credit, until it seemed possible the national interest would fall sacrifice to "this body [*corps*]" which had its own interests, "fantasies," and "whims." The company might have "succumbed to public hatred" and lost its privilege when it expired.[128] So we immediately understand that the *Histoire*'s attitude towards monopoly was a moral one and that it apparently had the support of the populace.

The *Histoire* presented a similar perspective on monopoly in its discussion of how the English could take the Cape of Good Hope from the Dutch in an effort to prevent the Dutch from resupplying their colonies in the Indies.[129] The English would be able to reap "enormous advantages" from a conquest of the Cape if only, the *Histoire* argued, people "could detach themselves from this spirit of monopoly." The monopolistic spirit, the text emphasised, was one against which "humanity and reason have forever cried-out."

The same condemnatory tone pervaded a discussion of the "bizarre laws" and prohibitions passed by Henry VIII to restrict and define the company of traders established in London.[130] These laws regulated prices on various commodities, limited workers' salaries, and set interest rates on loans. Even the export of horses was prohibited.[131] Finally,

---

"Isaac le maire et le commerce des actions de la compagnie des indes orientales" *Revue d'histoire moderne* 10, no.16 (1935): 5–21.

[127] *HDI* (1780), book 2, 420.

[128] Ibid.

[129] Ibid., 230.

[130] Ibid., book 3, 11.

[131] Ibid., 10. According to the *Histoire*, they were "not enlightened enough to see that this prohibition would lead to the neglect of both the multiplication and the improvement of the species."

"corporations" were established in all of the towns, meaning "[t]he State authorised all those who followed a single profession to make rules that they judged useful for their exclusive prosperity." These forms of exclusivity were called a "type of monopoly" by the *Histoire*, an "arrangement so contrary to universal industry" that the "nation [continues to] tremble."[132]

Here, we find the first of several examples in which the authors of the *Histoire*, acting as spokespersons for "reason" and "humanity," equated state control over local industries with monopoly. This equivalence broadened the scope of the definition, and consequently the critique of monopoly, to include all forms of apparent restrictions on freedom. In this way, the *Histoire* widened both the content and the stakes of monopoly into the moral and political realm.

As is often the case in the *Histoire*, the reader is then invited to consider an alternative and distant time, or, in this case, a distant place: eighteenth-century Persia and Russia. "Elton," described as an "adventurous and industrious" English merchant, had built an enormous fleet in the Caspian Sea to transport English goods to Persia via Petersburg and the Volga.[133] But his close alliance with a Persian ruler ultimately caused his demise, and as a result, a "jealous Moscovia" revoked all conceded privileges and prohibited English caravans from crossing Russia. This caused the ruin of many investors, including Elton, who was murdered by the jealous Persians after they toppled their ruler. Although the English East India Company had unsuccessfully opposed Elton's scheme, its monopoly ultimately survived because Parliament conceded its privilege in the light of Elton's debacle.[134]

This debacle did not put an end to public animosity towards the English East India Company. Later, we hear again of a "general outcry" against the company.[135] Accused of "weakening the naval forces through a great consumption of men" and "reducing without compensation the expeditions to the East and Russia," the company was exposed to "violent" animosity from the nation. By 1618, fearing these outcries, the company requested that the government examine the nature of its commerce and, if it was found to be contrary to the interest of the state, have Parliament

---

[132] Ibid.

[133] The reference is to Captain John Elton, "the last British merchant in Iran," who died there in 1751. Peter Avery et al., *The Cambridge History of Iran: From Nadir Shah to the Islamic Republic* (Cambridge: Cambridge University Press, 1991), 352.

[134] Ibid., book 5, 147–48.

[135] Ibid., book 3, 46–47.

prohibit it. But if the government found the company's commerce favourable to the state, then "a public declaration" should be made. Time did not soften national opposition; eventually, those "less rigid in their speculations" consented that the commerce of the Indies should exist, but they maintained that "it ought to be opened to the entire nation."

Here we find the English speaking for what appear to be the views of the authors of the *Histoire*: "An exclusive privilege appeared to them as a deliberate attempt on freedom." In the *Histoire*'s summation of English thought, the people established a government to "provide for the general good"; however, this government and the general good were threatened when, by way of "odious monopolies," public interest was sacrificed in favour of private interests. "This principle," deemed "fertile and incontestable" by the *Histoire*, had been strengthened by "recent experience."

The *Histoire* so caged its account of the argument against monopoly. One of its more ambiguous narratives detailed the ways in which the English monopoly trading companies survived the English Civil War and the republican revolution. We learn that Cromwell renewed the monopoly and that this monopoly ultimately gained legitimacy because of its mechanisms of support rather than because it emanated from an absolute royal authority. In the *Histoire*'s view, because the English companies had the support of Parliament, they furthered the interests of all Englishmen and not just the privileged, as in the French case. Indeed, in the early eighteenth century, as the *Histoire* recounted, critics of this exclusive privilege in the Indies argued that "the privilege was null because it was granted by kings who had no power to do so."[136] Thus, the "nation in general" approved of this "project to make commerce free" and to annul the company's privilege at the very least. The *corps*, which is how the *Histoire* often referred to the company, thereby equating it with the institutions of "Old Regime" privilege, opposed this project. A fiery dispute ensued in which a range of "factions" clashed impetuously and "without distinction of rank, age or sex." But despite the strong opposition to the monopoly, both houses of the British Parliament ultimately pronounced in favour of certain individuals allowed to engage solely or collectively in trade with India. They associated to form a new company, and in the end the former company obtained permission to continue until the expiration of its charter.[137]

---

[136] Ibid., 48.
[137] Ibid., 49.

True to form, the *Histoire*'s disparagements of monopoly are accompanied by occasional approbations for it. For example, Raynal explained that England possessed two East India Companies that were authorised by Parliament and stood therefore in contrast to the French company established by royal authority.[138] The suggestion that authorisation by Parliament made the English companies more legitimate is immediately countered, however, by an account of how these two *corps* sought to destroy each other before overcoming their differences to unite their funds in 1702. Only good things came from this merged company, according to the *Histoire*, as it found "happiness" from never having missed any of its engagements and from credits larger than its needs. Finally, its privilege was "less violent," since it had received the "sanction of the laws and obtained the protection of Parliament." The *Histoire* could condone this monopoly because it was the product of a decision made by democratically elected representatives. The means – in this case public authorisation and thereby legitimisation – justified the monopoly. The politics of the decision legitimised the economic entity.

Turning to the New World, a situation developed wherein monopolies failed even as commercial entities, and "monopoly rapidly replaced another monopoly." In the first reference to monopoly in book 15 we learn that none of the settlements in New France prospered because they were ruled by exclusive companies with neither the talent to select the best sites nor sufficient funds to allow them to await repayment. As a result, the different *corps* ruined themselves "one after the other," leaving the state empty-handed.

Not until Samuel de Champlain "threw" himself on the shores of the St. Lawrence River did Quebec finally become "the crib, the centre, and the capital of New France, or Canada." But it was not long before a growing "languor" took hold in the settlements. According to the *Histoire*, this was the fault of the Exclusif, which "planned less to create a national presence for France in Canada than to enrich itself with the commerce of furs."[139] By now, the *Histoire*'s refrain was familiar: "To cure this ill, one had only to substitute liberty to this monopoly." But "the time for such a theory had not yet come." Instead, the government chose to substitute this company with "an association" more numerous and composed

---

[138] The text continued: "Ever since this period the right to grant exclusive privileges, to limit them, to extend them or abolish them, has lain with the representatives of the nation." Ibid., 49–50.

[139] *HDI* (1780), book 15, 80.

of wealthier and more credit-worthy shareholders – 700 shareholders in total, 12 of whom obtained letters of nobility. This association was given a vast range of rights, "including access to the settlements formed or to be formed in Canada, and the authority to wage war or make peace according to its interests."

Here, we have a precise example of the vast political powers afforded monopoly-trading companies in the period.[140] Whereas the cod and whale fisheries remained free for all citizens, all commerce that could be carried out on land and by sea was granted to the company, including the lucrative trade in beaver pelts granted in perpetuity. The company was allowed to send or receive all sorts of goods without being assessed the slightest duty. Practicing any kind of trade in the colony for six years "gave rights to subsequently practice commerce freely in France." Finally, all manufactured goods were allowed to enter these faraway countries freely.

This "singular arrangement," whose motives, the *Histoire* concluded, were not easily understood, gave the workers of New France "incomparable advantage" over the workers of France, who were "enveloped by tolls, letters of mastery, branding fees, and all of the shackles that ignorance and avarice multiplied infinitely." In 1628, the first year of its privilege, the company sought to respond to this inequity by bringing from France 200 to 300 workers from the most useful professions. By 1643, it had brought over as many as two thousand men. Even these attempts were futile, however.[141] The monopoly did not fulfil any of its commitments, but its privileges were nonetheless prolonged. The deputies charged with painting the horror of the situation were never able to arrive at the foot of the throne, where silence was imposed by way of threats and punishments. This result, which equally harmed humanity, private interests, and politics, led to the consequences that naturally derived from it. Exchanges between the New World and the Old became rare because communications were too dangerous. The "savages," ill supported by their French allies, "fled continually before the ancient enemy they were accustomed to fear." The Iroquois, recovering their superiority, bragged that they would force the foreigners to leave their country after having taken away their children in order to replace those they had lost. The French themselves were "forgotten by their metropole" and, without the means to harvest their weak crops without risking their lives, were

---

[140] On the English equivalent of this argument, see Philip J. Stern, *The Company-State: Corporate Sovereignty and the Early Modern Foundations of the British Empire in India* (Oxford: Oxford University Press, 2011).
[141] *HDI* (1780), book 15, 82.

determined to abandon their poorly sustained settlements. The "misery and degradation" of the colony were such that it "subsisted with no more than the charity that missionaries received from Europe." The *Histoire* went on to explain that the French ministry sent 400 troops to New France in 1662, and these troops, later reinforced by the Carignan regiment, slowly defeated the Iroquois. By 1668, they had brought peace to the colony. This peace was the "seed of prosperity" that the liberty of commerce later caused to blossom.

Here, the *Histoire* made an obvious elision between prosperity and the liberty of commerce in the colonies, which indicates how profound the connection was between the two in the authors' minds. It followed with the argument that this "revolution in business fermented industry." The former colonists paid more attention to their plantations, cultivating and expanding them with greater success and confidence. Their new "spirit of life and activity" multiplied the exchanges that the "savages" had with the French, and as a result, "[C]ommerce revived the ties between the two worlds."[142] The administrators of the colony sought to live in harmony with their neighbours, and in an area of 400 to 500 leagues not a "single act of hostility" was committed. This was unprecedented in North America, seemingly the political consequence of military effectiveness and the liberty of commerce.

Book 15 also contains repeated references to the monopoly over the beaver trade. We find mention of the fact that whereas the "commerce of the beaver" was always free among the "savages," among the French it was enslaved to the "tyranny" of monopoly.[143] With time, restrictions upon the "passion" for trapping (*courir les bois*) were lifted slightly, and twenty-five permits to cross the colony's boundaries were granted yearly. The "ascendance" of New York rendered these leaves to cross boundaries more frequent, and they became their own "type of exclusive privilege."[144] The pelts were traded, and the revenue generated by the permits was distributed by the colony's governor.

The same book moves beyond the trapping to an account of the loss of the "almost exclusive branch of industry" that the colony presented to the metropole: the "*preparation* of beaver." At first, this trade fell under the yoke and shackles of "monopoly." The Company of the Indies made

---

[142] Ibid., 87.

[143] Ibid., 124.

[144] Ibid., 125. "C'étoient des especes de privileges exclusifs qu'on exerçoit par soi-même ou par d'autres. Ils duroient un an ou même au-delà. On les vendoit; et le produit étoit distribué par le gouverneur de la colonie."

pernicious use of its privilege, so that what it bought from the "savages" was paid for primarily with crimson cloths and woollen fabrics from England that "these peoples liked to adorn themselves with."[145] Since the Indians found that the English offered them twenty-five per cent and thirty per cent more for their goods than the (French) Company of the Indies, the "savages" kept what they could away from the company's agents and exchanged their beavers directly with the British for cloths from England or calicoes from the Indies. The *Histoire* concluded that, by way of the abuse of an institution that France was not obliged to maintain, France had lost for itself the "double advantage" of procuring primary goods for some of its manufacturers and ensuring outlets for the productions of others. Thus, the one remaining monopoly was also judged by its negative repercussions in the metropole.

A diatribe on the lot of "civil man" versus the lot of "savage man" followed. The reader learned of the "wretched farmer" and the "tenant or subject," who was "doubly a slave": If he has a few acres, "a lord will gather what he has not sown"; if he has a team of horses or cattle, they are forced into harness for the "*corvée*"; and if "he has only his person," the prince "takes him away for war."[146] The result: "Masters everywhere and humiliations always." That was the lot of the countryman. In the cities, the worker and the artisan "submit to the laws of greedy and lazy masters" who, through "the privilege of monopoly," possess "the power to have industry work for nothing" and to sell their works "at very high prices."

At this point, the author, probably Diderot, raised the spectre of luxury. Thus, the *Histoire* reported that "the people have but the spectacle of luxury," of which they were "doubly the victim." This was not only because of the taxing labour its pursuit demanded, but also the "insolence" of the "splendour" which "humiliated and crushed them." We can imply from this a causal connection between a society and an economy characterised by monopoly – here once again equated with privilege – and the inequalities in the society manifested as the existence of a harmful luxury.

This volume of the *Histoire* ends with an assertion that Rousseau had most famously included in his *Second Discourse* over twenty years before: that an "infinite distance" lay between "the lot of civilised man and that of savage man."[147] Quite simply, the difference between the two, "entirely to

---

[145] Ibid., book 16, 270.
[146] *HDI* (1780), book 17, 346–47.
[147] Cf. *Discours sur les origines de l'inégalité parmi les hommes* (1755).

the disadvantage of the social state," was "the inequality of fortunes and of conditions."[148] Monopoly was deemed to be that which "offended" all "artisans, and workers" to whom "the right to work freely and without the need to buy masterships is denied."[149] Labourers were destined to be "held bent over in a workshop to enrich a privileged entrepreneur."

The equation of labour with despotism was made even more explicit when army officers were next addressed: They served "as the instrument of despotism," but they were also its "victim," for they were not allowed to "sell [their] blood freely to whoever pays for it." Not only was the link to despotism made explicit here, but the reader was enjoined (not without sarcasm) to "[d]are to tremble," for "your cries will be fended off and lost at the bottom of a dungeon; flee, you will be followed, even beyond mountains and rivers; you will be sent back or delivered with feet and wrists tied by torture to the eternal difficulties to which you were condemned by birth." This is one of several examples in which the *Histoire* equated the life of the worker to that of the serf, and even to that of the African slave.[150]

When the *Histoire* returned to its account of the beaver trade in New France, the reader learned that in this economy, the beaver had become "the common measure for exchange." In an "authorised tyranny," two otter skins or three marten (a type of weasel) skins were demanded for a beaver skin. This was linked to another form of "tyranny," which, if not authorised, was "at least tolerated": the so-called Indians were "habitually cheated" on the measure, the weight, and the quality of what was delivered to them.[151] This "methodical robbery" necessarily led to the assumption that commerce in Hudson's Bay was "subjected to monopoly." This equation of robbery and monopoly is here suggested again.

The reader is then offered data to support the argument: the famous "figures" with which Raynal so bored his companions in the *salons*. The company in question (clearly the Hudson's Bay Company) possessed thirty-five hundred pounds in funds. These "modest advances" gave a return of forty to fifty thousand skins of beavers or other animals and precious objects with "exaggerated benefits" that "excited the envy and the murmurs of the nation." Two-thirds of these "beautiful furs" were consumed by the "three kingdoms" or else used by "national manufacturers," while the rest went to Germany, "where the climate offered advantageous

[148] *HDI* (1780), book 17, 348.
[149] Ibid., book 18, 182–83.
[150] Ibid., 183–84.
[151] Ibid., book 17, 366–67. The text added that the "lesion" was about one-third.

prospects."[152] By 1745, the search for the Northwest Passage to the West Indies ended with a resolution to promise a "considerable reward" to successful navigators. According to the *Histoire*, the "English ministry" understood that neither the efforts of the state nor those of any individual would achieve the goal until "commerce on Hudson's Bay [became] entirely free."[153] Having exercised its privilege since 1670, the company had not taken a single measure to discover the passage, and what's more, it had "stifled, with all of its powers, what the love of glory and all other motives pushed toward this great enterprise." Once again, the work concluded that the handicap was a result of the "spirit of iniquity" that forms the "very essence of monopoly."[154] Yet again, we find an indication of the ways in which the peculiar redundancy "exclusive privilege" functioned as a synonym for monopoly in the *Histoire*.

Exclusivity and privilege were indeed central targets of the *Histoire*'s critique of monopoly, as were the moral qualifications of monopoly evident in the use of terms like "iniquity" to describe it. Monopoly was largely construed as a *commerce odieux* in the *Histoire*, but it is also portrayed as the most dangerous threat to France's liberty, wealth, and well-being. It was not only odious but an "obvious attack against liberty."[155] Monopoly was "contrary to universal industry."[156] Yet establishing a simple dichotomy between advocates of free commerce and those opposed to it is not the only way to explain monopoly's place and role in the discourse of commerce in eighteenth-century France. As Diderot reminds us, a more complex attitude towards monopoly manifested itself in the period. Exposed in the *Histoire* and in Diderot's five reflections on the debate over the French Company of the Indies, the discourse conflated internal and external trade. This relationship comes to the fore when we study the 1769 polemic over the Company of the Indies' privilege and understand Diderot's conclusions about it. Not only does it suggest that French concerns were as much Indian as they were Atlantic in this period, we also find two connected critiques at work: The first, a critique of aberrant forms of commerce, was joined to a second and growing political critique of privileges in the prerevolutionary period. The well-being of the French polity was tied to its international commerce, both *doux* and *odieux*.

---

[152] Ibid., 367.
[153] Ibid., 371.
[154] Ibid., 375
[155] Ibid., book 3, 47.
[156] Ibid., book 3, chap. 1, 10.

Conclusion

Commerce and Its Discontents (bis)

The *Histoire*'s accounts of monopoly agitated a vast range of readers, as did the work as a whole. As I have shown, the *Histoire* was widely read, and its reception is now well documented.[1] But this did not mean its message was uniformly understood. Nor was its "author," the abbé Raynal.

Exiled in 1781 when the *Histoire* was condemned to be "whipped and burned," the abbé Raynal returned to Paris in 1791. A revolution was in full swing. The *Histoire* had rendered him a "Defender of Liberty" just as it endeared him to the Jacobins. Yet the author would ultimately disappoint the revolutionaries by delivering an address to the new National Assembly in which he offered a devastating critique of the new constitution and what he viewed to be the anarchic turn the Revolution had taken.[2] It took almost no time for irate former supporters to turn against him.[3] A colourful anecdote about his speech's reception reports that, upon hearing about it, the Jacobins of Marseille dragged the bust of Raynal, which had previously adorned their hall, through the streets of Marseille until it fell to pieces.

At the same time that he was being hounded in the metropole, Raynal was cheered in the colonies. Toussaint l'Ouverture (1743–1803), leader

---

[1] See Hans-Jürgen Lüsebrink and Manfred Tietz, eds., *Lectures de Raynal* (Oxford: Voltaire Foundation, 1991), and Hans-Jürgen Lüsebrink, and Anthony Strugnell, eds., *L'Histoire des deux Indes: Réécriture et polygraphie* (Oxford: Voltaire Foundation, 1995).

[2] *Adresse de Guillaume-Thomas Raynal, Remise par lui-même à M. le Président, le 31 mai 1791, et lue à l'Assemblée le même jour.* Imprimée sur le manuscrit de l'auteur. A Paris, Chez Gattey, libraire, au Palais-royal, nos 13 et 14.

[3] *G.T. Raynal démasqué, ou Lettres sur la vie et les ouvrages de cet écrivain* (n.p., 1791).

of the first, successful 1791 slave revolt in what is now Haiti, cited him at length.[4] A famous 1797 portrait of Jean-Baptiste Belley (1747–1805), the first deputy for Saint-Domingue (present-day Haiti) in the French National Assembly, also commemorated Raynal's role in the denunciation of the trade in slaves, if obliquely. Its painter, Anne-Louis Girodet-Troison (1767–1824), depicted Belley gazing upwards (towards Saint-Domingue perhaps) and leaning on a pedestal from which a severe bald-headed white marble bust glowered in an opposite direction. The inscription beneath read: "G.T.Raynal." Staring sternly into the distance, the Raynal represented here is the first outspoken critic of the slave trade in France, evoking those passages in the *Histoire* decrying that "odious commerce."[5] Shortly thereafter, a full copy of the *Histoire* – the ten volumes of text and two volumes of maps in-8° – accompanied an ambitious Corsican general on his 1798 Egyptian campaign. Napoleon is said to have drawn on the work as a model for planned imperial success.[6] From the revolutionary leader of rebellions against colonial masters to

---

[4] Raynal's posterity was fostered in Anglophone historiography by C. L. R. James's classic work, *The Black Jacobins: Toussaint L'Ouverture and the San Domingo Revolution* (1938, 1963). Rev. 2nd edition. (New York: Vintage, 1989). An efflorescence of scholarly attention has since continued the trend, parallel with the renewed interest in the Haitian Revolution sparked by the works of Michel-Rolph Trouillot, Laurent Dubois, Jeremy Popkin, and Doris Garraway, to name but a few.

[5] Helen D. Weston's nuanced reading of the portrait – first listed as "*Portrait de nègre*" at the *Exposition d'Elysée* in 1797 – invites us to understand the two figures in it as equals (due to their levelled heads), but also as "contrasts of the man of intellect with his exaggerated cranium and the man of nature with his exaggerated genitalia; as contrasts of freedom of thought and liberty of conscience in the academic field and freedom of the person and civil liberties fought for on the battlefield and in the political arena." Helen D. Weston, "Representing the Right to Represent: The 'Portrait of Citizen Belley, Ex-Representative of the Colonies' by A.-L. Girodet," *RES: Anthropology and Aesthetics*. 26 (1994): 88, 99. Susan Ross kindly brought this article to my attention. Mary C. Bellhouse also notes the many "competing signifiers" on the canvas (765), proposing that with the painting's title indicating that Belley is a citizen, his "uniform of an officer in the French army" and his "sash of a representative," Girodet's portrait "is an image of a new kind of French manliness: the Republican citizen-soldier." See "Candide Shoots the Monkey Lovers: Representing Black Men in Eighteenth-Century Visual Culture," *Political Theory* 34, no. 6 (2006): 764.

[6] A letter dated 28 mars 1798 to "Citoyen J-B Say" outlines the books Napoleon wanted assembled in a "bibliothèque portative." He allocated ten thousand francs for the purchase of over 300 volumes. Included among those books (divided into "Sciences and Arts," "Geography and Travels," "Histories," "Poetry," "Novels," and "Morals and Politics") were twelve volumes of the "Histoire Philosophique des Indes" [*sic*]. Cf. Alexandre Keller, *Correspondance, bulletins et ordres du jour de Napoléon*. 4 vols. (Paris: A. Méricant, 1909–12), vol. 4, and *Napoléon, Correspondance de Napoléon 1er*. I am indebted to Wayne Hanley for sharing these details with me.

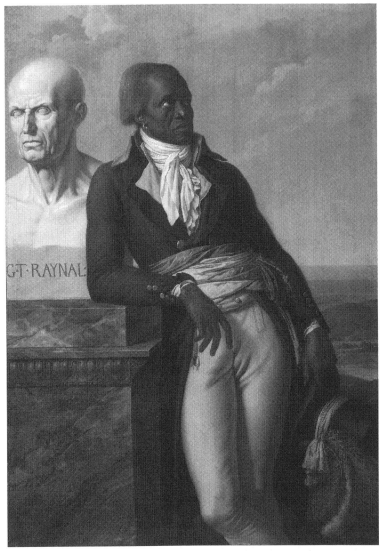

FIGURE 5.   Jean-Baptiste Belley with G.T. Raynal. *Portrait of C.(itizen) Jean-Baptiste Belley, Ex-Representative of the Colonies* by Anne Louis Girodet de Roussy-Troison. Dated "Year V" (1797). Oil on canvas, 158 x 111 cm, Châteaux de Versailles et de Trianon, Versailles.
Courtesy of the Réunion des Musées Nationaux/Art Resource, NY.

the imperialist *par excellence*, the immediate uses of the *Histoire* were clearly multiple.

This multiplicity of interpretations is not surprising. As I have sought to show, this text, vast both in scope and in reach, was replete with multiple messages, many of them contradictory. Yet the prevailing tension within the *Histoire* lay between an ideal of *doux* commerce and recognition of commerce's *odieux* potential. The debate over luxury, which was also a debate over commerce, highlighted the ambivalence about commerce in the *Histoire* and throughout Europe at the time. Any careful reading of this influential text reveals three categories of commerce that were neither civilising nor equalising, neither pacifying nor moralising. These three categories – slavery, piracy, and monopoly – provide the dissonance within the triumphant discourse of commerce in the *Histoire*, even if they do so in different ways. The trade of humans was deemed immoral by the *Histoire*, but its condemnation was amplified through an analogy made between feudal slavery, political slavery, and the trade in Africans. The accusation of hypocrisy on the part of European intellectuals who bemoaned their servitude to despots at the same time that they perpetuated the enslavement of Africans was sustained in the *Histoire*'s account of piracy. The foundations of international jurisprudence rested on the distinction between an individual, the pirate, and an action, piracy, the latter of which was deemed acceptable and redescribed as good seizure when undertaken by colonial powers. This was, according to the *Histoire*, a most odious form of commerce, because it rested on a double standard that favoured those with power over those without it. So, too, the *Histoire*'s critique of monopoly, a third form of odious commerce, was structured around the conflation of two otherwise distinct spheres: the international monopolies of the commercial trading companies and the domestic monopolies of the *corps*, or corporations, of tradesmen.

Each governed by a politics of definition, these categories were combined in the *Histoire* and beyond it. Far from being independent problems, luxury, slavery, piracy, and monopoly were together embedded within the discourse of commerce. In other words, slavery could not be understood as distinct from commerce, just as commerce could not be understood without its connection to slavery. Eighteenth-century French public intellectuals thus recognised a much denser and more varied discourse of commerce than the *doux commerce* thesis allows.

To be sure, even Albert Hirschman eventually recognised the coexistence of two distinct attitudes towards commerce.[7] He eventually reframed his discussion of commerce as a dialectic and literally mapped out a matrix of the relations between what, for the purposes of his chart, he deemed the *doux commerce* and self-destruction theses, the latter of which he identified as the "obverse" of the former. The self-destruction thesis maintained that commerce "exhibits a pronounced proclivity toward undermining the moral foundations [of society]."[8] To explain the genesis of the self-destruction thesis, Hirschman focused on Karl Marx and John Maynard Keynes. Yet in doing so, he overlooked the eighteenth-century origins of this dynamic which I have sought to uncover in this book, including one of the best-known examples of the thesis. This was Jean-Jacques Rousseau's famous *Discourse on the Origins of Inequality among Men* (1755), also referred to as the *Second Discourse*, wherein Rousseau famously countered the prevailing notion that "civilisation," here equated with commercial society, was a positive outcome for humanity.[9] For Rousseau, the trappings of civilisation were at best empty glitter. Civilisation, the consequence of societies of commerce, made men slaves to money, foreigners to virtue, and, worst of all for Rousseau, feminized them.[10] Less prominent in twenty-first-century undergraduate syllabi but more widely read in the eighteenth century, the *Histoire des deux Indes* offered an alternative perspective. It combined a triumphant praise of commerce with appalled consternation at its abuses and immoral potential. Both views structured the discourse of commerce in eighteenth-century France.

Since the early twentieth century, this position of simultaneous love and hatred has been labelled "ambivalence." The origins of this category are of course psychoanalytic. But the founder of psychoanalysis also offers an alternative perspective on the social promise of commerce. In the spirit of finding political economy where it has not traditionally been observed, I close with reflections on Sigmund Freud's essay *Civilization and Its Discontents*.[11] By the twentieth century, the promise of civilisation

---

[7] Albert O. Hirschman, "Rival Interpretations of Market Society: Civilizing, Destructive, or Feeble?" *Journal of Economic Literature* 20, no. 4 (1982): 1463–84.

[8] Ibid., 1466.

[9] Cf. Rousseau, *Origines de l'inégalité*.

[10] See Dena Goodman's analysis of Rousseau's *Lettre à d'Alembert* on this account in *The Republic of Letters: A Cultural History of the French Enlightenment* (Ithaca, NY: Cornell University Press, 1994), 53–56.

[11] The phrase "Civilization and Its Discontents" is a famously unsatisfactory translation of *Das Unbehagen in der Kultur*. The essay's original title was *Das Unglück in der Kultur*,

had become equivalent to the promise of *doux commerce*. If civilisation had formerly been understood as the set of social conditions characterised by "polish, gentleness, and softness," Freud offered an explanation of how this very promise of *douceur*, of sweetness and gentleness, in fact generated aggression and conflict. He explained that civilisation thus comprised both sweetness and odiousness. We are faced with a situation of simultaneous desire and rejection of civilisation. We are thus ambivalent about civilisation.

Freud's essay offers a paradigm through which to understand how the triumphant narrative of commerce could coexist with a deep sense of its hazards in eighteenth-century France. A sense of the sweet and gentle potential of commerce met with an understanding of its violent "discontents." Writing for the *Histoire*, Denis Diderot remarked at one point that commerce was the "soul of the moral world."[12] If this was true, then, as we have seen, the soul of the moral world was conflicted indeed.

---

or "Unhappiness in Civilization," but it was later altered to *Unbehagen*, a word for which it was difficult to choose an English equivalent, though the French *malaise* is close. Freud apparently suggested "Man's Discomfort in Civilization" in a letter to his translator, Mrs. Riviere, but it was ultimately she who found the phrase that was finally adopted. See Peter Gay's introduction to Sigmund Freud, "Civilization and Its Discontents." 1930. *The Standard Edition of the Psychological Works of Sigmund Freud*, edited by James Strachey, trans. Peter Gay (New York: W. W. Norton, 1989), 59–61. To be sure, this translation shifts the subject from "Man" to "Civilization," a move replicated in this book.

[12] *HDI* (1780), book 19, 243. Cf. Michèle Duchet, *Diderot et l'Histoire des deux Indes ou l'Écriture Fragmentaire* (Paris: A. G. Nizet, 1978), 166.

Bibliography

Primary Sources

Manuscript Sources

Bibliothèque de l'Arsenal
Pièces concernant l'histoire de la France: MS 3724
Mélanges historiques, critiques et littéraires par M. L'abbé Raynal: MS 9157–58
Bibliothèque nationale
Manuscrits français: 6429–35
Nouvelles acquisitions françaises: 9134, 18155, 15588
Chambre de Commerce de Marseille
CCIM LIII and *LIX*
France: Ministère des Affaires étrangères
Mémoires et Documents: Amérique, 16
Dossier du Personnel: No. 59

Printed Sources Originally Written or Published before 1800

Académie française. *Le dictionnaire de l'Académie française*. Paris: J. B. Coignard, 1694.
Anonymous. *Soupirs de la France esclave, qui aspire après la liberté*. Amsterdam: n.p., 1689.
Aristotle. *Nichomachean Ethics*. Edited by Roger Crisp. Cambridge: Cambridge University Press, 2000.
  The Politics and the Constitution of Athens. Edited by Stephen Everson. Cambridge: Cambridge University Press, 1996.
  Rhetoric. Translated by Edward Meredith Cope and John Edwin Sandys. Cambridge: Cambridge University Press, 2010.
Augustine. *The City of God against the Pagans*. Translated and edited by R. W. Dyson. Cambridge: Cambridge University Press, 1998.

Bachaumont, Louis Petit de. *Mémoires secrets pour l'histoire de la République des Lettres en France depuis 1762 par M. de Bachaumont.* Vol. 19. London: Adamson, 1777–89.

Barret-Kriegel, Blandine. *Les Académies de l'histoire.* Paris: Presses universitaires de France, 1988.

Boétie, Étienne de la. *Discours de la servitude volontaire.* Paris: J. Vrin, 2002.

Boucher d'Argis, Antoine-Gaspard. *Code rural; ou, Maximes et réglemens concernant les biens de campagne, notamment les fiefs, franc-aleux, censives, droits et justice ... par M... avocat au Parlement.* Paris: Prault père, imprimeur, 1749.

Traité des gains nuptiaux et de survie, qui sont en usage dans les païs de droit écrit, tant du ressort du Parlement de Paris, que des autres parlemens. Lyon: Duplain, 1738.

Boulainvilliers, Henri, comte de. *Histoire de l'ancien gouvernement de la France, avec XIV lettres historiques sur les Parlemens ou Etats-Généraux.* La Haye and Amsterdam: Aux dépens de la compagnie, 1727.

Boyer, Abel. *The Royal Dictionary, Abridged, In Two Parts: I. French and English, II. English and French.* Ninth edition. London: n.p., 1755.

Butel-Dumont, Georges-Marie. *Acte du Parlement d'Angleterre, connu sous le nom d'acte de navigation, passé en 1660, traduit littéralement de l'anglois, avec des notes [par G.-M. Butel-Dumont].* Amsterdam and Paris: C.-A. Jombert, 1760.

Essai sur les causes principales qui ont contribué à détruire les deux premières races des rois de France par l'auteur de la "Théorie du luxe." Paris: Vve Duchesne, 1776.

Recherches historiques et critiques sur l'administration publique et privée des terres chez les Romains, depuis le commencement de la République jusqu'au siècle de Jules-César. Paris: Vve Duchesne, 1779.

Théorie du luxe, ou Traité dans lequel on entreprend d'établir que le luxe est un ressort non seulement utile, mais même indispensablement nécessaire à la prospérité d'un état. London and Paris: Chez Jean-François Bastien, Libraire rue du Petit-Lion, 1775.

Butini, Jean-François. *Traité du Luxe.* Geneva: Chez Isac [*sic*] Bardin, Libraire au bas de la Cité, 1774.

Caraccioli, Domenico. *La vraie manière d'élever les princes destinés à régner.* Paris: n.p., 1788.

Cherhal Mont-Réal, Louis-François. *Éloge philosophique et politique de Guillaume-Thomas Raynal.* Paris: Deroy, 1796.

Cicero, Marcus Tullius. *De Officiis.* Translated by P. G. Walsh. Oxford: Oxford University Press, 2000.

On the Commonwealth and On the Laws. Translated and edited by James E. G. Zetzel. Cambridge: Cambridge University Press, 1999.

Condorcet, Jean-Antoine-Nicolas de Caritat. *Esquisse d'un tableau historique des progrès de l'esprit humain.* Edited by Alain Pons. Paris: Flammarion, 1988.

Monopole et monopoleur. 1775. In *Oeuvres de Condorcet.* Edited by Condorcet O'Connor and Arago, 11:35–38. Paris: Firmin Didot Frères, Libraires, 1847.

Constant, Benjamin. *Collection complète des ouvrages publiés sur le Gouvernement représentatif et la Constitution actuelle de la France, formant une espèce de cours de politique constitutionelle.* Paris: P. Plancher, 1818–20. In *Political Writings / Benjamin Constant.* Translated and edited by Biancamaria Fontana. Cambridge: Cambridge University Press, 1988.

Defoe, Daniel, Charles Johnson, pseud. *General History of the ... Pyrates.* Dublin: J. Watts, 1725.

Denisart, Jean-Baptiste. *Collection de décisions nouvelles et de notions relatives à la jurisprudence actuelle.* 3 vols. Paris: Vve Desaint, 1763–87.

Dictionnaire de Trévoux. Dictionnaire universel françois et latin. Paris: Libraires associés, 1743.

Diderot, Denis. *Correspondance.* Edited by Georges Roth and Jean Varloot. Paris: Éd. de Minuit, 1955–70.

Oeuvres. Edited by Laurent Versini. Paris: Éditions Robert Laffont, 1995.

Oeuvres complètes. Edited by Herbert Dieckmann, Jacques Proust, and Jean Varloot (*DPV*). Paris: Hermann, 1975.

Réfutation suivie de l'ouvrage d'Helvétius intitulé L'Homme. In *Correspondance,* vol. 5 of *Œuvres.* Edited by Laurent Versini. Paris: R. Laffont, 1997.

Diderot, Denis, and Jean Le Rond d'Alembert, eds. *Encyclopédie, ou Dictionnaire raisonné des sciences, des arts et des métiers, par une société de gens de lettres.* 17 vols. Paris: Chez Briasson; Neufchâtel: Chez Samuel Faulche et Compagnie, 1751–65.

Douin, Firmin de Caen. "Le Commerce, poëme. Qui a eu l'Accessit à l'Académie Françoise, en 1754." In *Amusemens poëtiques d'un philosophe, ou Poëmes académiques sur différens sujets, dont plusieurs ont été couronnés, et autres piéces fugitives.* Paris: Chez Cailleau, 1763.

"Le luxe, première cause de la décadence de Rome." In *Amusemens poëtiques d'un philosophe, ou Poëmes académiques sur différens sujets, dont plusieurs ont été couronnés, et autres piéces fugitives.* Paris: Chez Cailleau, 1763.

Dubucq, Jean-Baptiste. *Lettres critiques et politiques sur les colonies & le commerce des villes maritimes de France, Adressées à G.T. Raynal.* Geneva: n.p., 1785.

Du Coudray, Alexandre-Jacques, chevalier. *Le luxe, poëme en six chants; orné de gravures, avec des notes historiques et critiques, suivi de poésies diverses.* Paris: Chez Monory, Libraire de S.A.S. Monseigneur le Prince de Condé, 1773.

Émerigon, Balthazard-Marie. *Nouveau commentaire sur l'ordonnance de la marine du mois d'août 1681, par M*** [B.-M. Émerigon].* Marseille: J. Mossy, 1780.

Traité des assurances et des contrats à la grosse. Marseille: J. Mossy, 1783.

Exquemelin, Alexandre-Olivier. *Histoire des avanturiers qui se sont signalez dans les Indes.* Translated by M. de Frontigni è res. 2 vols. Paris: J. Le Febvre, 1686.

Falconer, William. *An [sic] Universal Dictionary of the Marine: or, A Copious Explanation of the Technical Terms and Phrases Employed in the Construction, Equipment, Furniture, Machinery, Movements, and Military Operations of A Ship.... To which is annexed, A Translation of the French Sea-Terms and Phrases.* London: T. Cadell, 1769.

Faure, Edgar. *La Banqueroute de Law*. Paris: Gallimard, 1977.

Febvé, abbé (chanoine de Vaudémont). *Essai philanthropique sur l'esclavage des nègres. Par Mr. L'abbé Febué Chanoine de Vaudemont: Membre de la Société du Philantrope*. n.p., 1778.

Ferrière, Claude-Joseph de. *Dictionnaire de droit et de pratique, contenant l'explication des termes de droit, d'Ordonnances, de Coutumes & de Pratique. Avec les jurisdictions de France...* Nouvelle édition, revue, corrigée & augmentée. Paris: Veuve Brunet, 1778–79.

France. *Arrest de la Cour de Parlement, qui condamne un imprimé, en dix vol. in-8, ayant pour titre, Histoire philosophique ... à être lacéré et brûlé par l'exécuteur de la Haute-Justice*. Paris: P. G. Simon, 1781.

Arrest de la cour de parlement, qui prive Thomas-Arthur de Lally de ses états, honneurs et dignités, et le condamne à avoir la tête tranchée,... pour avoir trahi les intérêts du roi, de son Etat et de la Compagnie des Indes... Extrait des registres du parlement, du 6 mai 1766. Paris: P. G. Simon, 1766.

Observations pour les citoyens Basterèche frères, négocians de Bayonne, sur un rapport fait par Cholet, député de la Gironde, au nom d'une commission spéciale, et à l'occasion d'une réclamation des citoyens Olivier et consorts du Havre. Paris: Baudoin impr., n.d.

Opinion sur la suppression des corsaires, prononcé par M. Kersaint, député de Paris, le 1er mai 1792. Paris: Impr. nat., n.d.

Ordonnance du Roi, Portant déclaration de guerre contre le Roi d'Angleterre. Du 9 Juin 1756. Fait à Versailles le neuf juin mil sept cent cinquante-six. Signé Louis. Signé M.P. de Voyer d'Argenson. Paris: Impr. royale, 1756.

Ordonnances des Rois de France, Règne de François 1er. Vol. 9, pt. 3. Paris: Éditions du CNRS, 1983.

Pétition pour les Armateurs du Corsaire "le Républicain" de Nantes. Paris: J. Grand impr., 1793.

Projet de décret sur la suppression des corsaires, présenté par M. Kersaint, député de Paris, le premier mai 1792. Imprimé par ordre de l'Assemblée nationale.

Rapport fait par C.-P. Claret-Fleurieu, au nom de la commission chargée de l'examen de la résolution du Conseil des Cinq-Cents, du 15 thermidor an V, relatif au message du Directoire exécutif concernant les prises faits dans les mers de l'Inde par le navire l'Emilie, capitaine SURCOUF. Séance du 17 fruct. an V. Corps législatif. Conseil des anciens. Paris: Imprimerie nationale, an V.

Réflexions d'un négociant et jurisconsulte Batave à l'occasion du rapport du citoyen Riou (pour la protection du commerce par mer contre les entreprises des corsaires), Riou, membre du Conseil des Cinq-cents, du 28 messidor. Paris: Impr. Antoine Bailleul, n.d.

Furetière, Antoine. *Dictionnaire Universel, contenant généralement les mots français, tant vieux que modernes, et les termes de toutes les sciences et des arts, etc*. Nouvelle édition. 5 vols. Paris: Vve Delaulne, 1732.

Gazette du commerce. Paris: n.p., 1763, 11 mai 1765.

Genty, Louis, abbé. *Discours sur le luxe, Qui a remporté le Prix d'Eloquence á l'Académie des Sciences, Belles-Lettres & Arts de Besançon, en 1783*. Orléans: Couret de Villeneuve, 1783.

Goethe, J. W. V. *Faust*. Part 2. Translated by Martin Greenberg. New Haven: Yale University Press, 1998.

Gournay, Vincent de. *Observations sur le rapport fait à M. le contrôleur général par M. de S*** le 26 juin 1755, sur l'état de la Compagnie des Indes, par feu M. de Gournay, Intendant du Commerce*. In l'Abbé Morellet, *Mémoire sur la situation actuelle de la Compagnie des Indes, juin 1769*. Paris: Desaint, 1769.

Grimm Friedrich Mechior, et al., eds. *Correspondance littéraire, philosophique et critique de Grimm et de Diderot depuis 1753 jusqu'en 1790*. Paris: Chez Furne, 1829–31.

Correspondance littéraire: Revue sur les textes originaux, comprenant outre ce qui a été publié à diverses époques, les fragments supprimés en 1813 par la censure, les parties inédites conservées à la Bibliothèque ducale de Gotha et à l'Arsenal à Paris. Edited by Maurice Tourneux. Tome deuxième. Paris: Garnier Frères, 1877, In Nendeln/Liechtenstein: Kraus Reprint, 1968.

Grotius, Hugo. *De iure praedae commentarius. Commentary on the Law of Prize and Booty*. 1604. Vol. 1. Translation of the original 1604 manuscript by Glwadys Williams. Vol. 2. Collotype reproduction of the original MSS of 1604. Oxford: Clarendon, 1950.

Mare liberum. Edited by Simone Goyard-Fabre. Caen: Centre de philosophie politique et juridique, 1990.

Guyot, Joseph-Nicholas, ed. *Répertoire universel et raisonné de Jurisprudence civile, criminelle, canonique et bénéficiale; ouvrage de plusieurs jurisconsultes…* Nouvelle édition corrigée, et augmentée tant des loix nouvelles que des arrêts rendus en matière importante pour les parlemens et les autres cours du royaume, depuis l'édition précédente. 17 vols. Paris: n.p., 1784.

Hume, David. *Discours politiques de Monsieur Hume traduits de l'anglois*. Translated by abbé Jean Bernard LeBlanc. Amsterdam: Michel Lambert, 1754.

"Of Refinement in the Arts." In *Essays Moral and Political*, 3rd ed. London: A. Millar, 1748. Translated into French by abbé LeBlanc as *Essais philosophiques sur l'entendement humain*, 2nd ed. Amsterdam: J.H. Schneider, 1761.

Political Discourses. Edinburgh: R. Fleming, 1752.

Lafontaine, Jean de. *The Complete Fables of Jean de la Fontaine*. Translated and edited by Norman B. Spector. Evanston: Northwestern University Press, 1988.

Les Fables de La Fontaine: Quatre siècles d'illustration. Edited by Alain-Marie Bassy. Paris: Éditions Promodis, 1986.

Lally-Tollendal, Thomas Arthur Comte de. *Memoirs of count Lally from his embarking for the East Indies, as commander in chief of the French forces in that country, to his being sent prisoner of war to England, after the surrender of Pondichery, consisting of pieces written by himself and addressed to his judges in answer to the charges brought against him by the attorney general of his M. C. M…. to which are added accounts of the prior part of his life, his condemnation and execution*. (No translator specified). London: F. Newbery, 1766.

Lauraguais, Louis-Léon-Félicité, duc de Brancas. *Mémoire sur la Compagnie des Indes, précédé d'un Discours sur le commerce en général, par M. le comte de Lauraguais*. Paris: Lacombe, 1769.

Lelong, Jacques (Père). *Bibliothèque historique de la France.* Paris: G. Martin, 1719.

Mallet. *Mémoire pour Jean Boucaux, Nègre, Demandeur. Contre le Sieur Verdelin, Défendeur.* Paris: L'Imprimerie de Claude Simon, Père, 1738.

Malouet. *Mémoire sur l'esclavage des nègres, dans lequel on discute les motifs proposés pour leur affranchissement, ceux qui s'y opposent, et les moyens practicables pour améliorer leur sort.* Neufchâtel: n.p., 1788.

Marat, Jean-Paul. *The Chains of Slavery, A Work wherein the Clandestine and Villanous Attempts of Princes to Ruin Liberty are Pointed Out, and the Dreadful Scenes of Despotism Disclosed.* Newcastle: n.p., 1774.

Melon, Jean-François. *Essai politique sur le commerce.* n.p., 1734.

Mercier, Louis-Sébastien. *L'an deux mille quatre cent quarante, rêve s'il en fût jamais.* London: 1771.

   L'An deux mille quatre cent quarante: Rêve s'il en fut jamais. Edited by Raymond Trousson. Bordeaux: Éditions Ducros, 1971.

   L'An 2440: Rêve s'il en fut jamais. Edited by Christine Marcandier-Colard and Christophe Cave. Paris: La Découverte, 1999.

   Tableau de Paris. 2 vols. Hambourg: Virchaux; Neufchâtel: S. Fauche, 1781.

   Tableau de Paris (1782–88). Edited by Jean-Claude Bonnet. Paris: Mercure de France, 1994.

Milton, John. *Milton: Political Writings.* Edited by Martin Dzelzainis. Cambridge: Cambridge University Press, 1991.

Montaigne, Michel Equyem de. *Essais* (1588). Edited by Pierre Villey. Paris: Quadrige/Presses universitaires de France, 1988.

Montesquieu, Charles-Louis de Secondat, baron de. *De l'Esprit des lois* (1748). Paris: Garnier; Flammarion, 1979.

   The Spirit of the Laws. Translated and edited by Anne M. Cohler, Basia Carolyn Miller, and Harold Samuel Stone. Cambridge: Cambridge University Press, 1989.

Morellet, André [abbé]. *Mémoire sur la situation actuelle de la Compagnie des Indes, juin 1769.* Paris: Desaint, 1769.

Necker, Jacques. *Réponse au Mémoire sur la situation actuelle de la Compagnie des Indes.* Paris: Imprimerie Royale, 1769.

Nemours, Dupont de. *Du Commerce et de la Compagnie des Indes, Seconde édition.* Amsterdam and Paris: Delalain, 1769.

Pansey, Henrion de. *Mémoire pour un Nègre qui réclame sa liberté.* n.p.: L'imprimerie de J. Th. Hérissant, Imprimeur du Cabinet du Roi, 1770.

Petit, Emilien. *Observations sur plusieurs assertions extraites littéralement de l'Histoire Philosophique des Etablissements des Européens dans les deux Indes, édition de 1770.* Amsterdam and Paris: Chez Knapen, Imprimeur de la Cour des Aides, au bas du Pont Saint Michel, 1776.

Pinto, Isaac de. *Essai sur le luxe*: Paris: Michel Lambert, 1762.

   "Lettre sur la jalousie du commerce, où l'on prouve, que l'intérêt des Puissances commerçantes ne se croise point, mais qu'elles on un intérêt commun à leur bonheur réciproque & à la conservation de la paix." In *Traité de la circulation et du crédit, contenant une 'Analyse raisonnée des Fonds d'Angleterre', & ce qu'on appelle Commerce ou Jeu d'Actions; un Examen critique de plusieurs*

Traités sur les Impôts, les Finances, l'Agriculture, la Population, le Commerce &c. précédé de l'Extrait, d'un Ouvrage intitulé 'Bilan général & raisonné de l'Angleterre depuis 1600 jusqu'en 1761'; & suivi d'une 'Lettre sur la Jalousie du Commerce', où l'on prouve que l'intérêt des Puissances commerçantes ne se croise point, &c. avec un Tableau de ce qu'on appelle 'Commerce', ou plutôt, 'Jeu d'Actions' en Hollande. Amsterdam: Chez Marc Michel Rey, 1771.

Pliny the Elder. *Natural History.* Translated by Harris Rackham. Vol. 3. Cambridge: Harvard University Press, 1967.

Raynal, Guillaume-Thomas. *Histoire philosophique et politique des établissements et du commerce des Européens dans les deux Indes.* Amsterdam: [n.p.], 1770.

Histoire … [des] deux Indes. Amsterdam: [n.p.], 1772.

Histoire … [des] deux Indes. The Hague: Chez Gosse fils, 1774.

Histoire … [des] deux Indes. Maestricht: Chez Jean-Edme Dufour, Imprimeur et Libraire, 1775.

Histoire … [des] deux Indes. Geneva: Chez Jean-Léonard Pellet, 1780.

Histoire … [des] deux Indes. Geneva: Chez Jean-Léonard Pellet, 1781.

Histoire … [des] deux Indes. Neuchatel and Geneva: Chez les Libraires Associés, 1783.

Histoire … [des] deux Indes, Édition critique. Vol. 1. Edited by Anthony Strugnell et al. Ferney-Voltaire: Centre international d'étude du XVIIIe siècle, 2010.

Rousseau, Jean-Jacques. *Les confessions.* Edited by J.-B. Pontalis. Paris: Gallimard, 1995.

Du contrat social. Amsterdam: Chez Marc Michel Rey, 1762.

Discours sur l'origine et les fondements de l'inégalité parmi les hommes. Amsterdam: M. M. Rey, 1755.

The Discourses and other Early Political Writings. Translated and edited by Victor Gourevitch. Cambridge: Cambridge University Press, 1997.

Œuvres complètes. Edited by Bernard Gagnebin and Marcel Raymond. Paris: Gallimard, 1981.

'The Social Contract' and Other Late Political Writings. Translated and edited by Victor Gourevitch. Cambridge: Cambridge University Press, 1997.

Rousseau, Thomas. *Les fastes du commerce: poème historique en douze chants.* Paris: Imprimerie le Couturier, 1784.

Savary des Bruslons, Jacques. *Dictionnaire universel de commerce: contenant tout ce qui concerne le commerce qui se fait dans les quatre parties du monde, l'explication de tous les termes qui ont rapport au négoce.* 3 vols. Paris: J. Estienne, 1723–30.

Dictionnaire universel de commerce, d'histoire naturelle et des arts et métiers… Ouvrage posthume du Sr Jacques Savary Des Bruslons,… continué… par M. Philémon-Louis Savary,… Nouvelle édition. 3 vols. Paris: Chez la Veuve Estienne et fils, 1748.

Dictionnaire universel de commerce, d'histoire naturelle et des arts et métiers… Ouvrage posthume du Sr Jacques Savary Des Bruslons,… continué… par M. Philémon-Louis Savary,… Nouvelle édition. 5 vols. Copenhague: Frères C. et A. Philibert, 1759–65.

Le Parfait négociant, ou Instruction générale pour ce qui regarde le commerce des marchandises de France et des pays étrangers. Paris: M. Guignard et C. Robustel, 1713.

Smith, Adam. *Correspondence of Adam Smith.* Edited by E. C. Mossner and I. S. Ross. Vol. 6 of *Glasgow Edition of the Works and Correspondence of Adam Smith.* Oxford: Oxford University Press, 1976.

——— *An Inquiry into the Nature and Causes of the Wealth of Nations.* 1776. 2 vols. Edited by R. H. Campbell and A. S. Skinner. Oxford: Oxford University Press, 1976.

Université de Paris. Faculté de théologie. *Determinatio sacrae facultatis Parisiensis in librum cui titulus: "Histoire philosophique et politique des établissemens des Européens dans les deux Indes," par Guillaume-Thomas Raynal, A Genève, chez Jean-Léonard Pellet, Imprimeur de la Ville & de l'Académie, M. DCC. LXXX.* Paris: Clousier, Jacques-Gabriel, 1781.

Valin, René-Josué. *Nouveau commentaire sur l'ordonnance de la marine du mois d'aout 1681. Où se trouve la Conférence des anciennes Ordonnances, des Us & Coutumes de la Mer, tant du Royaume que des Pays étrangers, & des nouveaux Réglemens concernans la Navigation & le Commerce maritime. Avec des Explications prises de l'esprit du Texte, de l'Usage, des Décisions des Tribunaux & des meilleurs Auteurs qui ont écrit sur la Jurisprudence nautique. Et des Notes historiques & critiques, tirées de la plupart de divers Recueils de Manuscrits conservés dans les dépôts publics.* 2 vols. La Rochelle: Chez Jerôme Legier, Imprimeur du Roi, au Canton des Flamands, 1766.

——— *Traité des prises ou principes de la jurisprudence française concernant les prises qui se font sur mer [...].* La Rochelle: Légier, 1763.

Voltaire (Arouet, François-Marie). *Dictionnaire philosophique.* [n.p.], 1764.

——— *Dictionnaire philosophique, nouvelle édition.* Amsterdam: Chez Marc-Michel Rey, 1789.

——— *Essai sur les moeurs et l'esprit des nations et sur les principaux faits de l'histoire depuis Charlemagne jusqu'à Louis XIII.* 1754. Edited by René Pomeau. Paris: Garnier frères (Bourges, impr. A. Tardy), 1963.

——— *Œuvres complètes.* Paris: Chez Antoine-Augustin Renouard, 1819–25.

——— *Oeuvres de Mr. de Voltaire Nouvelle édition Revue, corrigée et considérablement augmentée, avec des Figures en Taille-douce.* Tome Quatrième. Amsterdam: Étienne Ledet & Cie 1739.

Secondary Sources

Alimento, Antonella. "Entre animosité nationale et rivalité d'émulation: La position de Véron de Forbonnais face à la compétition anglaise." *GIM* (2009): 125–48.

Amat, Roman d' and R. Limouzin-Lamothe, eds. *Dictionnaire de Biographie française.* Vol 11. Paris: Librairie Letouzey et Ané, 1967.

Anderson, Wilda. *Diderot's Dream.* Baltimore: Johns Hopkins University Press, 1990.

Andries, Lise. "Les illustrations dans l'*Histoire des deux Indes.*" In *L'Histoire des deux Indes: réécriture et polygraphie,* edited by Hans-Jürgen Lüsebrink and Anthony Strugnell. Oxford: Voltaire Foundation, 1995.

Annequin, Jacques. "Métaphore de l'esclavage et esclavage comme métaphore." In *Esclavage, guerre, économie en Grèce ancienne*, edited by Pierre Brulé and Jacques Oulhen. Rennes: Presses universitaires de Rennes, 1997.

Antoine, Michel. "Le Conseil du Roi sous le règne de Louis XV." In *Mémoires et documents publiés par la Société de l'École des Chartes*. Vol. 19. Geneva and Paris: Droz, 1970.

Aravamudan, Srinivas. "Trop(Icaliz)ing the Enlightenment." *Diacritics* 23, no. 3 (1993): 48–63.

 Tropicopolitains: Colonialism and Agency, 1688–1804. Durham, NC: Duke University Press, 1999.

Atkins, Beryl T. et al. *Collins-Robert French-English English-French Dictionary.* Glasgow: William Collins and Dictionnaires Le Robert, 1987.

Avery, Peter et al. *The Cambridge History of Iran: From Nadir Shah to the Islamic Republic*. Cambridge: Cambridge University Press, 1991.

Baker, Keith Michael. *Condorcet: From Natural Philosophy to Social Mathematics.* Chicago: University of Chicago Press, 1975.

 ed. *The French Revolution and the Creation of Modern Political Culture.* Vol. 4. Oxford: Pergamon, 1994.

 Inventing the French Revolution: Essays on French Political Culture in the Eighteenth Century. Cambridge: Cambridge University Press, 1990.

 "Politics and Public Opinion under the Old Regime: Some Reflections." In *Press and Politics in Pre-revolutionary France*, edited by Jack R. Censer and Jeremy D. Popkin. Berkeley: University of California Press, 1987.

 "Transformations of Classical Republicanism in Eighteenth-Century France." *Journal of Modern History* 73, no. 1 (March 2001): 43–47.

Bancarel, Gilles. "La bibliographie matérielle et l'Histoire des deux Indes." In *L'Histoire des deux Indes: Réécriture et polygraphie*, edited by Hans-Jürgen Lüsebrink and Manfred Tietz. Oxford: Voltaire Foundation, 1995.

Bates, David W. *Enlightenment Aberrations: Error and Revolution in France.* Cambridge: Cambridge University Press, 2002.

Baudrillart, Henri. *Histoire du luxe privé et public depuis l'antiquité jusqu'à nos jours.* Paris: Hachette, 1878–80.

Beik, Paul H. *A Judgement of the Old Regime: Being a Survey by the Parlement of Provence of French Economic and Fiscal Policies at the Close of the Seven Years War.* New York: Columbia University Press, 1944.

Bell, David A. *The Cult of the Nation in France: Inventing Nationalism, 1680–1800.* Cambridge, MA: Harvard University Press, 2001.

Bell, David. "Un comparatiste au XVIIIe siècle: Balthazard-Marie Emerigon." *Revue internationale de droit comparé* 24, no. 2 (1972): 265–77.

Bellhouse, Mary L. "Candide Shoots the Monkey Lovers: Representing Black Men in Eighteenth-Century Visual Culture." *Political Theory* 34, no. 6 (2006): 741–84.

 "Femininity & Commerce in the Eighteenth Century: Rousseau's Criticism of a Literary Ruse by Montesquieu." *Polity* 13, no. 2 (1980): 285–99.

Bély, Lucien. *Dictionnaire de l'Ancien régime.* Paris: Presses universitaires de France, 2003.

Beneton, Phillipe. *Histoire des mots: Culture et civilisation.* Paris: Presses de la Fondation nationale des sciences politiques, 1975.

Benot, Yves. *Diderot, de l'athéisme à l'anticolonialisme*. Paris: François Maspéro, 1981.

"Diderot, Pechméja, Raynal et l'anticolonialisme." *Europe; revue littéraire mensuelle* 41 (Jan.–Feb. 1963).

La Révolution française et la fin des colonies. Paris: La Découverte, 1988.

Benveniste, Émile. "Civilisation: Contribution à l'histoire du mot." In *Hommage à Lucien Febvre: Éventail de l'histoire vivante*, 2 vols. Paris: Armand Colin, 1953.

Le vocabulaire des institutions indo-européennes. Paris: Éditions de Minuit, 1969.

Berg, Maxine. *Luxury and Pleasure in Eighteenth-Century Britain*. Oxford: Oxford University Press, 2005.

Berlin, Isaiah. *Concepts and Categories: Philosophical Essays*. Oxford: Oxford University Press, 1978.

Berry, Christopher J. *The Idea of Luxury: A Conceptual and Historical Investigation*. Cambridge: Cambridge University Press, 1994.

Best, Jacqueline and Matthew, Paterson eds. *Cultural Political Economy*. London and New York: Routledge, 2010.

Biondi, Carminella. *Ces esclaves sont des hommes: Lotta abolizionista e letteratura negrofila nella Francia del Settecento*. Pisa: Ed. Libreria Goliardica, 1979.

Blackburn, Robin. *The Making of New World Slavery: From the Baroque to the Modern, 1492–1800*. London: Verso, 1997.

Blom, Hans W., ed. *Property, Piracy, and Punishment: Hugo Grotius on War and Booty in De iure praedae – Concepts and Contexts*. Leiden: Brill, 2009.

Blum, Carol. *Strength in Numbers: Population, Reproduction, and Power in Eighteenth-Century France*. Baltimore and London: The Johns Hopkins University Press, 2002.

Booth, William James. "Household and Market: On the Origins of Moral Economic Philosophy." *Review of Politics* 56, no. 2 (1994).

Households: On the Moral Architecture of the Economy. Ithaca, NY: Cornell University Press, 1993.

Borschberg, Peter. "Hugo Grotius, East India Trade and the King of Johor." *Journal of Southeast Asian Studies* 30, no.2 (1999): 25–248.

Bossenga, Gail. "Financial Origins of the French Revolution." In *From Deficit to Deluge: The Origins of the French Revolution*, edited by Thomas E. Kaiser and Dale K. van Kley, 37–66. Stanford, CA: Stanford University Press, 2010.

Boulle, Pierre H. "French Mercantilism, Commercial Companies and Colonial Profitability" in *Companies and Trade: Essays on Overseas Trading Companies during the Ancien Régime*, edited by Léonard Blussé and Femme Gaastra. The Hague: Martinus Hijhoff, 1981.

"In Defense of Slavery: Eighteenth-century Opposition to Abolition and the Origins of a Racist Ideology in France." In *History from Below: Studies in Popular Protest and Popular Ideology*, edited by Frederick Krantz. Oxford: Basil Blackwell, 1988.

"Slave Trade, Commercial Organization and Industrial Growth in Eighteenth-Century Nantes." *Revue française d'histoire d'outre-mer* **59**, no. 214 (1972): 70–112.

Bouton, Cynthia A. *The Flour War: Gender, Class and Community in the Late Ancien Régime*. University Park: Pennsylvania State University Press, 1993.

Brewer, John, and Roy Porter, eds. *Consumption and the World of Goods*. London: Routledge, 1993.

Bromley, John. *Corsairs and Navies, 1660–1760*. London and Ronceverte: Hambledon Press, 1987.

Burkert, Walter. *Greek Religion*, translated by John Raffan. Cambridge, MA: Harvard University Press, 1985.

Campbell, R. H., and A. S. Skinner, eds. Introduction to *The Glasgow Edition of the Works and Correspondence of Adam Smith*. Oxford: Clarendon Press, 1976.

Caradonna, Jeremy. "Prendre part au siècle des Lumières: Le concours académique et la culture intellectuelle au XVIIIe siècle en France." *Annales. Histoire, Sciences Sociales*, **64**, no. 3 (2009), 633–62.

Carrière, Charles. *Négociants marseillais au XVIIIe siècle. Contribution à l'étude des économies maritimes*. Marseille: Institut historique de Provence, 1973.

Carpenter, Kenneth E. *The Dissemination of "The Wealth of Nations" in French and in France, 1776–1843*. New York: Bibliographical Society of America, 2002.

Casid, Jill H. *Sowing Empire: Landscape and Colonization*. Minneapolis: University of Minnesota Press, 2005.

Charles, Loïc. "French Cultural Politics and the Dissemination of Hume's Political Discourses on the Continent, 1750–1770." In *Essays on David Hume's Political Economy*, edited by Margaret Schabas and Carl Wennerlind. New York: Routledge, 2006.

——— Jean-Claude Perrot, and Christine Théré, eds. "Introduction des éditeurs." In *François Quesnay, Œuvres économiques complètes et autres textes*. Paris: INED, 2005.

Chartier, Roger. *Les origines culturelles de la Révolution française*. Paris: Éditions du Seuil, 1990.

Chassagne, Serge. *Oberkampf, un entrepreneur capitaliste au siècle des Lumières*. Paris: Aubier, 1980.

Cheney, Paul B. "History and the Science of Commerce in the Century of Enlightenment: France, 1713–1789." PhD dissertation, Columbia University, 2001.

——— *Revolutionary Commerce: Globalization and the French Monarchy*. Cambridge, MA: Harvard University Press, 2010.

Churchill, Winston. *The Age of Revolution*. Vol. 3, *A History of the English-Speaking Peoples*. New York: Dodd, Mead, and Company, 1957.

Cioranescu, Alexandre. *Bibliographie de la littérature française du dix-huitième siècle*. Paris: Éditions du Centre national de la recherche scientifique, 1969.

Citton, Yves. *Portrait de l'économiste en physiocrate: Critique littéraire de l'économie politique*. Paris: L'Hartmann, 2000.

Clark, Henry C. "Commerce, Sociability, and the Public Sphere: Morellet vs. Pluquet on Luxury." *Eighteenth-Century Life* 22, no. 2 (May 1998): 83–102.

Compass of Society: Commerce and Absolutism in Old Regime France. Lanham, MD: Lexington, 2007.

Creech, James. "'Chasing after Advances': Diderot's Article 'Encyclopedia.'" *Yale French Studies* 63 (1982): 183–97.

"Diderot and the Pleasure of the Other: Friends, Readers, and Posterity." *Eighteenth-Century Studies* 11, no. 4 (1978): 439–56.

Crouzet, François. "Politics and banking in revolutionary and Napoleonic France" in *The State, the Financial System, and Economic Modernization*, edited by Richard Eugene Sylla, Richard H. Tilly, and Gabriel Tortella Casares. New York: Cambridge University Press, 1999.

Cullen, Louis M. "History, Economic Crises, and Revolution: Understanding Eighteenth-Century France," *Economic History Review* 46, no. 4 (1993): 635–57.

Curran, Andrew. "Diderot and the *Encyclopédie*'s Construction of the *Nègre*." In *Diderot and European Culture*, edited by Frédéric Ogée and Anthony Strugnell, 35–56. Oxford: Voltaire Foundation, 2006.

Daire, Eugène. *Économistes-financiers du XVIIIe siècle.* Paris: Guillaumin, 1843.

Darnton, Robert. *The Corpus of Clandestine Literature in France, 1769–1789.* New York and London: W.W. Norton & Company, 1995.

Édition et sédition: L'univers de la littérature clandestine au XVIIIe siècle. Paris: Gallimard, 1991.

Davis, David B. *The Problem of Slavery in Western Culture.* Ithaca, NY: Cornell University Press, 1966.

Delon, Michel. "L'appel au lecteur dans l'Histoire des deux Indes." In *L'Histoire des deux Indes: Réécriture et polygraphie*, edited by Hans-Jürgen Lüsebrink and Anthony Strugnell. Oxford: Voltaire Foundation, 1995.

ed. *Dictionnaire européen des Lumières.* Paris: Presses universitaires de France, 1997.

Depitre, Edgard. *La toile peinte en France au XVIIe et au XVIIIe siècle.* Paris: M. Rivière, 1912.

Derrida, Jacques. "*Hors livre* / Outwork." In *Dissemination*, translated by Barbara Johnson. Paris: Editions du Seuil, 1972. Reprint. New York: Continuum, 2004.

Desan, Philippe. *Les Commerces de Montaigne: le discours économique des Essais*, Paris: A.-G. Nizet, 1992.

Dickey, Laurence. "Doux-Commerce and Humanitarian Values: Free Trade, Sociability and Universal Benevolence in Eighteenth-Century Thinking." *Grotiana* 22–23: 272–83.

"*Doux-Commerce* and the 'Mediocrity of Money' in the Ideological Context of the Wealth and Virtue Problem." In *An Inquiry into the Nature and Causes of the Wealth of Nations*, by Adam Smith, abridged with commentary by Laurence Dickey. Indianapolis: Hackett, 1993.

Dieckmann, Herbert. *Inventaire du Fonds Vandeul et inédits de Diderot.* Geneva: Droz; Lille: Giard, 1951.

Ditz, Toby. "Shipwrecked; or, Masculinity Imperiled: Mercantile Representations of Failure and the Gendered Self in Eighteenth-Century Philadelphia." *Journal of American History* 81, no. 1 (1994): 51–80.

Dobie, Madeleine. *Trading Places: Colonization and Slavery in Eighteenth-Century French Culture*. Ithaca, NY: Cornell University Press, 2010.

Dorigny, Marcel, ed. *Les Abolitions de l'esclavage de L.F. Sonthonax à V. Schoelscher, 1793, 1794, 1848*. Paris: Éditions UNESCO and Presses universitaires de Vincennes, 1995.

Douay, Françoise. "Valorisation/dévalorisation des corsaires, forbans et pirates dans la rhétorique du 18e siècle (pratiques et théorie)." Paper delivered at the 13ᵉ Colloque International du CRLV, "L'Aventure maritime: Pirates, corsaires et flibustiers." Château de La Napoule, May 2000.

Dubois, Laurent. *Avengers of the New World: The Story of the Haitian Revolution*. Cambridge, MA: Harvard University Press, 2004.

Les esclaves de la République: L'histoire oubliée de la première émancipation, 1789–1794. Paris: Calmann-Lévy, 1998.

Duchet, Michèle. *Anthropologie et histoire au siècle des lumières: Buffon, Voltaire, Rousseau, Helvétius, Diderot*. Paris: Maspéro, 1971. Reprint. Paris: Albin Michel, 1995.

Diderot et l'Histoire des deux Indes ou l'Écriture Fragmentaire. Paris: A. G. Nizet, 1978.

"*L'Histoire des deux Indes*: Sources et structure d'un texte polyphonique." In *Lectures de Raynal*, edited by Hans-Jürgen Lüsebrink and Manfred Tietz, 9–15. Oxford: Voltaire Foundation, 1991.

Dulac, Georges. "Dossier de la Compagnie des Indes (été 1769)." In *DPV*, 20:212.

"Les Gens de lettres, le banquier, et l'opinion: Diderot et la polémique sur la Compagnie des Indes." *Dix-huitième siècle* 26 (1994): 194–99.

"Introduction au 'Dossier de la Compagnie des Indes.'" *DPV*, 20:197, 200.

"Observations sur le Nakaz." In *Dictionnaire de Diderot*, edited by Roland Mortier and Raymond Trousson. Paris: Honoré Champion, 1999.

"Pour reconsidérer l'histoire des *Observations sur le Nakaz* (à partir des réflexions de 1775 sur la physiocratie)." In *Éditer Diderot: Études recueillies par Georges Dulac*, 467–514. Oxford: Voltaire Foundation, 1988.

Dunn, John, ed. *The Economic Limits to Modern Politics*. Cambridge: Cambridge University Press, 1994.

Edelstein, Dan. "War and Terror: The Law of Nations from Grotius to the French Revolution." *French Historical Studies* 31, no. 2 (2008): 229–62.

Ehrard, Jean. "L'Encyclopédie et l'esclavage: Deux lectures de Montesquieu." In *Enlightenment: Essays in Memory of Robert Shackleton*. Oxford: Voltaire Foundation, 1988.

"L'esclavage devant la conscience morale des lumières françaises: indifférence, gêne, révolte." In *Les Abolitions de l'esclavage*, edited by Marcel Dorigny. Paris: Éditions UNESCO and Presses universitaires de Vincennes, 1995.

Ette, Ottmar. "La mise en scène de la table de travail: poétologie et épistémologie immanentes chez Guillaume-Thomas Raynal et Alexander von Homboldt" In *Icons, texts, iconotext: Essays on Ekphrasis and Intermediality*, edited by Peter Wagner, 175–212. Berlin: De Gruyter, 1996.

Faccarello, Gilbert. "Galiani, Necker and Turgot: A Debate on Economic Reform and Policy in Eighteenth-Century France." In *Studies in the History of French Political Economy*, edited by Gilbert Faccarello. London: Routledge, 1998.

Fairchilds, Cissie. "The Production and Marketing of Populuxe Goods in Eighteenth-Century Paris." In *Consumption and the World of Goods*, edited by John Brewer and Roy Porter. London: Routledge, 1993.

Fassin, Éric. "Actualité du harcèlement sexuel." *Le Monde*. 22 February 2002.

Febvre, Lucien. "Civilisation, évolution d'un mot et d'un groupe d'idées." 1929. In *Lucien Febvre: Pour une histoire à part entière*. Paris: Service d'édition et de vente des publications de l'Éducation nationale, 1962.

Feugère, Anatole. *L'abbé Raynal. Bibliographie critique*. Angoulême: Impr. ouvrière, 1922.

———. *Un précurseur de la Révolution: L'abbé Raynal (1713–1796)*. Angoulême: Impr. ouvrière, 1922.

———. "Raynal, Diderot et quelques autres historiens des deux Indes." *Revue d'Histoire Littéraire de la France* 20 (1913): 345.

Fontana, Biancamaria, ed. and trans. *Political Writings / Benjamin Constant*. Cambridge: Cambridge University Press, 1988.

Fox-Genovese, Elisabeth. *The Origins of Physiocracy: Economic Revolution and Social Order in Eighteenth-Century France*. Ithaca, NY: Cornell University Press, 1976.

Freud, Sigmund. "Civilization and Its Discontents." 1930. *The Standard Edition of the Psychological Works of Sigmund Freud*, edited by James Strachey, translated by Peter Gay. New York: W. W. Norton, 1989.

Fumaroli, Marc. *Le poète et le roi: Jean de La Fontaine en son siècle*. Paris: de Fallois, 1997.

Galliani, Renato. *Rousseau, le luxe, et l'idéologie nobiliaire, étude socio-historique*. In *Studies on Voltaire and the Eighteenth Century*, vol. 268. Oxford: Voltaire Foundation, 1989.

Garrigues, André. *Musée de la compagnie des Indes: Guide du visiteur*. Morbihan: Citadelle de Port-Louis, 1993.

Garraway, Doris. *Tree of Liberty: Cultural Legacies of the Haitian Revolution in the Atlantic World*. Charlottesville: University of Virginia Press, 2008.

Gauthier, Florence, ed. *La Guerre du blé au XVIIIe siècle*. Paris: Editions de la Passion, 1989.

———. "Le rôle de la députation de Saint-Domingue dans l'abolition de l'esclavage." In *Les Abolitions de l'esclavage de L.F. Sonthonax à V. Schoelscher, 1793, 1794, 1848*, edited by Marcel Dorigny, 199–211. Paris: Éditions UNESCO and Presses universitaires de Vincennes, 1995.

Ghachem, Malick. "The Age of the Code Noir in French Political Economy." In *A Vast and Useful Art: The Gustave Gimon Collection on French Political Economy*. Edited by M. J. Parrine, 66–76. Stanford: Stanford University Libraries, 2004.

———. "Sovereignty and Slavery in the Age of Revolution: Haitian Variations on a Metropolitan Theme." PhD dissertation, Stanford University, 2002.

Gibbon, Edward. *The History of the Decline and Fall of the Roman Empire*. 6 vols. London: n.p., 1776–88.

Gilroy, Paul. *The Black Atlantic: Modernity and Double Consciousness.* Cambridge, MA: Harvard University Press, 1993.

Goggi, Gianluigi. *Denis Diderot, Pensées détachées, Contributions à 'L'Histoire des deux Indes.'* 2 vols. Siena: Tip. del Rettorato, 1976–77.

Denis Diderot, Fragments politiques échappés du portefeuille d'un philosophe. Paris: Hermann, 1991.

"L'Histoire des deux Indes et l'éloquence politique." *SVEC*, 7 (2003): 123–61.

"Quelques remarques sur la collaboration de Diderot à la première édition de l'*Histoire des deux Indes.*" In *Studies on Voltaire and the Eighteenth Century* 286, 21–26. Oxford: Voltaire Foundation, 1991.

Goldschmidt, Victor, ed. *De l'Esprit des Lois.* Paris: Garnier-Flammarion, 1979.

Goodman, Dena. *Criticism in Action: Enlightenment Experiments in Political Writing.* Ithaca, NY: Cornell University Press, 1989.

The Republic of Letters: A Cultural History of the French Enlightenment. Ithaca: Cornell University Press, 1994.

Gordon, Daniel. *Citizens without Sovereignty: Equality and Sociability in French Thought, 1670–1789.* Princeton: Princeton University Press, 1994.

Gosse, Philip. *The History of Piracy.* London: Longmans, Green, 1932.

Goubert, Jean-Pierre. *Du luxe au confort.* Paris: Éditions Belin, 1988.

Granderoute, Robert. "Goût et réflexion pédagogique au XVIIIe siècle." In *L'Encyclopédie, Diderot, l'esthétique: Mélanges en hommage à Jacques Chouillet*, edited by Sylvain Auroux, Dominique Bourel, and Charles Porset. Paris: Presses universitaires de France, 1991.

Groenewegen, Peter. *Eighteenth Century Economics: Turgot, Beccaria and Smith and their contemporaries.* London and New York: Routledge, 2002.

Haakonssen, Knud. *Natural and Moral Philosophy. From Grotius to the Scottish Enlightenment.* Cambridge: Cambridge University Press, 1996.

The Science of a Legislator: The Natural Jurisprudence of David Hume and Adam Smith. Cambridge: Cambridge University Press, 1981.

Haggenmacher, Peter. "Genèse et signification du concept de 'ius gentium' chez Grotius." *Grotiana*, no. 2 (1981): 44–102.

Halpern, Jean-Claude. "L'Africain de Raynal." In *Raynal, de la polémique à l'histoire*, edited by Gilles Bancarel and Gianluigi Goggi, 235–42. Oxford: Voltaire Foundation, 2000.

Harms, Robert. *The Diligent: A Voyage through the Worlds of the Slave Trade.* New York: Basic, 2003.

Haudrère, Philippe. *La compagnie française des Indes au XVIIIe siècle (1719–1795).* Vol. 1. Paris: Librairie de l'Inde, 1989.

"L'État et les négociants: Deux mémoires sur la situation de la compagnie française des Indes en 1730." In *État, Marine et Société: Hommage à Jean Meyer*, edited by Martine Acerra, Jean-Pierre Pousson, Michel Vergé-Franceschi, and André Zysberg. Paris: Presses de l'Université de Paris-Sorbonne, 1995.

Higgs, Henry. *Bibliography of Economics, 1751–1775.* Prepared for the British Academy. Cambridge: Cambridge University Press, 1935.

The Physiocrats: Six Lectures on the French "Économistes" of the Eighteenth-Century. London: Macmillan, 1897.

Hilaire-Pérez, Liliane. *L'Expérience de la mer: Les Européens et les espaces maritimes au XVIIIe siècle.* Paris: Éditions Seli Arslan, 1997.

Hirschman, Albert O. *The Passions and the Interests: Political Arguments for Capitalism Before Its Triumph.* 1977. 20th anniversary edition. Princeton, NJ: Princeton University Press, 1997.

"Rival Interpretations of Market Society: Civilizing, Destructive, or Feeble?" *Journal of Economic Literature* 20, no. 4 (1982): 1463–84.

Hobsbawm, E. J. *Bandits.* London: Weidenfeld and Nicolson, 1969.

Holdworth, Deryck W. "The Country-House Library: Creating Mercantile Knowledge in the Age of Sail." In *Geographies of the Book,* edited by Miles Ogborn and Charles Withers, 133–56. Farnham: Ashgate, 2010.

Hollander, Samuel. "Malthus as Physiocrat: Surplus versus Scarcity." *In The Literature of Political Economy: Collected Essays II,* 289–316. London and New York: Routledge, 1998.

Hont, Istvan. "The Early Enlightenment Debate on Commerce and Luxury." In *The Cambridge History of Eighteenth-Century Political Thought,* edited by Mark Goldie and Robert Wokler, 379–418. Cambridge: Cambridge University Press, 2006.

"Free Trade and the Economic Limits to National Politics: Neo-Machiavellian Political Economy Reconsidered." In *The Economic Limits to Modern Politics,* edited by John Dunn. Cambridge: Cambridge University Press, 1994.

Jealousy of Trade: International Competition and the Nation-State in Historical Perspective. Cambridge, MA: Harvard University Press, 2005.

"The Language of Sociability and Commerce: Samuel Pufendorf and the Theoretical Foundations of the 'Four-Stages Theory.'" In *The Languages of Political Theory in Early-Modern Europe,* edited by Anthony Pagden. Cambridge: Cambridge University Press, 1989.

"The Permanent Crisis of a Divided Mankind: 'Contemporary Crisis of the Nation State' in Historical Perspective." In *Jealousy of Trade: International Competition and the Nation-State in Historical Perspective,* 447–528. Cambridge, MA: Harvard University Press, 2005.

Hont, Istvan, and Michael Ignatieff, eds. *Wealth and Virtue: The Shaping of Political Economy in the Scottish Enlightenment.* Cambridge: Cambridge University Press, 1983.

Höpfl, Harro M. "From Savage to Scotsman: Conjectural History in the Scottish Enlightenment." *Journal of British Studies* 17 (1978): 19–40.

Hulliung, Mark. *The Autocritique of the Enlightenment.* Cambridge, MA: Harvard University Press, 1998.

Hundert, E. J. "Bernard Mandeville and the Enlightenment's Maxims of Modernity." *Journal of the History of Ideas* 56, no. 4 (1995): 577–93.

The Enlightenment's Fable: Bernard Mandeville and the Discovery of Society. Cambridge: Cambridge University Press, 1994.

"The Thread of Language and the Web of Dominion: Mandeville to Rousseau and Back." *Eighteenth Century Studies* 21, no. 2 (1987–88): 169–91.

Hutchison, Terence W. *Before Adam Smith: The Emergence of Political Economy, 1662–1776.* Oxford: Basil Blackwell, 1988.

Iannini, Christopher. "'The Itinerant Man': Crèvecoeur's Caribbean, Raynal's Revolution, and the Fate of Atlantic Cosmopolitanism." *William and Mary Quarterly* 61 (2004): 201–34.

Isanga, Joseph M. "Countering Persistent Contemporary Sea Piracy: Expanding Jurisdictional Regimes." *American University Law Review* 59, no. 5 (June 2010): 1267–1319.

Ittersum, Martina Julia van. "Hugo Grotius in Context: Van Heemskerck's Capture of the Santa Catarina and its Justification in De Jure Praedae (1604–1606)." *Asian Journal of Social Science* 31, no. 3 (2003): 511–48.

"Preparing *Mare liberum* for the Press: Hugo Grotius' Rewriting of Chapter 12 of *De iure praedae* in November – December 1608." In *Property, Piracy, and Punishment: Hugo Grotius on War and Booty in De iure praedae – Concepts and Context*, edited by Hans W. Blom, 246–80. Leiden: Brill, 2009.

Jaeger, Gérard A., ed. *Vues sur la piraterie: Des origines à nos jours*. Paris: Librairie Jules Tallandier, 1992.

James, C. L. R. *The Black Jacobins: Toussaint L'Ouverture and the San Domingo Revolution*. 1963. Rev. 2nd edition. New York: Vintage, 1989.

Jennings, Jeremy. "The Debate about Luxury in Eighteenth- and Nineteenth-Century French Political Thought." *Journal of the History of Ideas* 68, no. 1 (2007): 79–105.

Jones, Colin, and Rebecca Spang. "*Sans-culottes, sans café, sans tabac*: Shifting Realms of Necessity and Luxury in Eighteenth-Century France." In *Consumers and Luxury in Europe, 1650–1850*, edited by Maxine Berg and Helen Clifford, 37–62. Manchester: Manchester University Press, 1999.

Kafker, Frank A., and Serena L. Kafker. *The Encyclopedists as Individuals: a Biographical Dictionary of the Authors of the Encyclopédie*. Oxford: Voltaire Foundation, 1988.

Kaiser, Thomas E. "The Evil Empire? The Debate on Turkish Despotism in Eighteenth-Century French Political Culture." *Journal of Modern History* 72, no. 1 (2000): 6–34.

"Money, Despotism and Public Opinion in Early Eighteenth-Century France: John Law and the Debate on Royal Credit." *Journal of Modern History* 63, no. 1 (1991): 1–28.

Kaiser, Thomas E., and Dale K. van Kley, eds. *From Deficit to Deluge: The Origins of the French Revolution*. Stanford: Stanford University Press, 2010.

Kaplan, Steven L. *Bread, Politics and Political Economy in the Reign of Louis XV*. 2 vols. The Hague: Martinus Nijhoff, 1976.

La fin des corporations, Translated by Béatrice Vierne. Paris: Fayard, 2001.

Keller, Alexandre. *Correspondance, bulletins et ordres du jour de Napoléon*. 4 vols. Paris: A. Méricant, 1909–12.

Kessler, Amalia D. *A Revolution in Commerce: The Parisian Merchant Court and the Rise of Commercial Society in Eighteenth-Century France*. New Haven: Yale University Press, 2007.

Khadhar, Hédia. "La description de l'Afrique dans l'*Histoire des deux Indes*." In *L'Histoire des deux Indes: Réécriture et polygraphie*, edited by Hans-Jürgen Lüsebrink and Anthony Strugnell. Oxford: Voltaire Foundation, 1995.

Kors, Alan. *D'Holbach's Coterie: An Enlightenment in Paris.* Princeton, NJ: Princeton University Press, 1976.

Kwass, Michael. "Consumption and the World of Ideas: Consumer Revolution and the Moral Economy of the Marquis de Mirabeau." *Eighteenth-Century Studies* 37, no. 2 (2004).

Labrosse, Claude. "Réception et communication dans les périodiques littéraires (1750–1760)." In *La diffusion et la lecture des journaux de langue française sous l'ancien Régime,* edited by Hans Bots. Amsterdam: APA-Holland University Press, 1988.

Lacapra, Dominick. *Writing History, Writing Trauma.* Baltimore: Johns Hopkins University Press, 2001.

Larrère, Catherine. *L'Invention de l'économie au XVIIIe siècle: Du droit naturel à la physiocratie.* Paris: Presses universitaires de France, 1992.

Lebris, Michel. *L'aventure de la flibuste: Actes du colloque de Brest, 3–4 mai 2001.* Paris: Hoëbeke/ Abbaye de Daoulas, 2002.

Lewis, Charlton T., and Charles Short. *A Latin Dictionary.* Oxford: Clarendon Press, 1880.

Lexicon Iconographicum Mythologiae Classicae. Vol. 5, 1. Munich: Artemis Verlag, 1990.

Livesey, James. "Agrarian Ideology and Commercial Republicanism in the French Revolution." *Past & Present* 157 (1997): 94–121.

Lüsebrink, Hans-Jürgen. "L'Histoire des deux Indes et ses Extraits: un mode de dispersion textuelle au XVIIIe siècle." *Littérature* 69 (1988), 28–41.

Lüsebrink, Hans-Jürgen, and Anthony Strugnell, eds. *L'Histoire des deux Indes: Réécriture et polygraphie.* Oxford: Voltaire Foundation, 1995.

Lüsebrink, Hans-Jürgen, and Manfred Tietz, eds. *Lectures de Raynal.* Oxford: Voltaire Foundation, 1991.

Lüthy, Herbert. *La Banque protestante en France.* 2 vols. Paris: SEVPEN: J. Touzot, 1959–70.

Mandeville, Bernard. *The Fable of the Bees, or, Private Vices, Publick Benefits.* 2 vols. Oxford: Clarendon Press, 1924. Reprint. Indianapolis: Liberty Classics, 1988.

Marcel, Gabriel, ed. *Mémoire inédit de Grossin sur le Madagascar.* Paris: Institut géographique de Paris, chez Delagrave, 1883.

Margairaz, Dominique. "Luxe." In *Dictonnaire européen des lumières,* edited by Michel Delon. Paris: Presses universitaires de France, 1997.

Martin, Dale B. *Slavery and Salvation: The Metaphor of Slavery in Pauline Christianity.* New Haven, CT: Yale University Press, 1990.

Marx, Karl. *Capital: A Critique of Political Economy* (1867). Vol. 1. Translated by Ben Fowkes. London: Penguin Classics, 1990.

Theories of Surplus Value. 3 vols. Moscow: Progress Publishers, 1969–71.

Masselman, George. *The Cradle of Colonialism.* New Haven: Yale University Press, 1963.

Massiet Du Biest, Jean. *La Fille de Diderot, Mme de Vandeul.* Tours: l'auteur, 48, rue Jehan-Foucquet, n.d.; (Laval: Impr. de Barnéoud frères), 1949.

Maza, Sarah. *The Myth of the French Bourgeoisie: An Essay on the Social Imaginary, 1750–1850.* Cambridge, MA: Harvard University Press, 2003.

McCloskey, Dierdre. *The Bourgeois Virtues: Ethics for an Age of Commerce.* Chicago: Chicago University Press, 2006.

Meek, Ronald L. *The Economics of Physiocracy: Essays and translations.* Cambridge, MA: Harvard University Press, 1963.

"Smith, Turgot, and the 'Four Stages' Theory." In *Smith, Marx and After: Ten Essays in the Development of Economic Thought.* London: Chapman & Hall, 1980.

Social Science and the Ignoble Savage. Cambridge, MA: Cambridge University Press, 1976.

Merrick, Jeffrey. "Male Friendship in Pre-revolutionary France." *GLQ: A Journal of Lesbian and Gay Studies* 10, no. 3 (2004).

Meyssonnier, Simone. *La balance et l'horloge: la genèse de la pensée libérale en France au XVIIIe siècle.* Montreuil: Editions de la Passion, 1989.

Michaud, L. G. *Biographie universelle ancienne et moderne ....* Nouvelle édition. 45 vols. Paris: Madame C. Desplaces et M. Michaud, 1854–65.

Mijolla, Alain de, ed. *International Dictionary of Psychoanalysis.* Detroit: Thomson Gale, 2005.

Miller, Judith. "Economic Ideologies, 1750–1800: The Creation of the Modern Political Economy." *French Historical Studies* 23, no. 3 (2000): 497–511.

Mastering the Market: The State and the Grain Trade in Northern France, 1700–1860. Cambridge: Cambridge University Press, 1999.

Morineau, Michel. *Les Grandes compagnies des Indes orientales (XVIe-XIXe siècles).* Paris: Presses universitaires de France, 1994.

Morize, André. *L'Apologie du luxe au XVIIIe siècle et "Le Mondain" de Voltaire.* Paris: H. Didier, 1909. Reprint. Geneva: Slatkine, 1970.

Mortier, Roland, and Raymond Trousson, eds. *Dictionnaire de Diderot.* Paris: Honoré Champion, 1999.

Mousnier, Roland. *The Institutions of France under the Absolute Monarchy, 1589–1789,* translated by Arthur Goldhammer. Chicago: University of Chicago Press, 1984.

Muthu, Sankar. *Enlightenment against Empire.* Princeton, NJ, and Oxford: Princeton University Press, 2003.

Murphy, Antoin E. *John Law: Economic Theorist and Policy-maker.* Oxford: Oxford University Press, 1997.

Richard Cantillon: Entrepreneur and Economist. Oxford: Clarendon Press, 1987.

Napoléon. *Correspondance de Napoléon 1er: Publiée par ordre de L'Empereur Napoléon III.* 32 vols. Paris: H. Plon, 1858–70.

Negroni, Barbara de. "Diderot et le bien d'autrui." In *Oeuvres philosophiques/Diderot,* edited by Michel Delon and Barbara de Negroni. Paris: Gallimard, 2010.

O'Connor, Condorcet, and M. F. Arago, eds. *Oeuvres de Condorcet.* 12 vols. 1847–49. Paris: Firmin Didot Frères, Libraires, 1847.

Ogborn, Miles, and Charles Withers, eds. *Geographies of the Book.* Farnham: Ashgate Publishing Limited, 2010.

Ogée, Frédéric, and Anthony Strugnell, eds. *Diderot and European Culture.* Oxford: Voltaire Foundation, 2006.

Pagden, Anthony. "The 'Defence of Civilization' in Eighteenth Century Social Theory." *History of the Human Sciences* 1 (1988): 33–45.

——. *European Encounters with the New World.* New Haven, CT: Yale University Press, 1993.

——. ed. *The Languages of Political Theory in Early Modern Europe.* Cambridge: Cambridge University Press, 1989.

——. *Lords of all the Worlds: Ideologies of Empire in Spain, Britain, and France c.1500-c.1800.* New Haven: Yale University Press, 1995.

Pardailhé-Galabrun, Annick. *La Naissance de l'intime: 3000 foyers parisiens, XVIIe – XVIIIe siècles.* Paris: Presses universitaires de France, 1988.

Patalano, Rosario. "Il Dictionnaire universel de commerce dei Savary e la fondazione dell' autonomia del discorso economico." In *Storia del pensiero economico.* Florence: Florence University Press, 2001.

Peabody, Sue. *There Are No Slaves in France: The Political Culture of Race and Slavery in the Ancien Régime.* New York: Oxford University Press, 1996.

Pérotin-Dumon, Anne. "The Pirate and the Emperor: Power and the Law on the Seas, 1450–1850." In *Bandits at Sea: A Pirates Reader*, edited by C. R. Pennell. New York: New York University Press, 2001.

Perrot, Jean-Claude. "Les dictionnaires de commerce au XVIIIe siècle." *Revue d'histoire moderne et contemporaine* 28 (1981): 36–67.

——. *Une histoire intellectuelle de l'économie politique, XVIIe – XVIIIe siècle.* Paris: Éditions de l'École des Hautes Études en Sciences Sociales, 1992.

Perrot, Philippe. "De l'apparat au bien-être: les avatars d'un superflu nécessaire." In *Du luxe au confort*, edited by Jean-Pierre Goubert. Paris: Éditions Belin, 1988.

——. *Le luxe: Une richesse entre faste et confort, XVIIIe – XIXe siècle.* Paris: Éditions du Seuil, 1995.

Pistoye, Alphonse de, and Charles Duverdy. *Traité des prises maritimes dans lequel on a refondu en partie le Traité de Valin en l'appropriant à la législation nouvelle.* Paris: Auguste Durand, Libraire, 1855.

Pocock, J. G. A. *Barbarism and Religion. Volume I: The Enlightenments of Edward Gibbon, 1737–1764.* Cambridge: Cambridge University Press, 1999.

——. *The Machiavellian Moment: Florentine Political Thought and the Atlantic Republican Tradition.* Princeton, NJ: Princeton University Press, 1975.

——. "The Political Economy of Burke's Analysis of the French Revolution." In *Virtue, Commerce, and History: Essays on Political Thought and History, Chiefly in the Eighteenth Century.* Cambridge: Cambridge University Press, 1985.

Pointon, Marcia. "Jewelry in Eighteenth-Century England." In *Consumers and Luxury in Europe, 1650–1850*, edited by Maxine Berg and Helen Clifford, 120–46. Manchester: Manchester University Press, 1999.

Polak, Jean. *Bibliographie maritime française.* Grenoble: Éditions des 4 seigneurs, 1976.

Popkin, Jeremy. *Facing Racial Revolution: Eyewitness Accounts of the Haitian Insurrection.* Chicago: University of Chicago Press, 2007.

——. *You Are All Free: The Haitian Revolution and the Abolition of Slavery.* Cambridge: Cambridge University Press, 2010.

Pothier, Robert Joseph. *Oeuvres de Pothier: Traité du contrat d'assurance*. Paris: Letellier, 1810.

Reddy, William. *The Rise of Market Culture: The Textile Trade and French Society, 1750–1900*. Cambridge: Cambridge University Press, 1987.

"The Structure of a Cultural Crisis: Thinking About Cloth in France Before and After the Revolution." In *The Social Life of Things: Commodities in Cultural Perspective*, edited by Arjun Appadurai, 261–84. New York: Cambridge University Press, 1986.

Rediker, Marcus. *Between the Devil and the Deep Blue Sea: Merchant Seamen, Pirates, and the Anglo-American Maritime World, 1700–1750*. Cambridge: Cambridge University Press, 1987.

Reinert, Sophus. "Lessons on the Rise and Fall of Great Powers: Conquest, Commerce, and Decline in Enlightenment Italy." *American Historical Review* 115, no. 5 (2010): 1395–1425.

The Virtue of Emulation: International Competition and the Origins of Political Economy. Cambridge, MA: Harvard University Press, 2011.

Rétat, Pierre. "Luxe." *Dix-huitième siècle* 26 (1994): 79–88.

Rey, Alain, et al. *Dictionnaire historique de la langue française*. Paris: Dictionnaires Le Robert, 1998.

Rey, Alain, and Josette Rey-Debove. *Le Nouveau Petit Robert*. Paris: Dictionnaires Le Robert, 1994.

Rich, E. E. and C. H. Wilson, eds. *The Cambridge Economic History of Europe*. Vol. 4. Cambridge: Cambridge University Press, 1967.

Riley, James C. *The Seven Years War and the Old Regime in France: The Economic and Financial Toll*. Princeton, NJ: Princeton University Press, 1986.

Ritchie, Robert. "Government Measures against Piracy and Privateering in the Atlantic Area, 1750–1850." In *Pirates and Privateers: New Perspectives on the War on Trade in the Eighteenth and Nineteenth Centuries*, edited by David J. Starkey, E. S. van Eyck van Heslinga, and J. A. de Moor, 10–28. Exeter: University of Exeter Press, 1997.

Roche, Daniel. *La Culture des apparences: Une Histoire du vêtement, XVIIe–XVIIIe siècle*. Paris: Fayard, 1989.

France in the Enlightenment, translated by Arthur Goldhammer. Cambridge, MA: Harvard University Press, 1998.

"Négoce et culture dans la France du XVIIIe siècle." *Revue d'histoire moderne et contemporaine* 25 (1978): 375–95.

Røge, Pernille. "'La Clef de Commerce' – The changing role of Africa in France's Atlantic empire c. 1760–1797." *History of European Ideas*, Special issue on "New Perspectives in Atlantic History," 34, no. 4 (December 2008): 431–43.

Rosenblatt, Helena. *Rousseau and Geneva: From the First Discourse to the Social Contract, 1749–1762*. Cambridge: Cambridge University Press, 1997.

Rosanvallon, Pierre. *Le capitalisme utopique: histoire de l'idée de marché*. 3rd ed. Paris: Éditions du Seuil, 1999.

Le libéralisme économique: histoire de l'idée de marché. Paris: Éditions du Seuil, 1989.

Rothkrug, Lionel. *Opposition to Louis XIV: The Political and Social Origins of the French Enlightenment.* Princeton: Princeton University Press, 1965.

Rothschild, Emma. *Economic Sentiments: Adam Smith, Condorcet and the Enlightenment.* Cambridge, MA: Harvard University Press, 2001.

Russo, Elena. "Virtuous Economies: Modernity and Noble Expenditure from Montesquieu to Caillois." *Historical Reflections/Réflexions Historiques* (1999): 25: 251–278.

Roudinesco, Elisabeth, and Michel Plon, eds. *Dictionnaire de la psychanalyse.* Paris: Fayard, 1997.

Sala-Molins, Louis. *Les Misères des lumières: Sous la raison, l'outrage.* Paris: R. Laffont, 1992.

Schabas, Margaret. *The Natural Origins of Economics.* Chicago: University of Chicago Press, 2006.

Schonhorn, Manuel, ed. *A General History of the Pyrates.* Columbia: University of South Carolina Press, 1999.

Scott, Joan Wallach. *Gender and the Politics of History.* New York: Columbia University Press, 1988.

Sekora, John. *Luxury: The Concept in Western Thought.* Baltimore: Johns Hopkins University Press, 1977.

Sen, Amartya. Foreword to *The Passions and the Interests* by Albert O. Hirschman. Princeton: NJ Princeton University Press, 1997.

On Ethics and Economics. Oxford and New York: Basil Blackwell, 1987.

Sgard, Jean. *Dictionnaire des journaux, 1600–1789.* Oxford: Voltaire Foundation; Paris: Université de Paris, 1991.

Shklar, Judith. *Men and Citizens: A Study of Rousseau's Social Theory.* Cambridge: Cambridge University Press, 1969.

Shovlin, John. "The Cultural Politics of Luxury in Eighteenth-Century France." *French Historical Studies* 23, no. 4 (Fall 2000): 578–84.

"Emulation in Eighteenth-Century French Economic Thought." *Eighteenth-Century Studies* 36, no. 2 (2003): 224–230.

"Luxury, Political Economy, and the Rise of Commercial Society in Eighteenth-Century France." PhD dissertation, University of Chicago, 1999.

"Nobility and Economy." In *The Political Economy of Virtue.* Ithaca, NY: Cornell University Press, 2006.

The Political Economy of Virtue: Luxury, Patriotism, and the Origins of the French Revolution. Ithaca, NY: Cornell University Press, 2006.

Skinner, Andrew. "Natural History in the Age of Adam Smith." *Political Studies* 15 (1967): 32–48.

Vision of Politics: Regarding Method. Cambridge: Cambridge University Press, 2002.

Skrzypek, Marian. "Le commerce instrument de la paix mondiale." In *Raynal, de la polémique à l'histoire,* edited by Gilles Bancarel and Gianluigi Goggi, 243–54. Oxford: Voltaire Foundation, 2000.

Smith, Jay. "Between Discourse and Experience: Agency and Ideas in the French Pre-Revolution." *History and Theory* 40, no. 4 (2001): 116–42.

Nobility Reimagined: The Patriotic Nation in Eighteenth-Century France. Ithaca, NY: Cornell University Press, 2005.

"No More Language Games: Words, Beliefs, and the Political Culture of Early Modern France." *American Historical Review* 102, no. 5 (1997): 1413–40.

"Social Categories, the Language of Patriotism, and the Origins of the French Revolution: The Debate over *noblesse commerçante*." *Journal of Modern History* 72 (2000): 339–74.

Soboul, Albert. *La Civilisation et la Révolution française. Vol. 1, La Crise de l'Ancien régime*. Paris: Arthaud, 1970.

Sonenscher, Michael. *Before the Deluge: Public Debt, Inequality, and the Intellectual Origins of the French Revolution*. Princeton, NJ: Princeton University Press, 2007.

"The Nation's Debt and the Birth of the Modern Republic." In *Political Studies* 42 (1994): 166–231.

Spang, Rebecca L. "Review of Paul Cheney's Revolutionary Commerce: Globalization and the French Monarchy." *H-France Review* 11 (2011), no. 86: 1.

Spector, Céline. "Économie et politique dans l'oeuvre de Montesquieu." Doctorat de Nouveau Régime, Université de Paris X-Nanterre, 2001.

"'Il est impossible que nous supposions que ces gens-là soient des hommes': la théorie de l'esclavage au livre XV de L'Esprit des lois." *Lumières* 3 (2004): 15–51.

"Le concept de mercantilisme." *Revue de métaphysique et de morale* 3 (2003): 289–309.

Montesquieu: Pouvoirs, richesses et société. Paris: Presses universitaires de France, 2004.

"Rousseau et la critique de l'économie politique." In *Rousseau et les sciences*, edited by Bernadette Bensaude-Vincent and Bruno Bernardi. Paris: L'Harmattan, 2003.

Stalnaker, Joanna. *The Unfinished Enlightenment Description in the Age of the Encyclopédie*. Ithaca, NY: Cornell University Press, 2010.

Starobinski, Jean. "Diderot et la parole des autres." *Critique* 296 (1972): 3–22.

Le remède dans le mal: Critique et légitimation de l'artifice à l'âge des Lumières. Paris: Gallimard, 1989.

Steiner, Philippe. "L'Esclavage chez les économistes français (1750–1830)." In *Les abolitions de l'esclavage*. Paris: UNESCO, 1995.

La "Science nouvelle" de l'économie politique. Paris: Presses universitaires de France, 1998.

Stern, Philip J. *The Company-State: Corporate Sovereignty and the Early Modern Foundations of the British Empire in India*. Oxford: Oxford University Press, 2011.

Stiglitz, Joseph E. *Globalization and its Discontents*. New York: W. W. Norton, 2002.

Stoler, Ann Laura. *Carnal Knowledge and Imperial Power: Race and the Intimate in Colonial Rule*. Berkeley: University of California Press, 2002.

Strugnell, Anthony. "Matérialisme, histoire et commerce: Diderot entre le réel et l'idéal dans l'Histoire des deux Indes." In *Être matérialiste à l'âge des Lumières [Texte imprimé]: hommage offert à Roland Desné*, edited by Béatrice Fink and Gerhardt Stenger. Paris: Presses universitaires de France, 1999.

Sykes, J. B., ed. *The Concise Oxford Dictionary of Current English*. Based on *The Oxford English Dictionary and its Supplements*. 7th ed. Oxford: Clarendon Press, 1982.

Tarrade, Jean. *Le commerce colonial de la France à la fin de l'Ancien Régime: L'évolution du régime de l'"Exclusif" de 1763 à 1789*. 2 vols. Paris: Presses universitaires de France, 1972.

Taylor, Charles. *Sources of the Self: The Making of the Modern Identity*. Cambridge, MA: Harvard University Press, 1989.

Teichgraeber, Richard. *Free Trade and Moral Philosophy: Rethinking the Sources of Adam Smith's Wealth of Nations*. Durham, NC: Duke University Press, 1986.

Terjanian, Anoush. "Savage Encounters with the Old World: The Imported Criticism of Eighteenth-Century France." M.Phil. dissertation, University of Cambridge, 1996.

Théré, Christine. "Economic Publishing and Authors, 1566–1789." In *Studies in the History of French Political Economy: From Bodin to Walras*, ed. Gilbert Faccarello, 1–56. London: Routledge, 1998.

Thomas, Hugh. *The Slave Trade*. London: Picador, 1997.

Thomasseau, Jean-Marie. *Commerce et commerçants dans la littérature*. Bordeaux: Presses universitaires de Bordeaux, 1988.

Thomson, Ann. "Diderot, Roubaud, et l'esclavage." *Recherches sur Diderot et sur l'Encyclopédie* 35 (2003): 69–93.

Thomson, Erik. "Commerce, Law, and Erudite Culture: The Mechanics of Théodore Godefroy's Service to Cardinal Richelieu." *Journal of the History of Ideas* 68, no. 3 (July 2007): 407–27.

"France's Grotian Moment? Hugo Grotius and Cardinal Richelieu's Commercial Statecraft." *French History* 21, vol. 4 (2007): 377–94.

Thomson, Janice E. *Mercenaries, Pirates and Sovereigns: State-Building and Extra-Territorial Violence in Early Modern Europe*. Princeton, NJ: Princeton University Press, 1994.

Tomaselli, Sylvana. "On labelling Raynal's *Histoire*: reflections on its genre and subject." Paper presented at "Raynal's 'Histoire des deux Indes': Colonial Writing, Cultural Exchange and Social Networks in the Age of the Enlightenment," Cambridge, July 1–3, 2010.

Trésor de la langue française: Dictionnaire de la langue du XIXe et du XXe siècle (1789–1960). Paris: Éditions du Centre national de la recherche scientifique, 1977–80.

Trouillot, Michel-Rolph. *Silencing the Past: Power and the Production of History*. Boston: Beacon Press, 1995.

Trumble, William R., and Angus Stevenson, eds. *Shorter Oxford English Dictionary on Historical Principles*. 5th ed. Oxford: Oxford University Press, 2002.

Tuck, Richard. Introduction to *The Rights of War and Peace*, by Hugo Grotius. Indianapolis: Liberty Fund, 2005.

Philosophy and Government, 1572–1651. Cambridge and New York: Cambridge University Press, 1993.

The Rights of War and Peace: Political Thought and International Order from Grotius to Kant. Oxford: Oxford University Press, 1999.

Tully, James. *Imperialism and Civic Freedom.* Vol. 2, *Public Philosophy in a New Key.* Cambridge: Cambridge University Press, 2008.

Turcan, Isabelle. "Les flibustiers de la lexicographie française des 17ᵉ et 18ᵉ siècles." Paper delivered at the Colloque du CRLV, May 2000.

Turley, Hans. *Rum, Sodomy and the Lash: Piracy, Sexuality, and Masculine Identity.* New York: New York University Press, 1999.

Tuttle, Leslie. *Conceiving the Old Regime: Pronatalism and the Politics of Reproduction in Early Modern France.* New York: Oxford University Press, 2010.

United States. *Eighth public hearing of the National Commission on Terrorist Attacks upon the United States.* Staff Statement No. 5 Diplomacy. 23 March 2004.

Vardi, Liana. "Physiocratic Visions." In *The Super-Enlightenment: Daring to Know Too Much,* edited by Dan Edelstein. Oxford: Voltaire Foundation, 2010.

——— "Rewriting the Lives of Eighteenth-Century Economists." *American Historical Review* 114, no. 3 (2009): 652–61.

Van Dillen, J. G. "Isaac le maire et le commerce des actions de la compagnie des indes orientales." *Revue d'histoire moderne* 10, no.16 (1935): 5–21.

Venayre, Sylvain. "Le pirate dans 'l'aventure coloniale,' 1850–1940." *L'Ull critic* 11 (2007): 157–68.

Viguerie, Jean de. *Histoire et Dictionnaire du Temps des Lumières.* Paris: Robert Laffont Bouquins, 1995.

Villiers, Patrick. *Les corsaires du Littoral: Dunkerque, Calais, Boulogne, de Philippe II à Louis XIV (1568–1713).* Paris: Presses universitaires du Septentrion, 2000.

Viner, Jacob. *Essays on the Intellectual History of Economics.* Edited by Douglas A. Irwin. Princeton: Princeton University Press, 1991.

Vovelle, Michel, ed. "Révolution aux Colonies" in *Annales historiques de la révolution française,* no. 293–94 (1993): 345–509.

Vries, Jan de and A. M. Van der Woude. *The First Modern Economy: Success, Failure, and Perseverance of the Dutch Economy, 1500–1885.* Cambridge: Cambridge University Press, 1997.

Waquet, Françoise. "Qu'est-ce que la République des Lettres ? Essaie de sémantique historique." *Bibliothèque de l'Ecole des Chartes* 147 (1989): 473–502.

Weber, Henry. *La compagnie française des Indes.* Paris: A. Rousseau, 1904.

Weiss, Gillian. "Back from Barbary: Captivity, Redemption and French Identity in the Seventeenth- and Eighteenth-Century Mediterranean." PhD dissertation, Stanford University, 2001.

Weston, Helen D. "Representing the Right to Represent: The 'Portrait of Citizen Belley, Ex-Representative of the Colonies' by A.-L. Girodet." *RES: Anthropology and Aesthetics.* 26 (1994): 83–99.

Weulersse, Georges. *Le Mouvement physiocratique en France, de 1756 à 1770.* 2 vols. Paris: Alcan, 1910.

La Physiocratie à l'aube de la Révolution, 1781–1792. Paris: École des hautes études en sciences sociales, 1985.

La Physiocratie à la fin du règne de Louis XV, 1770–1774. Paris: Presses universitaires de France, 1959.

Whatmore, Richard. *Republicanism and the French Revolution: An Intellectual History of Jean-Baptiste Say's Political Economy*. Oxford: Oxford University Press, 2000.

Wilder, Gary. *The French Imperial Nation-State: Negritude and Colonial Humanism between the Two World Wars*. Chicago: University of Chicago Press, 2005.

Williams, David. *Condorcet and Modernity*. Cambridge: Cambridge University Press, 2004.

Willens, Liliane. "L'esclavage est-il réformable? Les projets des administrateurs coloniaux à la fin de l'Ancien Régime." In *Les Abolitions de l'esclavage de L.F. Sonthonax à V. Schoelscher, 1793, 1794, 1848*, edited by Marcel Dorigny. Paris: Presses universitaires de Vincennes, 1995.

"Lafayette's Emancipation Experiment." *Studies in Voltaire and the Eighteenth Century* 242 (1986): 354–62.

Winch, Donald. *Adam Smith's Politics: An Essay in Historiographic Revision*. Cambridge: Cambridge University Press, 1978.

Riches and Poverty: An Intellectual History of Political Economy in Britain, 1750–1834. Cambridge: Cambridge University Press, 1996.

Withers, Charles. *Placing the Enlightenment: Thinking Geographically about the Age of Reason*. Chicago: University of Chicago Press, 2007.

Wokler, Robert and John Hope Mason, eds. *Diderot's Political Writings*. Cambridge: Cambridge University Press, 1992.

Wolf, Edwin, and Kevin Hayes. *The Library of Benjamin Franklin*. Philadelphia: American Philosophical Society, 2006.

Wolpe, Hans. *Raynal et sa machine de guerre: "L'Histoire des deux Indes" et ses perfectionnements*. Paris: M. Th. Litec, cop., 1956.

Yacou, Alain, and Michel Martin, eds. *De la Révolution française aux révolutions nègres et créoles*. Paris: Éditions Carribéennes, 1989.

Index

52016713R00145

Made in the USA
Columbia, SC
25 February 2019